NARCO WARS

How British Agents Infiltrated
the Colombian Drug Cartels

TOM CHANDLER

Milo Books

Published in November 2018 by Milo Books

ISBN 978-1-908479-92-1

Typeset by e-type

Printed in Great Britain by CPI Group (UK) Ltd,
Croydon, CR0 4YY

MILO BOOKS LTD

www.milobooks.com

t
A
and
than any other British customs officer. He was awarded the
MBE, medals from the Colombian Government and Security
Service, and the Cruz Blanca from the Spanish National Police.

To my best friends, Chris, Jezz, Ben, Ki and Nicky, who share a love of travel and adventure. We have had fantastic times together in many different countries. Keep travelling, push boundaries and live your dreams.

CONTENTS

A CUBAN CRISIS

A T 10 P.M. ON Saturday, 28 September 1996, a small freighter flying a Honduran flag cast off from its mooring in Barranquilla, on the north coast of Colombia, and quietly set sail. The night air was hot and sticky after an afternoon of heavy rain. Black storm clouds still glowered overhead, blocking out any light from the moon, and the dark blue hull of the seventy-metre vessel was barely visible as it eased down the Magdalena river and northwards into the Caribbean Sea. The thumping bass and salsa music booming from Barranquilla's bars slowly faded away. The sea was calm, and having checked his marine forecasts the Colombian captain was relieved to know that good weather and easy sailing lay ahead. He was carrying a cargo of waste paper to offload in Havana, on the north coast of Cuba. He also had on board another cargo, one that he and his crew would secretly hand over to speedboats at a prearranged rendezvous at sea, under the cover of night, before his arrival in port: cocaine.

Fair weather and a calm sea would make the job much safer. In high winds and choppy waves, the task of transferring drugs to small boats was hazardous for the crews and highly dangerous for the captain himself. If any was lost into the sea, he would be held responsible. One missing bale would cost him his entire payment for the trip, or even his life if the cartel didn't accept his explanation. Until the drugs were handed over, any problems were his sole responsibility.

The captain mulled over the possibilities as he sailed slowly northward. He prayed that with fine conditions and good luck, the contraband would soon be delivered without any glitches, sent on its way to the Florida Keys and from there to the table tops and noses of wealthy Americans.

It was not until late the following morning that Pacho telephoned to give me the update.

'Señor,' he panted, out of breath and excited. 'The *Limerick* has gone. It left last night and is on its way. We need to act quickly.'

I was at home in Bogotá, enjoying a quiet Sunday morning with my family. I stopped what I was doing, reached for my notebook and pen, and told Pacho to take his time and calmly give me as much detail as he could.

'This is the run, señor. For certain. They loaded the drugs last night and then it left at about ten o'clock. I think it's about three tonnes, and it's hidden in two secret compartments in the water tanks, or beneath them.'

Pacho was one of my network, and he was good. He had been working for me as an informant for ten months and had managed to sniff out top-quality information about large cocaine shipments by sea. He knew he could call me anytime, night or day, to pass it on. He had first heard about the cargo ship called *Limerick* several months earlier when it was moored at Palermo, a small jetty on the Magdalena river on the outskirts of Barranquilla. Palermo was away from the main port and had no loading facilities, and there was no reason at all for a legitimate cargo vessel to anchor there. He had heard rumours that it was killing time, waiting for traffickers to bring a large quantity of drugs before moving to a commercial jetty to take on legitimate cargo. Pacho had been patiently gathering intelligence about the ship since then and had even managed to infiltrate deep into the transport organisation.

I managed to calm Pacho down a little and get him to tell me the story in more detail. He said the *Limerick* had sailed from Barranquilla and was heading to Cuba with a cargo of waste-paper. He couldn't say the exact quantity of drugs on board, but he knew for certain that it was huge, perhaps more than three tonnes, maybe even five. He gave me a description of the two places where it was concealed deep within the ship: a secret compartment beneath the fresh water tanks at the front, and another somewhere beneath the main cargo hold. The crew knew how to open hidden hatches and get to the coke, and he warned me that it would be difficult to find without their help. The drugs were to be handed over to speedboats known as 'go-fasts' the night before the *Limerick* reached Cuba.

The *Limerick* had a head start of about thirteen hours, so I needed to act. Every minute that passed would make it harder to find a small ship in the vast expanse of the Caribbean. And just because it had declared that it was sailing to Havana didn't mean it would go straight there. Often the captains of drug ships told port authorities that they were going in a certain direction to a specified port, then took a different route or went somewhere else to thwart surveillance.

suddenly appeared and came charging down towards me, followed by an equally frightening accomplice. From behind them came a stream of shouts.

'Help!'

'Stop them!'

'We've been robbed!'

What happened next was not a question of me being courageous, far from it, I just couldn't get out of their way. The two intruders were in their early twenties, built like athletes, and came rushing down the narrow stairway towards me. I was a small, nine-stone obstacle blocking their escape. The first one smashed into me and we both crashed down the stairs, head over heels, in a jumble of flailing arms and legs. Fortunately when we hit the bottom I landed on top of him, and somehow was able to pin him down, with his face into the floor and his right arm pulled behind his back. His accomplice jumped over me and made his escape through the doorway.

For fifteen long minutes I somehow held him down, pressing my knee as hard as I could into his back and keeping his arm wedged up behind his shoulder. I knew that if I loosened my grip and he got free, I would be in deep trouble. He did not stop screaming vile abuse the whole time, threatening to do the most horrendous and painful things to me once he got free. Fortunately he didn't. The police finally arrived, cuffed him and took him away, and I gave a statement. Then I finished my VAT visit and left.

I had made my first ever arrest. I felt quite chuffed with the way things had turned out, but for a long time afterwards I kept a cautious eye out for Mr Tyson whenever I ventured back to Notting Hill.

A week later I was summoned by the Collector, the regional director of HMCE responsible for all customs activities in North and West London. To me he was one small step down from God at the time. The Collector had received letters from the company and from the local police praising my actions in arresting one of the thieves. He normally only got letters of complaint from the public, so he was extremely pleased. He asked how I saw my career going forward and if there was anything I needed. I grasped the opportunity.

'Do you think it would be possible to get a secondment to the Collection Investigation Unit?' I politely asked. Without hesitation he picked up the telephone and the following week I started a twelve-month secondment to the London North and West Collection Investigation Unit, or CIU.

It was 1981 and at that time HMCE had a two-tier investigation service. The Investigation Division, known as the ID, dealt with the bigger cases at a national and international level. It had about eight hundred investigators, most of whom were based in London. The Collection Investigation Units, or CIUs, were twenty-one regional teams that dealt with local investigations within their respective regions, although they sometimes joined forces to do bigger jobs. I had a fantastic time working with North and West CIU, and gained my first insight into what customs investigation work was about: carrying out covert observations from the back of a van, making 'bin runs' to dig evidence from criminals' rubbish in the middle of the night, tailing suspects without being spotted, and launching raids on premises. I was quickly hooked on the excitement of investigation work, and so applied to join HMCE's elite investigation service and make my one-year secondment permanent. The bar to recruitment was set high, but I cleared it and was accepted.

During the next six years, I worked in London, North Wales and the Midlands, investigating for various regional CIUs. We dealt with the whole spectrum of HMCE work: tobacco smuggling, illegal alcohol stills, betting duty scams, VAT frauds, and smaller drug cases such as importations by parcel post. In those days we did everything ourselves, so one day we might be doing surveillance on villains, the next day interviewing company directors about a complex fraud, the next day kicking in doors following the delivery of a parcel of drugs from Amsterdam. It was fantastic work.

But in the back of my mind I always knew that the biggest and most interesting investigations were handled by the Investigation Division in London. The ID had a national and international remit and dealt with the major criminals and larger, more complex investigations. I had always wanted to work on international drugs cases, so in 1987 I transferred to the ID. I went with two aspirations: to become a motorbike surveillance rider, and to investigate big cocaine importations from South America. I was lucky and got to do both, and much more. I promised my wife, Luisa, that I would only work in London for a few years and then we could return to a more tranquil life in the provinces. But I got hooked on the thrill of anti-drugs work.

TWO YEARS LATER, I was working a night shift with Merv Mullins, the SIO of the Golfs, a heroin team, as we ran a live operation in north London. Merv pointed out a job advert in the *IDWO*, the ID's internal staff newsletter.

'Hey, Tom, they need someone who speaks Spanish. This one's got your name on it.'

He passed me the newsletter and urged me to put in for it. They needed a senior investigator with experience in drugs work, who spoke Spanish, and who was willing to go to Peru for two to four years as the drug liaison officer, or DLO. I thought about it, and applied.

A week later I was invited to attend a selection interview with Dick Lawrence, the Chief Investigation Officer and head of the ID, in his office at 3.30 p.m.

'Would you like tea, or something stronger?' Dick asked as I entered his office and he invited me to sit in one of the comfortable chairs by his coffee table.

'Err, tea, please,' I replied. I wondered whether I'd just failed the first test.

After what turned out to be a very pleasant interview, he gave me the job. In later years HMCE would introduce a far more sophisticated and robust selection process for DLOs, involving paper sifts, advanced vetting, a demanding two-day assessment centre and then final interviews, but back then it was done by personal recommendation and a one-to-one interview over tea and biscuits with the Chief. By then I had been doing investigation work for about ten years, had been promoted twice and gained a great deal of experience. I loved the job. But not once had I been able to use my knowledge of Spanish. In South America I would at last be able to do an exciting job, probably the best in the whole of HMCE, and could put my Spanish to some use. I was buzzing with excitement and enthusiasm and couldn't wait to get there.

During the late 1980s the influx of drugs to the UK was

fast increasing. Addiction and cases of HIV and AIDS spread by the sharing of contaminated needles were growing at an alarming rate. Public concern about the social impact of drug abuse was rising, fuelled by fears about the arrival of highly addictive crack-cocaine in our inner cities and an associated rise in drug-related crime and violence. In response, the government of Margaret Thatcher increased funding to the War on Drugs and made it a national priority. There was pressure to reduce supply by taking action in the key source countries as well as at home, and the ID decided to send DLOs overseas. The first was sent to Pakistan, then the main source for most of the heroin reaching the UK, in 1984. The first British DLOs in South America went to Venezuela and Peru in 1986, by which time there were four in India and Pakistan and another in Jamaica.

The idea was simple: rather than relying on officers to detect drugs when they arrived at our ports and airports, the DLOs in the source countries would work with local law enforcement and other agencies to gather intelligence in advance about drugs being sent. The aim was to seize more of the stuff before it could reach the streets of Britain, to disrupt the supply and transport routes, and to target the criminal organisations responsible. Those first officers proved that the concept worked, and in the following years the DLO network was expanded.

During my years in Peru the DLO network was still relatively small. There were just ten of us around the world in 1989 but we supplied a huge flow of intelligence to the UK and stopped a lot of drugs from arriving. For four years I worked alone as the sole DLO in Peru, operating from the British embassy in Lima, coordinating investigations with the Peruvian authorities and recruiting my own inform-ants. Peru was the number one source of coca leaf and *pasta basica*, the cocaine base, which was then sold on to the Colombian narcos to produce cocaine hydrochloride. It was also in the grip of an insurgency from the Maoist Shining Path guerrilla movement, which made for some very interesting times. Occasionally they would blow up police stations or power supply lines, and it wasn't unusual to go for days without electricity and even water. I also had responsibility for working in five other countries, Ecuador, Bolivia, Chile, Paraguay and Argentina, and so spent a lot of time travelling. It was great experience of working on my own initiative, developing international drug cases, navigating untold hurdles and sussing out who I could and couldn't trust to work with.

In 1993, after four years in Peru, I was asked by the ID if I would move to Colombia. I didn't hesitate to say yes. As far as I was concerned it was *the* plum posting for a drugs investigator: the source of most of the world's cocaine, and home to the richest and most powerful criminal organi-sations known to man. The first DLO had been sent to Colombia in 1990. Des set up the post and developed our early relationships with the Colombian agencies, and I now hoped to build upon this. Des had since been joined by another officer, Dan, so when I took over in early 1994 there would two of us.

In December 1993, just weeks before I took up post, Pablo Escobar the fugitive head of the Medellin Cartel, was shot dead by the Colombian Police. Headlines around the world proclaimed that the most notorious narco of all time was now dead. Whilst this was a major success for law enforcement, in reality his trafficking empire had already been taken over by other mafias, and his death would have little or no effect upon the flow of cocaine to Europe. Indeed, it enabled the Cali Cartel to consolidate their control over the global supply of cocaine, and to grow into the most powerful and evil criminal organisation ever known.

2

THE POWER OF THE CARTELS

EFORE GOING TO Colombia, I received detailed briefings from HMCE and the intelligence agencies about the drug cartels. During the 1980s and 1990s, the Medellin and Cali cartels dominated the cocaine trade, helping to make Colombia one of the most violent countries on earth, with one of the highest murder rates. The Medellin Cartel was founded by the three Ochoa brothers, Fabio, Juan and Jorge, together with Pablo Escobar, Carlos Lehder and Jose Rodriguez Gacha. It eventually came to be firmly controlled by Escobar, who personally micro-managed the business from production through to transport and sale at destination. At its peak the Medellin Cartel controlled over seventy per cent of the world's supply and was said to generate an income of more than $420 million dollars a week, or $22 billion a year.

Escobar was an uncontrollable gangster who became renowned for his ruthlessness. His cartel waged war against the Government and assassinated ministers, politicians and judges. He was responsible for ordering the blowing up of an Avianca airliner in mid-flight, killing all 107 passengers on board, in a failed attempt to kill the presidential candidate Cesar Gaviria. He hired international mercenaries to train an army of gunmen, or *sicarios*, who enforced his wishes and eliminated opponents without compunction. One of his leading hitmen, John Jairo Velasquez, alias 'Popeye', later admitted to personally murdering three hundred people and ordering the deaths of over three thousand more.

The Cali Cartel was founded in the late 1970s by the brothers Gilberto and Miguel Rodriguez Orejuela, along with Jose Santacruz Londoño. They were joined later by Helmer 'Pacho' Herrera, who became the fourth member of their management board. Known as *'los señores de Cali'* – 'the gentlemen of Cali' – they were from a higher social background than Escobar and considered themselves to be better educated and more professional. They trafficked throughout the 1980s but managed their business in a more sophisticated manner. They were also more discreet and, unlike Escobar, sought to maintain a low profile and avoid publicity. Instead of attacking the Colombian state as Escobar did, the Cali Cartel tried to blend with it, investing money in businesses and banks and discreetly corrupting government officials and institutions.

The two cartels initially co-existed, with Medellin supplying Miami and Cali controlling New York, the two main US distribution hubs. But conflict between them grew during the mid-1980s when the Orejuelas became alarmed by Escobar's political aspirations and thirst for publicity, as well as his increasing violence and hostility towards the Colombian government. By the early 1990s Escobar's power had been weakened by the years of conflict and he started to lose control. The Medellin Cartel splintered in 1992 when Escobar murdered two of his closest associates, Moncada and Galeano. The Ochoas, Don Berna and other Medellin traffickers separated from Escobar and created a paramilitary group called Los Pepes (People Persecuted by Pablo Escobar), which aligned itself with the Cali Cartel to attack their former partner. Cali took advantage of this instability and consolidated its control over a larger share of the cocaine trade. It also secretly collaborated with the Colombian and US authorities in their efforts to destroy the Medellin Cartel and hunt down Escobar. When he was finally killed in December 1993, the remnants of his cartel crumbled and Cali took over its trade.

Thus by the end of 1993, the men from Cali dominated the global trade and had immense power. They were said to control eighty percent of the world's cocaine supply. This would last for a further two years, until late 1995, when Miguel and Gilberto Orejuela were both arrested. Other key leaders, such as Jose Santacruz, Victor Patiño and Henry Loaiza, surrendered themselves to the authorities to negotiate more lenient sentences. For a period, the king-pins continued to manage business from inside jail, but the multiple arrests and seizure of assets during 1995 effectively led to the end of the Cali Cartel in its existing form. Pacho Herrera, the last Cali kingpin still at large, handed himself in to the authorities in September 1996. There followed an abrupt period of violence while rival sub-groups fought over different parts of the cartel's empire.

But by late 1996 the fragmentation was resolved, and a dominant new conglomerate emerged: the North Valley Cartel, or Norte del Valle. It comprised several powerful traffickers, including Orlando Henao, Juan Carlos

Ramirez Abadía (alias 'Chupeta'), Wilber Varela, Diego Montoya and Ivan Urdinola. They had previously conducted business under the umbrella of the Cali Cartel, but splintered from them in 1995 when the Orejuelas suggested a negotiated surrender to the Government. Now they took control. The North Valley Cartel would assume the Cali Cartel's transport and distribution routes and would be the leading force in Colombia's coke trade for the next ten years, but there was no longer one single organisation controlling the entire process from production to source. Instead, there were various criminal groups and 'mini-cartels' involved, each of them powerful and independent but collaborating together for specific enterprises. In addition to the North Valley there were several smaller syndicates such as the Bogotá Cartel, headed by Pastor Perafan and the North Coast Cartel, operating from Barranquilla and Cartagena.

The death of Escobar meant that when I arrived in Bogotá in January 1994, the Cali Cartel was in the ascendancy. Indeed it was at its peak. They were no less violent than Escobar had been, but were far more organised, intelligence-driven and efficient. They had developed a powerful counter-intelligence infrastructure that they used to identify their opponents and others who were a threat. They then had teams of *sicarios* and mercenaries to torture and murder the traitors or suspected informants. Thousands of people in Colombia were assassinated or simply disappeared.

I was forewarned that Cali had purchased sophisticated eavesdropping systems and would be able to listen to our telephone conversations. They would target not only the Colombian police but also foreign drug liaison officers and the US Drug Enforcement Administration (DEA) to find out what we were investigating and to identify informants. I was told that they might also put us under surveillance to identify our homes and families. The cartels and had a vast network of contacts and informants. They had infiltrated the police and DAS, and even the government up to the very highest levels. It would later be discovered that they had contributed $8 million to the campaign of President Ernest Samper, with a view to buying political favour and ensuring their own immunity from prosecution. In addition to the large numbers of officials on their payroll, they were said to have thousands of sources such as taxi drivers and airport workers, all feeding information back.

It was frightening to know that the cartel had such power, would be monitoring my phone calls, possibly following me to identify my family, and that many of the people who I worked with would be on their payroll and telling them details of my work. The outlook was daunting, and I knew it was going to be difficult to know whom I could trust and work with. I had been warned that they might even send false informants to approach us. There were several reasons why they might do this; perhaps to see who the British DLOs were, to get our descriptions and photographs, and to find out about how we operated. They might also try to get information about how we handled our informants, how much we paid for information, and identify our meeting places, telephone numbers and security measures. Or maybe they would just waste our time and distract us.

I could fully understand all of these motives, but nonetheless I never expected that they would actually go to such lengths. I was wrong. My first taste of Cali's counter-intelligence tactics came soon after my arrival.

I WAS THREE months into the job when an unknown Colombian male telephoned the embassy in Bogotá and said he needed to speak urgently with the official dealing with drugs. The receptionist passed the call on to me. The man sounded both scared and excited. He said he was from Cali and had information about a large cocaine shipment being sent to the UK, but he could not give me details by telephone. He wanted to meet me in a nearby park. I declined and asked him to come to the embassy, where we could talk safely without anyone seeing us. He refused, claiming that it was far too dangerous for him to be seen visiting the embassy. He would only meet me elsewhere, either in a park or a bar.

The problem with meeting an unknown person offering information is that it could simply be a ruse to harm or kidnap a British diplomat, or specifically a DLO. Even if he was genuine, there was a risk that he could be suspected of informing and might be under surveillance by the bad guys, in which case I could walk into a trap. Or he could simply be some deranged person looking for attention. Either way, it was highly dangerous to meet an unknown 'walk-in' on your own in Bogotá, away from the security of the embassy. We always had first encounters with walk-ins in a meeting room at the embassy, where visitors were filmed and identified on entry and where I had armed guards as back-up.

I explained to 'Manuel', which was the codename I allocated to him, that he could give me the information by telephone, write it down and fax it, or we could meet at the British embassy. He replied that he knew about a shipment of seven tonnes of cocaine that the cartel would send in the coming days to the UK, and that he was only in Bogotá for one day and could meet me in the park to tell me about it, but would not come to the embassy. Seven tonnes was a huge amount, unheard of for a direct shipment to the UK. I was highly sceptical, very uncomfortable about this guy, and inclined to refuse to meet him. On the other hand, what if it was true? I could be about to turn away what would be the biggest UK-bound drugs seizure ever.

Common sense prevailed.

'No, I'm sorry, I can't do that,' I told him. 'The embassy really is the safest place. How about this? You come in and say you want to apply for a travel visa. I will make sure that you are discreetly taken aside into an interview room, where I will meet you. It won't look suspicious, and we can talk in complete security.'

'No, no, señor. It is impossible. Someone can see me going into the embassy. It is too dangerous. They will kill me.'

We said goodbye. For the next few weeks I lived with the niggling doubt that I may have just turned away both a highly valuable informant and the biggest case ever. It was not a nice thought.

Our DLO in Quito, the capital city of Ecuador, was Martin. I had known him for years, and in my new post I was officially his regional manager, so we spoke regularly. In early May, Martin telephoned to say he had been offered an informant who had a massive case for the UK. This new walk-in wanted to meet him to give information about a six-tonne consignment of cocaine that the Cali

Cartel was shipping to the UK, but he wouldn't come in to the embassy and wanted to meet somewhere in downtown Quito. Martin had told him to call back later, and wanted my advice as to whether he should agree to the meet.

It all sounded familiar, and after comparing details it became clear that this was the same person as Manuel. We both knew that it could be dangerous to meet him, as he clearly had some unknown, ulterior motive for contacting us. Martin came up with a sensible proposal. He would arrange a rendezvous in a local bar, but would be accompanied by a trusted colleague from the Ecuadorian drugs police, and would have an armed police backup team nearby.

Martin duly met Manuel. He gave vague details of the alleged, impending shipment, and asked Martin lots of questions about the reward money the British paid for information, how much per kilo seized, whether the informant could 'participate' in the crime, how many DLOs we had in Ecuador, and so on. After the meeting, the drugs police followed the man, and pulled him in for questioning. They presumably had very effective interrogation techniques because Manuel broke down and confessed everything.

He said a trafficker in Cali called Cruz was paying him to approach the various drug attachés based in embassies to find out information. He had been to the Americans, the British and the Germans in Bogotá, and was now visiting the British and Germans in Quito. His task was to gather as much information as he could about us, including our names and telephone numbers, physical descriptions, how much reward we paid, and how and where we met informants. He was also instructed to waste as much of our time and resources as possible by inventing fictitious shipments that we would report back to our agencies. He was basically an envoy from the Cali Cartel, paid by them to learn about us and muddy the waters. I later spoke with DEA and German colleagues in Bogotá and they confirmed that he had also approached them. The DEA had even registered him as an informant and paid him some money for expenses.

This was my first false informant. Fortunately we had realised what he was before he could do any harm. It was a useful lesson to learn in my early months in Colombia, and a chilling reminder that the warnings I had been given were true: the Cali Cartel would be watching us. Over the next two years I would get several other walk-ins from the city of Cali, offering information. I never knew whether they appeared under instructions from a trafficking cartel or were acting on their own, but the scenario was always the same. They came, offered vague information and asked lots of questions. They gave me nothing of any value, and I gave them nothing in return. Then I would then never see them again. It was all part of the deadly game.

DAN AND I worked from an office within the British embassy in Bogotá and had official titles as, respectively, First and Second Secretaries within the Chancery. Being posted as diplomats gave us full diplomatic cover, which was vital for our work. For a start, it meant that we and our families had diplomatic immunity, so we could not be arrested or threatened by corrupt police. If things ever got too dangerous we could leave the country at any time and no bent Colombian official would be able to detain or stop us. At another level, it gave us the seniority and diplomatic status to engage with ministers, heads of police and other agencies when we needed to. It also gave us a cover story. When meeting people, we could present ourselves as British diplomats working at the embassy, dealing with trade or political matters. We only told those people who really needed to know about our true work.

At the visible official level, our role was to work closely with the Colombians to share information and coordinate joint investigations, the overall objective being to disrupt the flow of drugs to the UK. The problem with running joint investigations, however, was that the Colombian authorities had been so heavily infiltrated by the drug cartels that it was risky to share anything sensitive with them. We always had to assume that the people we worked with might pass our information to the traffickers. This fear was confirmed several years later when the Cali Cartel was finally dismantled; documents and payroll records seized from business offices in the city of Cali itself showed that large numbers of the Colombian Police, DAS and judiciary had been on their payroll.

Colombia had several law enforcement agencies involved in the war – and over there it really was a war – on drugs. All of them had been infiltrated to some degree by the cartels and their staff could not always be trusted.

DIJIN, the Criminal Investigations Directorate, was the main police department responsible for criminal investigations. In theory, DIJIN was the lead agency, the one that we as DLOs should have worked with most closely. In practice, so many of its staff were untrustworthy that we had little to do with them.

DIRAN, the Antinarcotics Directorate, commonly

known as the Antinarcotics Police, or ANP, was the main police department dealing with drugs. However its primary focus was the eradication of coca plants and the destruction of cocaine-processing laboratories. The ANP did little proactive investigation work, but with assistance from the British DLOs they would in time develop a small intelligence and investigation unit.

The Fiscalia was the Colombian prosecution service. It could also conduct its own investigations, but in the 1990s it did little proactive intelligence work. Its function was limited to the preparation of cases for prosecution.

DAS, the Department of Administrative Security, was the Colombian security and intelligence service, broadly equivalent to our own MI5. It was responsible for immigration, liaising with Interpol, and state security. Whilst even elements of DAS had been infiltrated, it was the only Colombian agency that carried out effective intelligence work and intelligence-led investigations into the cartels.

DIAN, the Department of Tax and Customs, was the customs service. It had no remit to investigate drug smuggling, and its staff in the ports were highly corrupt.

The problem with all of these agencies was that we could not trust any of them at an institutional level. They were all riddled with corruption, often right up to the top. Our challenge as DLOs was to find specific individuals who were not double-dealing and with whom we could safely work. This we managed to do. We found small groups of honest individuals in DAS and the ANP, and over time built close working relationships with them. In DAS we dealt personally with the director of intelligence. He allocated a small number of trusted intelligence and counter-intelligence staff to work with us, and we came to trust them. Their Interpol unit was also reliable. In the ANP we worked with the director, Colonel Leonardo Gallego, who also nominated trusted officers to collaborate with us. These personal relationships with handpicked individuals were fundamental to the working model of the British DLOs, and enabled us to develop a unique and very successful partnership with Colombia.

Working with these small groups of trusted contacts within DAS and ANP, we exchanged information about suspect traffickers, developed intelligence, and carried out joint investigations. When police or customs officers in the UK investigated criminals importing cocaine from Colombia, they would pass us details of the Colombian telephone numbers and people in contact with their suspects, and we would develop the case at our end. DAS or ANP would gather intelligence about them, or open an official investigation, and give us information from their surveillance and telephone intercepts. These joint investigations often led to the identification and arrest of drug trafficking groups in both Colombia and the UK. But despite some excellent cases with the Colombian Police and DAS, our success would always be limited by high levels of corruption. For that reason, in addition to our official collaboration with their agencies, we also had to gather intelligence from other, non-official, sources. That required us to develop our own contacts – and to cultivate informants. This was by far the more dangerous aspect of our work, one that we had to do ourselves without the support of local agencies, often working alone.

Our main lifeline back to the UK was our dedicated desk

officer at the international section of Customs ID in London. 'Poddy', as he was known, was our direct link to the rest of British law enforcement. We were in touch with him on a daily basis, through a secure communications system. We would pass on intelligence and Poddy would then coordinate any necessary actions or investigations by HMCE, the police, or any European countries involved. Poddy, and later another desk officer, 'Shuggy', were key components in converting our intelligence into tangible results back home.

The volume of work that we would go on to generate from Colombia became so great that within two years the team would more than double in size. Anne arrived in October 1995 and was a lucky find. She spoke fluent Spanish and was very bright, with a bubbly outgoing personality and razor-sharp Liverpudlian wit. She had been doing a tedious desk-job in the VAT insolvency part of HMCE, (another round peg put into a square hole by the human resources department) and was so bored and under-tasked that she was about to resign when she saw the advert for Bogotá. Anne quickly became a fantastic asset to the team. Then Bernie came a few months later, followed by Steve, who replaced Dan in June 1996. Bernie and Steve had both worked on the Romeos, the ID's top cocaine target team in the UK, and also in Alpha, the secret telephone intercept unit. They were seasoned investigators with heaps of experience, and I was fortunate to lead a strong team of DLOs who worked really well together.

When I first arrived we had a couple of informants in Bogotá but none in any of the ports. I was determined to change that, and set myself a target. I would try to recruit a network of informers in the Colombian seaports, to focus on disrupting the shipments of cocaine by sea.

3

RECRUITING

M Y SHIRT WAS soaking wet and clung to my body. It was barely 11 a.m., but already the humidity and heat were stifling. I could feel trickles of sweat running down my back, and droplets fell from my brow into my eyes. I was standing in the searing morning sun, watching a large ship being loaded with containers. I had only recently arrived in Colombia and Señor Salas, the commercial director of Cartagena port, had kindly agreed to give me a tour so that I could see its operation first-hand.

A huge crane picked up containers from the quayside and raised them into the air before swinging them sideways and lowering them into the ship's hold. One after another, scores of containers destined for Europe were being loaded onto the *Sierra Express*. I tried to take in everything, watching the various people as they worked: the crane driver cranking control handles in his cabin above, a supervisor barking into his radio below, several forklift drivers and dockers loading loose cargo and provisions on the quayside, a couple of crewmen overseeing from the deck, security staff watching operations as they guarded the gangway to the ship. There were dozens of workers all going about their tasks.

But how many of these containers have drugs inside? I wondered. *How many of these people are involved in trafficking? Which of them know what is going on and could be good informants?* And more importantly, *How on earth can I get to meet these people?*

The cartels were extremely powerful, but not invulnerable. At the end of the day they had to get their product across the Atlantic Ocean. Colombia was producing around 900 tonnes of cocaine per year, of which about 350 went to Europe. Most of that would be transported by sea, so the ports were of vital strategic importance. There were only a handful of seaports in Colombia, and I reckoned that they must be natural choke-points for the huge flow of cocaine. I knew that this would be the weakest link in the chain, the cartels' Achilles' heel. My plan, audacious and daunting as it seemed at the time, was to try to recruit a network of informants in all of the Colombian seaports. If it worked, I aimed to infiltrate the cartel's transport systems and identify and seize their drug shipments.

Before I left the UK, I had discussed my plan with Phil, the ID's senior manager in London responsible for the Americas. Phil had a wealth of experience. He had spent years working on target teams investigating some of the major drug smugglers of the 1980s. He had also worked in Alpha, our secretive intelligence unit, and had been a DLO himself in Thailand. We got on well and had similar outlooks. He was always positive and energetic and was without doubt one of the better managers in London, one of those proactive ones who push actions forward and don't baulk at problems. But when I told him what I had in mind, I could see he had some reservations.

'Tom, that sounds like a fantastic idea and it makes sense,' he said, somewhat cautiously. 'But if it was that easy to recruit informants in the ports, the DEA would already be doing it. You'll need to take great care and move slowly, because that is going to be difficult. And extremely dangerous.'

At least he didn't say, 'No,' or think I was mad.

When I first arrived in Colombia, HMCE didn't have a single informant in any of the Colombian ports. It was not just us; no-one from any of the other overseas agencies seemed to be working the ports either. Up until then, the DLOs tended to wait passively for potential informants to come forward and contact them. But our embassy in Bogotá was over six hundred miles from Cartagena and the northern coast. It was unlikely that dockworkers, crewmen or shipping agents would travel all the way to Bogotá to talk to us. Yet no DLOs had tried going into the ports themselves to recruit informants. The DEA had scores of staff in its offices in Bogotá and Barranquilla, and numerous informants, but was focusing all of its efforts on arresting the cartel 'kingpins' rather than seizing shipments. In fairness, DEA agents were not customs officers and didn't really understand the fine detail of how ports operated and how smuggling was carried out. But the fact was that the DEA were doing nothing there and neither were any other foreign liaison officers; nor were DAS or the Colombian police. The ports were treated as a dangerous no-man's land, left to the control of the cartels.

To some extent it didn't matter which cartel was running the show at any given time, whether it was Medellin, Cali, the North Valley or one of the other major players: the ports had their own mafias, who controlled the movement of drugs and other prohibited goods through there. The Medellin Cartel had been the first to establish corrupt maritime transport networks as part of their wider empire. They paid key figures in the docks and the shipping authorities, and established a port mafia that could control and guarantee the safe passage of illicit shipments. The Cali Cartel set up their own networks, and then consolidated with those that they took over from Medellin. Later came the North Valley and others. But irrespective of who were the overall masters and owners of the drugs, the port mafias had themselves become powerful criminal groups who controlled maritime transport, and charged a hefty fee for doing so.

The Antinarcotics Police had tried to exert some control, but had been forced to close their units in the ports by a combination of corruption and threats. Colonel Leonardo Gallego, the head of the ANP, explained to me that whenever they sent a new *teniente*, or lieutenant, to command their unit in Cartagena or Buenaventura, within days that officer was approached and offered bribes to allow shipments through. If he declined, he was given the choice between *plata o plomo* – silver or lead. In other words, he could take a bribe or a bullet. If the lieutenant declined the bribe, he would suffer further threats not only to himself but to his family. It was difficult to imagine how a young officer, on a low salary, might withstand the pressure when the mafia showed him pictures of his wife and children, said they knew where they lived and went to school, and that a horrible 'accident' might befall them if he did not cooperate. The bribe or the bullet is a powerful threat, especially when the bullet option applies to your loved ones as well. Many officers took the money and kept quiet. Others pleaded with their managers for a transfer back to Bogotá. Colonel Gallego came to realise that when he posted staff to Cartagena and other ports, those who did not immediately report back threats and ask to be withdrawn had probably been corrupted.

The three biggest Colombian ports from which drugs went to Europe were Cartagena, Santa Marta and Buenaventura. The narcos controlled them completely, by corruption and fear, and could export securely and without risk or interference. Given the scale of the problem, I wondered where to begin. *How on earth do you start to recruit informants in a lawless foreign port?*

Of the three main container ports, Buenaventura, on the Pacific coast, was by far the least attractive option. Its name may mean 'good fortune' in Spanish but it was a dirty, sinister and inhospitable city, completely controlled by druglords and criminals. Its small airport was not in operation at that time, so to get there I would have to fly to Cali and then drive by car on the only road in or out. It also had only one decent hotel, La Estación, so it wouldn't be hard to find me if anyone came looking. It was by far the most perilous of the main ports and I had no wish to start there. Even in later years, I always felt vulnerable, apprehensive and a little scared when I went to Buenaventura. I knew that I stood out, that the bad guys almost certainly knew I was there, and that they could easily find me and do me harm if they wanted to.

Santa Marta was nicer but still very risky. Because it was a small town with fewer hotels, I would still stand out and have fewer options to keep a low profile.

Cartagena had the advantage that it was a big tourist location with numerous hotels. The large numbers of international visitors would give me cover. So I started there, purely because it was the safest. Some level of risk was inevitable, but I wanted to start in the least dangerous place.

In my first six months, I made several visits to Cartagena and met all the main agencies and authorities: police, customs, the Port Authority, port security, shipping companies, freight agents, in fact anyone who would talk to me and tell me about the business. The flight north from Bogotá took ninety minutes but I tried to go there once a month to begin with. My initial objective was simply to establish contacts and learn as all I could about the port and how it operated, how drugs were being shipped, and who the cartels would need to have on their payroll in order to guarantee their shipments.

I sometimes used my title as First Secretary at the embassy, rather than as a DLO, to gain access to people who might otherwise have been reluctant to meet. I would offer help with training and aid, and it was sometimes easier as a diplomat to get access to senior people without raising my profile too much. Then slowly, over a period of months, I broadened my circle of contacts and started to understand how the mafia circumvented the port controls. I analysed the various ways by which they were sending drugs from Cartagena, and for each method I looked at the process and the people involved. I tried to work out who I would use if I were a trafficker.

There are many ways to send drugs by sea. They include:

- Concealed within legitimate cargo inside containers
- 'Rip-ons', in which bags of drugs are secretly placed inside the doors of legitimate containers

- With crewmen
- Hidden onboard ships in various places
- Beneath the hulls of ships as parasitic attachments or in rudder housing or cooling intake vents
- On yachts and sailing boats
- By 'go-fast' speedboats

There are other methods but these were the main ones. Whichever method they used, when the cartels sent a large consignment they had to pay people to package it, conceal it, ship it, protect it, and ensure that it would not be seized. They didn't take chances with high-value consignments; their safe exit and transit was always paid for and guaranteed. Even though one in every ten containers leaving Cartagena was supposed to be searched by Customs, they somehow always searched the wrong ones. No drugs were ever seized. Safe passage meant safe passage, and no one dared interfere.

To identify possible sources, I needed to think like a trafficker. The cartels recruited corrupt people to facilitate their shipments; I needed to recruit people to tell me about them. We both needed contacts in the port, and ironically, we would sometimes use the same people, who played for both sides. While the high level of corruption in the port meant that no drugs were being seized, it also meant that many people knew about each shipment. Shipping agents, freight forwarders and customs agents would all be aware of the suspect exporters and containers. Some of them had worked in Cartagena for years and knew all the regular exporters well. It was relatively easy for them to spot the new ones, the unusual ones, or the 'businessmen' from

Medellin or Cali who turned up to export a container of fruit to Europe even though it was obvious that they knew nothing about such trade. But the shipping agents and other good people kept their mouths closed and their eyes averted. They were scared.

Customs and police were paid off so that certain containers were not searched. Stevedores and cargo handlers were paid to load drugs; port security and others were all bribed to look the other way. I reckoned that these were not all inherently bad people or criminals. They were just normal people who were terrified of the mafia, and it was safer for them to take the money and look the other way rather than refuse. Better the bribe than the bullet. I knew there must be dozens of people in the ports with minor roles who could identify drug shipments. All I had to do was find them, work out how to approach them, and then somehow overcome their fear and persuade them to work with me.

I slowly identified some possible useful contacts and I started spreading word that the UK would pay for information about illicit shipments, and that we would be discreet and protect the source. My early efforts were a bit scatter-gun, pitching to everyone I could. This was successful in so far as it generated some initial contacts, but it was a high-risk strategy that would come back to bite me.

THE FIRST BREAKTHROUGH came six months after my first visit to Cartagena. Each confidential informant, or 'CI', would be given a codename as part of the standard procedure to conceal their identity. CI Maribel made contact in October 1994. She would not speak with me directly at first, because she was terrified of someone finding out, but arranged to communicate anonymously via a trusted third party. She said that a cargo vessel called *Humboldt Express* had just left for Europe with a container on board full of drugs. Maribel gave me full details of the container, which was officially recorded as containing fifteen tonnes of pine-apple pulp, exported by a company called Exportadora de Frutas del Pacifico, in Cali. I did some quick checks and found out that the export company was not registered as a business, nor was it registered for tax, and did not seem to have a telephone number. Further checks showed that the firm's Cali address was a one-room apartment; not very credible for an international exporter of fruit. Maribel's information was looking good. I passed it on to Poddy, my desk officer in London, and he coordinated action for when the ship arrived.

Several weeks later, on November 1, the *Humboldt Express* berthed in Rotterdam. Several of the containers discharged from it were subject to a low-key and ostensibly routine inspection by Dutch Customs. The one identified by Maribel was among them. It was found to contain no less than twelve tonnes of marijuana. While it was infa-mous for cocaine, Colombia also exported huge quantities of its own, highly regarded strain of herbal cannabis. Twelve tonnes was a massive amount, and I was ecstatic. What a first result!

I was so pleased that I emphasised to London that we needed to get a reward to my new source very quickly, in order to reassure her. The process of applying for rewards was tediously slow and normally took several months. Not this time. I told CI Maribel of the seizure a few days afterwards, and within a month was meeting her for the first time and paying her a considerable sum of money, around six months' salary for the average Colombian. I hoped that our discreet handling of the information, plus the quick and generous reward, would lead to further intelligence. Sure enough, within a few weeks Maribel not only came back to me with more, but also introduced a friend, 'Patricia', as another informant.

In January 1995, CI Patricia passed on details of another container of pineapple pulp, again destined for Holland, on the vessel *Isla de la Plata*. The exporter was another Cali-based company, Lufa del Pacifico, and again the shipment was marijuana. My checks again showed that the company was not registered and was probably fictitious. Such was the confidence of the Colombian narcos that they made no effort whatsoever to conceal the drugs; they were simply stuffed into the container. When Dutch Customs opened the doors to look inside upon its arrival in Holland, it was packed with marijuana from top to bottom. This time it was twenty tonnes, one of the biggest seizures in Europe ever, with not a single pineapple as cover. Such audacity demonstrated that the cartels had no fear or expectation that anyone might open and search the container.

I was on a roll. Within weeks another new informant, CI Emilio, contacted me. Emilio was a very cool guy in his early thirties, who dressed elegantly in a sharp Italian suit, a white designer shirt open at the neck, and crocodile-skin shoes. He passed as a wealthy young executive, lived in a smart, middle-class area of northern Bogotá, and had business contacts with former members of the Medellin Cartel. Emilio gave me details of a container that had been shipped by powerful Medellin traffickers to a customer in the UK. It was supposed to contain a legitimate consignment of *hierbas* – herbs – and Emilio told me it did indeed contain herbs, but strictly illegal ones. I passed the intel to Poddy, and when the container arrived in Felixstowe on March 29 it was watched, then searched. Eight tonnes of herbal cannabis were inside. The British customers got away, but would be investigated and caught at a later date.

Then yet another new informant came forward and told me about a container on board the same ship as the first seizure, *Humboldt Express*. It led to another great result: more than twenty tonnes of marijuana, seized this time in Belgium. Again, the container was packed full of drugs, from floor to ceiling, without any attempt to hide it. From my first four informants, more than sixty tonnes of marijuana had been seized from four containers in the space of just a few months.

These early discoveries taught me several things. Firstly, the traffickers were so confident of guaranteed safe passage through the Colombian ports that they were sending huge consignments to Europe without making any effort to hide them. Secondly, the informants had told me only about marijuana, not cocaine. I assumed that this was because it was less dangerous, and the owners were perhaps less murderous than those of large cocaine shipments. Thirdly, it taught me that my plan could work, and that it was possible to recruit informers in the ports. It was just a question of getting my message to the right people.

However, I knew that my scatter-gun approach of spreading the word was high-risk. I needed to be more focused, to take time to identify specific individuals who were well-placed to give me the best information. Then I would have to find a way to contact them and gain their trust before making my pitch.

IN MY EARLY EFFORTS to recruit, I had some spectacular and dangerous failures. I approached one major shipping agency in Bogotá which had offices in all the main ports. I had analysed exports to the UK and knew that this agency handled a large volume of containers going out. They would certainly know their regular, legitimate customers and could easily spot the suspicious ones. I arranged a meeting with the managing director by playing my 'First Secretary at the embassy' card and saying I wanted to discuss their trade to the UK. Had I said I was a drugs liaison officer, he would never have agreed to meet. I went to his office and we chatted for some time about the numbers of containers going to the UK, the main exports, and other pleasantries. It seemed to be going well, so I took the plunge and revealed that I was in fact a HM Customs liaison officer.

He didn't flinch or look concerned, which was encouraging. But when I got down to detail and suggested that he and his staff might pass me information, his tone changed to angry.

'Do you realise that the mafia in Buenaventura and Cartagena kill people when they lose a load of drugs?' he said. 'And one of the first people they suspect of being an informer is always the shipping agent?'

His voice got louder as he became more agitated.

'Two of my employees were murdered during the past year in Buenaventura, and my staff are all living in fear.

They know that this could happen to them, without any warning, at any time. A load of drugs gets seized in Europe and, bang, without any warning, that's it.'

I tried to calm him down and defuse the situation.

'Yes, I understand, believe me. But we work in a very discreet manner and I can assure you that we would not do anything that might put you or your staff at risk.'

That went straight over his head.

'Do you realise that just by being in my office today, by visiting me and speaking with me, you are putting my life at risk and the lives of all my staff? If a drugs seizure takes place in the coming weeks and word got out that you had been in my office, me and my staff might be suspected as informers and be killed.'

It was no use. I had blown it.

He finished by saying, in a loud voice so that his staff in the next room could hear, 'Please get out of my office, and never come back here or talk to me or my staff again.' Before he had even finished speaking, he was on his feet and ushering me towards the door.

It was not one of my most successful recruitment attempts, but I gained some useful pointers on how not to pitch a shipping agent. Through such early mistakes, I realised that I needed to first build trust in people before trying to recruit them. This would require patience. I also needed to think more carefully about motivation. Given the huge dangers of being an informant against the cartels, what would motivate someone to talk to me?

The main factor was, of course, money. Nearly everyone that I would recruit in Colombia did it for money. We paid well, and that compensated for the risks taken. But money was not always the sole reason, and sometimes informants were motivated by other considerations. Some had a hatred of drug traffickers and the violence that they caused, others sought personal revenge for the misfortune of a friend or family member, and others were even prompted by a genuine desire to do good and to help rid their country of the drug cartels.

CI Eddy was a businessman working in the maritime trade in Santa Marta. He was Colombian, lived in Colombia, and was married to a Colombian. But unknown to most people, his great-grandparents had been British, and he yearned to re-establish his ancestral links. He was a huge fan of the Royal family and loved the UK. When I first approached him, he was extremely receptive to the suggestion that he might be an informant for HM Customs. The thought of secretly working for the British government enthralled him. Deep down inside, I think he wanted to be a spy, and I played on this.

Within a few months, Eddy told me about a container of handicrafts that had been shipped from Santa Marta on the vessel *Caribia Express* and was bound for the UK. He had carefully researched the people behind the shipment and was confident that they were traffickers. A customs rummage team was waiting when the ship arrived in Felixstowe, and they found 3.6 tonnes of marijuana inside the container. I assumed that a quick payout for this first seizure would encourage Eddy to give me more, so I immediately applied for a reward and had it approved by London.

A few weeks later, I flew to Santa Marta and met Eddy in the Hotel Irotama. But when I told him that we would pay him for the result, he seemed displeased.

'What's the matter?' I asked. 'Is everything OK? Were you expecting more than the figure I've mentioned?'

'Tom,' he said wearily. 'I must tell you that you have upset me. I feel deeply offended by what you've just said.'

I was thrown. 'Eddy, I don't understand. I'm sorry if I have offended you. You put yourself at risk to pass me this information, so I assumed that you would welcome some payment in return. It was a fantastic result, and HM Customs are happy to pay you a reward for it.'

'Tom, I am not doing this for financial gain, and I don't want your money. I'm happy to help you get information about drug trafficking because it is the right thing to do. And because I want to help the British Government in its fight against drugs. It is very kind of Customs to offer me money, but I will never accept money from you.'

His reaction was so strong that I feared that I had completely undone the recruitment. I was gobsmacked. It was the only time I ever had to return reward money to London saying that the CI didn't want it.

Eddy continued to work with us and provided useful material over the following years, but he would never take payment. The only benefit that he ever accepted was an invitation to a gala event at the British ambassador's residence in Bogotá, where he enthusiastically mingled with the diplomats and visiting dignitaries.

In only one other case was I completely surprised by the motivations of an informant. It took me more than six months to recruit CI Fidel. I didn't know him at first, didn't even know his name, but I had identified that a certain person who held a senior position within a specific shipping company in Cartagena must be well-placed to spot suspect containers, and set about finding the person who had this role. Then I looked for an opportunity to meet him. I obtained his name through another contact, telephoned him one day and asked if we could meet. Then slowly, over several months, meetings and lunches, I managed to win his friendship.

He was a nice guy, a family man with children who held strong Christian values. To begin with we talked not only about shipping but about family, work, sport and other things we had in common, and I worked hard to earn his trust, as well as to understand what might motivate him to subdue any possible fear and work with me. Overcoming fear was always my biggest hurdle. Everyone working in the ports lived under a cloud of terror. Whenever drugs were seized, people were killed. Sadly it was often the wrong people, innocents who just happened to be on the margins. I knew that in order to convince someone to work with me, I would have to breach this barrier.

Over a casual lunch one day, I found out what might motivate Fidel. His company shipped containers of bananas and other produce to Europe. Traffickers frequently hid drugs inside legitimate containers of his clients' goods, or inside the refrigeration units of the banana containers. Occasionally the drugs were found, and several of his containers had been seized during the past year in Belgium. Fidel explained that the Belgian Police or Customs not only confiscated the drugs but also impounded the legitimate cargo and the container itself. Because of lengthy legal proceedings, it sometimes took more than a year before they released the container. By then the cargo was rotten and he had to pay for its disposal. Even worse, the container had often rusted and was not fit for use. Refrigerated containers were very expensive, and these incidents were causing considerable financial damage to his company. It lost valuable containers and incurred expensive legal fees in having lengthy disputes with the Belgian authorities.

I asked what he would like to see happen differently.

'I wish the Belgians would just take the drugs, and not my bloody containers!' he said.

I told Fidel that if we worked together I could solve his problem. I proposed that in future, if he notified me of suspect containers going to Europe, I would ensure that the authorities would seize only any drugs they found, and would release the company's legitimate cargo and container immediately. I assured him that furthermore we would act discreetly and no-one would ever know of his involvement. Fidel was very interested.

Several weeks later, he passed me his first tip-off about a container going to Belgium. When Poddy gave the details to the police in Antwerp, he stressed how important it was that they took out only the drugs. Poddy could not explain why, but said that if they did this we would be able to provide them with more information about shipments in future.

The Belgians examined the container and found twenty tonnes of marijuana inside. As requested, they left the container, and it was released back to the shipping company within days. CI Fidel was delighted. He became a long-term and reliable informant, secretly giving us many large seizures over the next five years, totalling more than a tonne of cocaine and sixty tonnes of marijuana. To put this into perspective, that would surpass the entire amount seized in the whole of the UK in 1995 – and all from a single informant. Just as importantly, more than seventy-four traffickers were arrested and numerous criminal organisations in Europe dismantled because of Fidel's intelligence.

I applied this same slow, targeted approach to recruitment over the following two years: first identifying people in key positions, carefully selecting the ones who would have access to information, then approaching them, befriending them, winning their confidence, working out what might motivate them – and then, after many months, making a pitch. It was painfully slow but it reaped unprecedented rewards.

FOLLOWING THE EARLY marijuana seizures, my next breakthrough came via a series of training courses. I needed an excuse to approach and speak to more people working in the ports, such as security staff, customs officers and police. I decided on the idea of offering a series of training courses for these staff in the four main ports, Cartagena, Santa Marta, Barranquilla and Buenaventura. With support from my embassy colleagues, I secured an agreement that the Foreign Office would fund the courses and HM Customs would provide trainers.

Ostensibly we were offering training to the Colombian authorities to help them detect illicit cargoes and improve their security. The real purpose, however, was so that I could spend more time in the ports and meet key staff without attracting attention. We duly arranged a series of two-week courses in each port. The planning for them, as well as the courses themselves, gave me an excellent excuse to talk to the right people. In Cartagena I was even given a port security pass so that I could come and go as I pleased.

The contacts that I made were further developed over the following year by regular visits.

It was always understood by myself and the trainers that the course participants, or at least a large number of them, might be corrupt. That didn't matter too much, as we would not train them in anything advanced or sensitive. The idea was not only to sow seeds amongst the attendees, but also to have them disperse my message to their colleagues. Some I would try to recruit directly myself over the following months. Others passed on the word, and would indirectly generate informants over the following years. My message was simple: British Customs will pay good rewards for information about cocaine shipments to Europe, and we will always work in a discreet manner to protect you. There is no need to be afraid.

The large marijuana seizures continued, and a small but expanding cluster of well-placed informants passed me information about them regularly. Over the next few years our intelligence led to the seizure of over two hundred tonnes of Colombian marijuana, most of it in the UK and Netherlands, worth £800 million at street level. In the first two months of 1996 alone, over twenty tonnes were seized at Felixstowe in two separate containers. This was a British record. Colombian marijuana had been flooding in for several years without being detected, but at last we were seizing a large part of it.

Not every case went to plan though. On one occasion CI Marta said that a container was being shipped to Holland packed with another twenty tonnes of cannabis. She gave me the container number and the exporter, the ship it was on, and said that when it arrived it would be stored in the port for several days, as the importer would not collect it immediately. However, she said that the night after it arrived, criminals would go into the port with a lorry and steal the container. We warned the Dutch. Poddy told them specifically that a criminal mafia working in their port was planning to steal the container, so they should take great care to secure it.

When the container was offloaded on arrival, Dutch Customs opened it and saw that it was indeed packed full of marijuana, just as we had said. From the size of the container and its contents, they estimated that it was about twenty tonnes, again as per our information. But it was already 5 p.m. on a Friday afternoon, and the Dutch officers knew it would take them several hours to unload such a large amount, secure it, and fill in all the paperwork – and their bosses would not be happy about paying them overtime to work late into the evening. So they closed the container, secured the doors with additional seals, and had it stacked high on top of two other containers, so that it could not be reached or tampered with. Then, despite our warnings, they all went home for the weekend.

When Poddy told me, I was furious. 'What? Are they stupid or do they just not believe us?' I responded. But there was nothing we could do.

Monday morning came and the Dutch Customs team turned up for work, ready to offload and formally confiscate twenty tonnes of marijuana.

'Oh Godverdomme, het is weg!' a senior customs officer shouted, breaking into a run as he approached the area where they had left the container. 'Oh Goddamn, it's gone! Where the hell is it?'

Surprise, surprise, the container was gone. The team frantically searched the rows of giant metal boxes, hundreds of them stacked three high, in the vain hope that it had been lifted onto another stack. They also checked the port IT systems but found no record of the container being moved. It had vanished.

How does someone make a twenty-foot shipping container, weighing twenty-five tonnes, disappear when it is stacked six metres high on top of others? Especially from a modern port with security guards patrolling, and security cameras watching, and security guards at the exit checking every lorry? Well, that's the port mafias for you. They can make things disappear just like magic, especially when those things are high-value goods or drugs. They bribe security guards, hack into IT systems, alter customs declarations and take what they want. Over the weekend, the container had been loaded onto a lorry and stolen, just as Marta had said would happen and just as we had warned them. That is the power of money and corruption. And it was happening almost every day in the ports of Rotterdam, Amsterdam and Antwerp, the biggest gateways for drugs into Europe.

I had come to Bogotá to disrupt cocaine trafficking but had not appreciated the importance and scale of Colombia's marijuana trade. During the 1970s and 1980s, it was the main supplier of marijuana to the USA and much of Europe. Santa Marta Gold was a variety grown on the slopes of Colombia's Sierra Nevada, a mountain range near Santa Marta. It has a sweet, intense aroma and a powerful psychedelic effect, and gained its reputation as a top-quality marijuana much preferred by discerning users. The early cocaine traffickers, such as Pablo Escobar and the Orejuela brothers, had started out by trafficking marijuana to the USA, before realising that the profit margins on cocaine were much higher. But throughout the 1990s and into the millennium, Colombia continued to cultivate and export many hundreds of tonnes of marijuana. Shipments to the USA diminished as the latter started to cultivate its own and eventually became self-sufficient, but it continued to export huge volumes to Europe.

I was a bit disappointed that the early seizures had mostly been marijuana and not cocaine. But I had recruited half a dozen informants in my first twelve months and that was a good start. By the following year we would have over twenty sources in all the main container ports, plus the coal ports and banana ports, and the flow of intelligence about shipments of cocaine to Europe would reach hitherto unparalleled levels.

4

THE CARTAGENA RIP-ON MAFIA

I VISITED CARTAGENA FOR the first time in May 1994 and fell immediately in love with the place. My Avianca flight from Bogotá flew over the city before heading out to sea and then circling back in a wide arc to land at the airport, and from my window seat I could see the large Bay of Cartagena, with the island of Tierra Bomba on one side and the industrial areas and mangrove islands on the other. Dozens of boats dotted the bay, some with short white tails trailing behind to show that they were moving, others at anchor. The modern Boca Grande area protruded like a long finger, with high-rise apartment blocks and palm trees lining the yellow-white beaches. As we flew over the main container port, I could see cranes moving, lifting little boxes coloured red, blue, white and yellow onto ships berthed in the docks below. It was beautiful. I felt a rush of excitement, intermingled with apprehension about what lay ahead.

I was about to arrive in one of the biggest cocaine shipment ports in South America. I would be there alone, in an unfamiliar place, with the aim of recruiting informants. And I would be starting from scratch, with no-one to help or back me up. It was a strange feeling, and I was uneasy.

I would fly to Cartagena scores of times over the coming years, but the view from the aircraft as it flies over the city would never cease to give me a buzz of excitement. Cartagena is an amazing city. It exudes a certain mystique, a sense of legend and romance, but with a dark undercurrent of danger. On the surface it is the jewel of Colombia's Caribbean coastline, with spectacular sandy beaches, tropical climate, and an awe-inspiring historic centre. Beneath the veneer lies a murky criminal world run by drug cartels, who rule what is the world's biggest cocaine gateway by corruption and fear. I would come to understand the darker side of Cartagena, and the workings of its underworld.

Cartagena de Indias is one of the oldest and most picturesque ports in South America. It lies at the mouth of a large natural bay that opens out into the Caribbean Sea, with stone fortresses guarding the entrance. The historic centre of the old town is a network of narrow cobbled streets and colourful colonial buildings, enclosed securely within thick walls of grey stone, with cannon batteries pointing outward to defend against marauding pirate ships. Cartagena was founded by the Spanish conquistador Pedro de Heredia, who arrived in 1533 with three ships and a force of just 150 men and twenty-two horses to conquer the New World that we now know as Colombia. Earlier attempts by the Spanish to settle here had been defeated by the ferocious Caribe natives, who occupied the coastal area, but Heredia had a cunning plan. He brought with him a local Caribe girl called Catalina. She had been abducted by a Spanish raiding party about twenty years earlier and carried off to Santo Domingo, where she was taught Spanish and converted to Christianity. Heredia used her as his ambassador to communicate with the Caribe tribesmen. She persuaded them that the Spanish wished them no harm, and would bring them great wealth. Heredia's plan worked, and through his diplomatic use of Catalina he was able to avoid fighting the Caribe and gain their support. With their help, Cartagena was established, and flourished into a bustling trading port. Within a few years it was the gateway to South America and the main port from which Spanish conquistadors shipped their treasures back to Spain. Great fleets of Spanish galleons came, bringing supplies from Europe and slaves from Africa, and taking away the gold that the Spanish plundered from the Incas and indigenous tribes of what is today Peru, Ecuador and Colombia.

During its early years, Cartagena was plagued by British and French pirates who repeatedly attacked the town, eager to capture its treasures and gold. The most famous of these was Sir Francis Drake, who arrived off Cartagena in 1586 with a force of twenty-three ships and 3,000 fighting men. Drake captured Cartagena after a fierce battle, plundered the town, and demanded a further ransom of 107,000 gold ducats from Spain before he would leave. Whilst English history books depict Drake as a great national hero, Colombian and Spanish students are taught, perhaps more accurately, that he was a greedy, bloodthirsty mercenary. It was because of these continuous pirate raids that the Spanish set about constructing an impressive system of fortresses, linked by thick walls and hidden tunnels, to protect the town. The entrance to the bay was also protected by fortresses and cannon emplacements, and hidden chains that could be drawn to trap attacking ships. When Admiral Vernon returned in 1741 with a huge armada of 124 English warships and 27,600 men, he was unable to capture Cartagena, and after a long, bloody siege he was obliged to return to England in shame, with his forces decimated.

When I arrived in 1994, some 408 years after Drake and 253 years after Vernon's failed invasion, Cartagena was still a lovely place. It was much bigger, of course, and a modern tourist resort had built up along the palm-lined shores of Boca Grande to the west. Luxurious hotels and apartments lined the beaches to accommodate the wealthy American and Canadian tourists who flocked there each winter. But the old town remained the same as I imagined it would have been hundreds of years before, frozen in time: a network of narrow streets with quaint courtyards and squares, lined by Spanish colonial houses painted in bright pastels and decorated with flowers. The old headquarters of the Spanish Inquisition were still intact, with deep cellars and torture chambers to make a visitor's skin shiver. The charm and colour of the streets was breathtaking, the buildings edged with elaborate wooden balconies draped with heavily scented bougainvillea, hibiscus and a mass of other tropical flowers with unknown names. It was a romantic haven of history, all safely enshrined inside thick stone walls.

The old port was too shallow for modern ships, and a large new port had been constructed further along the bay, with three separate container terminals to accommodate the daily flow of ships. Cartagena retained its status as the most important port in South America, but for different reasons. No longer famous for its galleons of Spanish gold, it was now important for another more highly valued cargo: cocaine. Cartagena had become the main port in South America from which the drug cartels shipped their 'white gold' to the USA and Europe.

COLOMBIAN CUSTOMS OFFICERS claim to check roughly one in every ten containers exported from their shores. When these same containers arrive in Europe, it is possible to search only a small percentage more, due to the sheer volume passing through. So officers at both ends need to prioritise. Automated profiling techniques are used to identify those deemed of the highest risk, for example where the exporter or importer is new, previously unknown or suspect. Traffickers are aware of these selection criteria and take measures to use containers that will not be chosen for search. The 'rip-on' technique is a well-organised system that involves concealing drugs inside legitimate containers without the owner's knowledge. It is one of the most effective methods used to send large consignments of drugs from South America to Europe.

When a trafficking group wants to ship cocaine, the rip-on organisation is contracted to arrange safe transit from the port of exit and safe delivery through customs controls at the port of destination. For this service, they charge a large fee. In Cartagena it worked as follows:

a. A corrupt employee, often working for a customs agency or port authority, was paid to identify a suitable container being shipped to the desired destination in the weeks ahead. The container had to be from a reputable exporter and consigned to a well-known, reputable importer, which would ensure that it passed all customs profiling and would not be examined on either departure or arrival. The corrupt employee provided details of the container and the type and serial number of the unique seals on its doors. (Seals are put on the doors when loaded to guarantee that the container has not been opened or interfered with.)

b. A local counterfeit specialist was paid to manufacture two duplicate counterfeit seals for each seal on the container.

c. The container would arrive in Cartagena a few days before the ship was due to load. The mafia would secretly bring the cocaine into the port area. This normally involved the participation of corrupt port workers, security guards and sometimes police.

d. On the night before departure, the workers cut the container seals, opened the doors and put the cocaine inside. The coke was normally in holdalls or canvas bags to make it easier to carry on and off. A set of duplicate seals were also put inside the container, for use by the rip-off team when it arrived. Port security were bribed to be absent at the time of the rip-on, or to turn a blind eye, and security cameras were disabled if necessary.

e. The container doors were closed and re-sealed with the duplicate seals. This completed the rip-on.

f. On arrival at destination in Europe, the rip-off team, normally port workers or corrupt police, would open the container, remove the coke and re-seal the doors with the duplicate seals left inside by the rip-on team. This was the rip-off. The drugs were then brought out of the secure port area by dockers, port security or others.

In such a scenario, the legitimate exporter and importer are never aware that their container has been used to carry drugs. Anyone checking the container at either end will see that the seals are intact and all appears to be in order. It is almost impossible for customs or the police to detect shipments sent by rip-on unless they have specific information from an informant. But to rip-on large quantities of cocaine into containers for Europe requires participation by a number of people, in strict sequence and all depending on each other. It also requires excellent communication and the organisation and coordination of people at both ends.

Considering the complex process involved, I looked for the vulnerable spots where it might be possible to recruit informants in Cartagena to infiltrate the rip-on organisations. I decided that security staff were probably the weakest link in the chain. I reckoned that they would play only a minor role in the process, perhaps just making themselves scarce at specific times when the rip-on was happening, and so would be less worried about self-incrimination if I approached them. I therefore tried to get close to security staff in the port to recruit them, but failed. Many months later I found out why. The port security staff did not just play a minor role, as I had thought, but were often the main organisers, and were key figures in the port mafia.

CI Mike was the first to infiltrate part of the group in late 1995 and to tell me how the rip-ons worked. He explained that the rip-on mafia in Cartagena port was an extremely powerful organisation that had corrupt police, port security and dockworkers on its books. They were shipping hundreds of kilos of cocaine each month to Europe, had successfully transported tonnes during the previous two years, and had never lost a single consignment. A highly efficient, well-oiled machine, it was one of the Cali Cartel's primary supply routes to its European customers.

Over the following months, CI Mike tried to infiltrate further, to identify the corrupt officials who were involved, and to pinpoint specific shipments. According to Mike, the rip-ons were organised for 'Chupeta', the alias of Juan Carlos Ramirez Abadia, a senior member of the Cali Cartel. Chupeta's main transport man on the north coast was a guy known as Willy, who came from Barranquilla. Willy arranged the rip-on with the head of port security in Cartagena, who in turn worked in coordination with a corrupt ANP officer. Between them they controlled the rip-on mafia within the port. They were paid huge sums to arrange safe shipments of 2–300 kg of cocaine at a time. Sometimes the drugs were even brought into the port area by the ANP in an official police vehicle.

I did not know for certain whether Mike's information was correct, but I did know the head of port security. I had met him many times, particularly when I arranged training courses. He had been helpful in facilitating the courses and had given me total access to the port. To all appearances, he was an honest man who cooperated with me and the authorities. But in addition to Mike's information, I had received separate intelligence that he was corrupt. Running the security in a Colombian port in the 1990s was an extremely dangerous job. It was like being the only sheriff in a Wild West town full of outlaws and gunslingers. To uphold the law rigorously would surely mean certain death, and then the town would be left without a sheriff and with no protection. If anyone in Cartagena port tried to stop the Cali Cartel and others from exporting cocaine, or became a serious impediment to their business, they would be killed. Surely the head of security would have been offered the bribe or the bullet? Surely he must have to cooperate, or at least turn a blind eye, in order to stay alive?

As I saw it, he may have been wholly corrupt, as some said, or partially so, or he might have been shrewdly pretending to be corrupt in order to keep himself alive and do his job. He may have been focussing on the top priority areas of his role, such as protecting cargo from theft and ensuring the physical security of the port installations, and perhaps ignored some other activities. Or indeed, he might have chosen the dangerous path of playing for both sides. Either way, over the next three years the head of security was helpful and collaborative, or at least pretended to be, and I pretended to believe that he was working for the right side. As with many people who I worked with in Colombia, there was always a huge doubt in my mind about whether he was genuine or fake, and I could never be sure which side he was really batting for. Like most of the people I had to work with, I could never trust him.

Over the following twelve months, CI Mike told me about five separate rip-on shipments to Europe. Each one was for 2–300kg. He continued to say that corrupt security and police were in charge of the process and arranged everything. He would give me the name of the ship, the date of departure, destination, and quantity of cocaine that had been loaded, but he could never get close enough to give me the container number. Each ship carried hundreds of containers, and without the number I could not do anything. Consequently, we were unable to stop any of them. It was immensely frustrating to hear about the constant flow of cocaine and yet not be able to seize any drugs.

It was not until a new source came forward, CI Barry, that we would truly penetrate the rip-on organisation. Barry was introduced to me by a police contact. He worked in the port and was willing to trade information for money. Barry had excellent access and was right in the thick of it. He seemed reliable and was easy to handle, insofar as he followed instructions and was calm and professional. Barry corroborated exactly what CI Mike had previously reported: he told me that the Cartagena rip-on mafia was a very powerful group that had been sending two or three shipments a month to Europe for the past two years. Each was between 200 and 300 kg. The rip-ons were organised by port security and police, and were mostly destined for Holland, from where much of the drugs went to the UK.

CI Barry told me that he could identify the next shipment, but he was scared. Given that the mafia had not lost a single load in two years, if we started seizing them they would immediately suspect an informant and go looking for him. I reassured him that we would take great care not to give any impression that the information had come from Colombia. He said he would trust me and see how the first one went.

In October 1996, Barry informed me that the vessel *Capitan Vilano* had sailed from Cartagena, and that just before it left a large quantity of cocaine had been ripped-on to a container of cocoa destined for Holland. He gave very detailed information, including the container number. When the container arrived in Rotterdam on 29 October, we arranged for Dutch Customs to carry out a 'routine' search as soon as it was offloaded, before any dock workers could get access to it. The Dutch found 300 kg of cocaine in holdalls just inside the doors of the container. This was the first rip-on success, and the breakthrough we had waited for.

Two weeks later, CI Mike reported that the container ship *Sierra Express* had just left Cartagena and that about 300 kg had been ripped-on to a container. As usual, he was not able to give enough detail to identify which container, so we could not act. However, Barry called me the following day with more detail: he said that the *Sierra Express* had 200 kg just inside the doors of a container of cocoa butter, again going to Holland. Although he did not know the container number, this was enough for us to work on. Discreet checks of the ship's manifest showed that there were two containers of cocoa butter on board, both for the same Dutch importer. However, Barry was scared about how the cartel would react if this second shipment was seized. I promised him that we would handle it discreetly.

The Dutch did a great job. When the *Sierra Express* arrived in Amsterdam, on 1 December, they identified the two suspect containers and watched them being offloaded, but did not go near or search them. Instead, covert customs staff observed from afar and waited. Later that day, they saw two dock workers approach one of the containers under cover of darkness, open it and remove bags. The dockers then closed the container doors, put fresh seals on them so that no one would know that they had been opened, put the bags into a vehicle and drove away. A short time later, as the vehicle came to leave the port, a security patrol challenged them and asked to do a routine search of the vehicle. The bags were found to contain 250 kg of cocaine. I was very pleased when I heard how the Dutch had handled it. Not only had they seized the drugs and arrested the Dutch rip-off team, but they had done it in a manner that would minimise risk to my informant. It was a fantastic result.

The owners of the cocaine, and the Cartagena rip-on group, were furious. Having never had a problem in the previous two years, they had now lost two successive consignments, worth around £80 million at street value. The cartel knew beyond doubt that they had a problem, but had no idea whether it was in Holland or Colombia. Nor did they know whether they had an informant in their midst, or whether the police in either country might have an investigation underway and might be tapping their telephones, or those of their customers in Europe. My sources told me that the cartel was in disarray and had ordered the suspension of all further rip-on shipments from Cartagena until they could resolve the problem. In the meantime, they had tasked their own informants within the police and intelligence services to find out where the leak was coming from – and to eliminate it. This was a very dangerous situation for us all, but especially for Barry and Mike. If the cartel discovered that they were behind the seizures they would be in grave danger, as would I.

Over the following two months, I kept contact with informants to a minimum. When we did need to speak, we took care to use only 'clean' telephones and employed counter-surveillance and tradecraft that had been agreed in advance. By January my sources reported that the rip-on activity was still suspended but that there was great pressure to start up again. The Cali suppliers had customers in Europe and USA who needed re-supplying after the Christmas holiday period, and if the organisation did not re-open the system through Cartagena, the Cali men would use other routes.

In February 1997, I received word from Barry that the rip-ons had started again. The *Sierra Express* had just left for Europe with another 300 kg in one of the containers on board. From the details he gave me, our freight analysts in London were able to identify the container in question, and the Dutch were waiting for it when it arrived. On 26 February, the *Sierra Express* reached Rotterdam, and once again the Dutch mounted covert surveillance based on our advance intelligence. Later that night, police officers watched as dock workers stealthily opened the container doors, took out bags and loaded them into a vehicle. The vehicle was followed and the police later arrested four members of the rip-off group and seized the coke they had removed. This was another massive blow to the cartel in Colombia.

I knew that there would be a violent reaction to the loss of a further 300 kg and the arrest of their rip-off team. I intended to again limit contact with Barry until the heat was off and things calmed down. But just one day after the seizure, I received a pager message from him.

'Urgent. I need to speak.'

I sent a message back and gave him a clean, previously unused mobile number to call. The phone rang a few minutes later.

'Señor, I need to meet you in person. There is something very big about to happen.'

'I can't come to Cartagena my friend, I am too busy. In any case, it's far too dangerous for us to be seen together at the moment. What's it about?'

The line was silent for a short while. He was not expecting a negative response.

'Señor, you must come. We have to meet face-to-face. I can't tell you about this by telephone, it is far too dangerous. This is big, much bigger than the other ones that we have seized. I can get you all the details, but I need to speak to you first about what the mafia will do if we seize it, and my safety. And we need to meet quickly, because the shipment is already on its way.'

Meeting an informant face-to-face so soon after a big seizure was not a good idea. I knew that the cartel was actively trying to identify the mole, and if we were seen together both of us would be in great danger. There was always a risk that Barry or I could already be under surveillance by either the transport group or by the suppliers in Cali or the North Valley. I also had to consider the possibility that Barry might have already been caught. Whilst unlikely, it was possible that under interrogation, or torture, or to save the lives of his wife and children, Barry had told them that I was responsible for their recent shipments going down. He could be luring me into a trap, to be captured by hitmen on Cali's payroll.

All of these possibilities had to be considered. I had to balance the risks of meeting him against the chance of getting important information about a big shipment, and against the need to maintain his trust. He had said it was urgent, and he desperately wanted to meet me. If I declined, it would damage his faith in me. So I agreed to meet. But I told him that we must both follow strict arrangements. I would also bring him to Bogotá, where I had more control and back-up in case of a problem.

On 28 February, Barry slipped away from home in the early hours and flew from Cartagena to Bogotá. Once in the capital, he followed a pre-agreed route that I had given him months in advance, specifically for just such a high-risk meeting. All along the route, Steve and I observed from hidden vantage points to make sure that he was alone and not being followed. Then, and only when we felt sure that there was no team following, did we pick him up in a car and take him to a safe apartment to talk.

Barry was nervous but also excited. He explained that Cali traffickers had brought two tonnes of cocaine to Cartagena a few weeks earlier for shipment to Miami. It was to be sent in two separate lots. Two days earlier, on 26 February, the *FLS Colombia* had set sail from the El Bosque container jetty in Cartagena. It was taking about eighty containers to Miami, and among them was a legitimate consignment of ceramic toilets and sanitary ware. Barry said that as much as a tonne of coke had been ripped-on and secretly put inside the container of ceramics on the night before the ship left. If it went through successfully, the rest would be sent by the same method over the coming weeks. But this was a race against time, as the vessel would probably arrive in Miami within the next thirty-six hours.

'But, señor,' said Barry at the end, 'please tell US Customs to act discreetly, and not go straight to that one container. Please get them to search many containers or do some kind of exercise. Otherwise the mafia will know straight away that there is an informant.' After a pause, he added, 'Even then, I think that after this seizure there will be some blood-letting in Cartagena.'

Within an hour of the meeting, I passed the information to Martin, our DLO in Miami, who coordinated action with US Customs. Martin urged them to be discreet and make any search appear routine, but when the FLS Colombia arrived in Miami, on 3 March, they had to act quickly to find the dirty container before any team could remove the drugs. A narcotics dog was taken on board the ship when it berthed and before it started unloading, for a 'routine' sniff around the ship and its containers. Fortunately it detected the scent of cocaine on a container from Colombia, although I'm not sure whether the dog really did find the smell or whether it was prompted by a discreet nudge from its handler. Either way, on the excuse of the dog's indication, US Customs searched that container and several others in the same area as soon as they were offloaded. Inside, along with the legitimate cargo of ceramic toilets and wash basins, there were dozens of hessian sacks which, when cut open, were found to contain just over 1,450 kg of pure cocaine. This was worth about $200 million at street value in the USA. It was the biggest rip-on cargo so far detected.

The combined seizures in Holland and Miami, within just days of each other, had a devastating impact on the rip-on organisation in Cartagena. Having shipped cocaine successfully for over two years without a single consignment being seized, they had now suffered five big seizures in six months. They had to compensate the suppliers for the lost shipments, which would involve paying many millions of dollars. More importantly, they had lost all credibility with their customers and could no longer offer secure, guaranteed transit via Cartagena.

It was a great feeling to know that we had caused such a massive loss to the traffickers. We had disrupted their system and stopped the flow of cocaine from one of the most important ports. Rip-ons were again suspended from Cartagena, and the cartels turned to other routes. But I knew that they would now be even more determined to hunt down the source of the problem. Until then, they had not known for certain whether the earlier seizures had been caused by leaks in Holland or in Colombia. Now there was no doubt whatsoever that the source of the problem lay at their end. The Miami seizure proved beyond any doubt that there was an informant, or informants, within their midst in Cartagena. And I knew that the mafia would stop at nothing until they hunted down the culprits and eliminated them. This would mean a period of huge danger for us all.

5

TRADECRAFT

B EFORE I WENT to Colombia I knew that the drug cartels were murderous and that personal security would have to be taken seriously. I received comprehensive intelligence briefings prior to taking up the post, not only from HM Customs but also from the US authorities and British intelligence services, about the capabilities of the Cali Cartel. Their power at that time was incredible – and terrifying. It was hard to comprehend how a criminal organisation could have developed such advanced and sophisticated intelligence systems, far better than those of any government in South America, in fact better than those of many European countries. They had developed large networks of corrupt officials within the Drugs Police (DIRAN), the Security Service (DAS) and other government agencies, who passed them intelligence about operations against them. These corrupt officials also informed about the activities of the DEA and other foreign agencies, such as the British DLOs. The cartel also paid corrupt prosecutors, judges and court officials to ensure that any prosecutions against cartel members failed. Even if arrested, the major traffickers were nearly always freed because flaws were found in the prosecution or important evidence went missing.

This corruption went to the very highest levels. Even senior managers of DIRAN and DAS were corrupted, as were many politicians and government ministers. The Cali Cartel had made large donations to political parties and election campaigns in order to buy favour, and they called in these favours when needed. The cartel had developed a powerful and effective counter-intelligence capability. They paid thousands of people such as taxi drivers, airport staff and hotel employees, to inform them about the movements of anyone involved in the fight against drugs trafficking. If the British DLOs, the DEA, or senior DAS and DIRAN officers travelled to Cali or Buenaventura, for example, the cartel would know about it, and would arrange surveillance to monitor what they were up to. If an investigation was commenced against them they would detect it and thwart it at the outset.

The cartel also had their own teams of intelligence experts to monitor official communications. Sophisticated IT systems had been set up so that the radio and telephone communications of the police and DAS were monitored. The scale of this was subsequently proven in late 1995 when the Colombian Police raided a modern office building in Cali. Inside, they found a huge $1.5 million IBM mainframe computer, networked to dozens of terminals manned by workers who monitored intercepted calls around the clock. The system contained the telephone numbers of DAS, police and Interpol officers involved in anti-narcotics work. They also had the details of the DEA, foreign embassies and overseas liaison officers working in Colombia, including not just office numbers but also mobile and home numbers.

The mainframe was linked to the Cali and Bogotá telephone systems, and by using state-of-the-art bulk data analytical tools they could identify any telephone calls to law enforcement agencies or the authorities. This incredible, multi-million-dollar intelligence system had been designed and set up by the Cali Cartel purely for their internal security and to identify informants and traitors. Whenever they lost a large drug shipment, they would conduct an internal investigation to identify who was to blame. If they identified the culprit, or an informant, they almost always killed them. Even if there was no specific evidence and they merely suspected certain people, they took the view that it was better to be safe than sorry, and would eliminate them all. Following large seizures in the USA or Europe, it was not unusual to read a week or so later of several people being murdered in Buenaventura, Cartagena or wherever the cargo had originated.

Once traitors were identified by the cartel, the terrible violence of their response was shocking. Suspected informants were brutally tortured and interrogated, often over several days, to find out what they had divulged to the authorities and to assess the damage. They would then be gruesomely murdered and their bodies dumped. For more serious traitors, the cartel unleashed a level of violence that was hard for any civilised person to comprehend, sometimes killing wives, children and even entire families, often in unspeakable ways.

One example of their reaction after a drug seizure sticks in my mind not only because of their ruthlessness but also because of the precise, almost military efficiency with which it was carried out. Approximately 100 kg of cocaine had been found at Bogotá Airport inside cargo that was about to be flown to Spain by Iberia Airlines. It was the result of an investigation led by DAS. In the days after the seizure all was quiet, while the mafia investigated who might be to blame. Then, four days later, five people who worked at the airport were simultaneously executed in different parts of Bogotá. The mafia had verified who was responsible for the seizure, then punished them to send a clear warning to others. They sent a team of *sicarios* on motorcycles and murdered all of those who they suspected might be responsible: a senior member of DAS at the airport, an Iberia employee, cargo handlers and others. All died on the same morning as they left their respective homes for work. Two were walking their children to school when they were gunned down, another was at a bus stop and the others were leaving their homes. It sent a shock wave of terror through the airport community and had the desired effect; the flow of information stopped.

Another example was the case of Victor Patiño Fomeque, a former police officer who left the force to work his way up to a senior rank in the Cali Cartel. He finally ran the security for their maritime operations. Patiño was arrested in 1995, and several years later was extradited to the USA, where he offered to cooperate with the DEA in return for a lighter sentence and safety for his wife and children. He gave the Americans a wealth of information about the Cali and North Valley cartels, their transport and distribution networks, and their property assets. He also gave evidence in US court proceedings against senior leaders. In revenge, they ordered their *sicarios* to execute Patiño's entire extended family in Colombia, and slaughtered more than thirty-five of his relatives, including cousins, nephews and nieces, as well as numerous others who had worked with him, such as lawyers, security guards, associates and friends. It was said that over fifty people were killed in total. Victor's half-brother Luis Ocampo Fomeque, his closest associate, was chopped into pieces and his body parts were thrown into the River Cauca. The same fate befell a woman and two children who were with him when he was taken.

PERHAPS THE INCIDENT of the cartel's violence that hit me hardest at a personal level was the murder of Mardoqueo Cuellar Camelo. Mardoqueo was the head of DAS Counter-Intelligence. He was an intelligent, dedicated and energetic senior agent, and a sociable and likeable young man. After graduating from university, he had joined DAS as an agent in 1988, when he was twenty-three years old, and quickly became one of their most well-respected high-fliers. He specialised in intelligence work and was promoted to head of Counter-Intelligence in January 1995, at the age of just thirty. His counter-intelligence teams were the most professional, experienced and trustworthy people in DAS. I had come to have faith in them, and respected their capabilities. We worked with them on some of our biggest and most sensitive cases, those where we needed top quality surveillance and intelligence-gathering work against important targets, by people who were sound. Mardoqueo was a very hands-on, energetic manager, and we worked with him to coordinate top cases.

On the night of Tuesday, 13 June 1995, Mardoqueo was working in the north of Bogotá when his red Chevrolet was intercepted by two vehicles. They blocked him in, one in front and one behind, and forced him to stop. They were clearly professionals: witnesses said that men jumped out and dragged Mardoqueo from his car before he could draw his firearm. He was taken to a rural location near Funza, to the north-west of Bogotá, where, DAS later informed us, he was horribly tortured. Then he was killed.

We had to assume, given his torture, that he had told his captors about the cases DAS were working on, including those with the British DLOs. Mardoqueo had been at my home just a few nights earlier, talking about some of our jobs. He knew where we lived, knew our families, and knew about our most important investigations with DAS against Cali Cartel traffickers. I doubted that he would have given up our personal details, but we had to assume the worst.

On a personal level, it was tremendously upsetting to lose a close colleague. It was particularly distressing because he was such a lovely person, a kind and honest man with a bright future ahead. On a professional level, it meant that we had to carry out a detailed risk assessment of the impact upon our current cases, and upon the security implications for ourselves and our families. London ID offered to immediately re-house us in new apartments, or to bring us back to the UK for a while if we wanted. After talking it over, Dan and I decided that we would continue working as normal, but with increased security arrangements for our wives and families.

My wife, Luisa, did not mind it at first, but she soon came to hate the oppressive feeling of being accompanied everywhere. A team of guards rotated so that a DAS close-protection officer was with her at all times. In addition to this visible bodyguard, a covert back-up team shadowed her from a distance whenever she went out, and tried to spot possible surveillance or threats. The role of this team was to identify any hit team who might be monitoring her movements and then take them out before they could attack. Luisa came to know her close-protection agent well. He was part of a small, elite team of DAS agents who had previously been given training by specialist units in the UK and by the SAS. He stayed in our apartment when she was at home and accompanied her everywhere when she went out. Luisa was a little disappointed, however, that he would never help her when she came from the supermarket struggling to carry heavy bags of groceries.

'Miguel, do you think you could help me carry some of these bags to the car please?' she once asked.

'Sorry, *señora*, I can't do that. My job is to protect you and I need to focus on what is happening all around us and keep my hands free so that I can react quickly. I can't protect you if I am carrying your shopping.'

We maintained this level of security for several months until we felt that the threat was no longer serious. Luisa was relieved when she could return to a normal life without agents closely following her every move. Meanwhile DAS offered a reward of thirty million pesos for information leading to the capture of those responsible for Mardoqueo's death.

BECAUSE OF THE Cali Cartel's ruthlessness in eliminating their opponents, and their sophisticated counter-intelligence systems, it was important that we took measures to protect ourselves and our informants. Tradecraft is the generic name for the various techniques that agents and informant handlers use to avoid being detected. It includes such things as counter-surveillance and the techniques used to meet and communicate securely with others without being caught.

The specialist training I had received before taking up my post had included exercises with the Secret Intelligence Service, more commonly known as MI6, the experts in handling covert sources overseas. This took place at a discreet location on the south coast of England and I found it both useful and very enjoyable. One of the techniques we learned was the dead letterbox – a way to exchange secret messages without physically meeting. An agent discreetly leaves documents, or perhaps a computer disk or USB stick, in a pre-agreed secret hiding place. At a later time or date, the handler collects the item without having to actually meet the source, which is very useful if you are both under surveillance by hostile forces. Real cases have been reported where the dead letterboxes were such things as a hole in a tree, a loose brick in a wall, or more elaborate props such as a fake rock.

The hard bit is to drop off or collect the item without being seen. During training we had tremendous fun practising how to drop and collect messages for each other whilst avoiding detection by surveillance teams intent on spotting us. This is without doubt a useful technique if you are dealing with a nuclear scientist who wants to pass a microchip with details of the next generation bomb. However, it is not much use when you are dealing with a poorly educated Colombian docker who wants to tell you about an impending drug shipment, especially when the docker can't read or write and struggles to follow simple instructions, let alone anything as complex as a dead letterbox routine. More importantly, details of shipments often need to be passed on very quickly, and DLOs need to ask questions to clarify events and the role of the source, so while it was fun to learn, I never made use of the dead-letterbox technique and am not aware of any other DLO having done so.

That apart, the training was excellent preparation. SIS specialists taught us counter-surveillance, agent recruitment and other covert activities. Experts gave additional training in evasive driving and how to react in kidnap situations. We spent a lot of time learning how to carry out counter-surveillance and to check that we were clean before meeting informants. I was not particularly good at this, and knew that it was a weakness. In one exercise I spent hours walking around pre-arranged routes in a town centre, trying to spot possible surveillance on me before meeting a contact in a pub. I had carefully designed the route myself earlier, with several quiet stretches where I could easily see anyone behind me, a few dead-ends where I would double-back on myself, then a detour into a shopping centre, where I could wander up escalators and down lifts, all designed to force any officers following me to 'show out'. After several hours spent cleansing myself in this way, I felt confident that all was clear, and did the meeting. At the debriefing the next morning I felt confident until a group of six complete strangers came into the room. I had never seen any of them before. I was horrified to hear them relate all of my movements of the previous afternoon. They described in great detail every shop that I went into, every person I spoke with or stood close to, my clever switchbacks, and how they saw me then go to a pub to meet someone. Then they produced photographs to back it all up.

It brought it home to me how difficult it is to detect a

well-trained surveillance team, and also how useless I was at this. I had failed to spot a single one of them. Indeed, in all my time working in South America, I only once noticed surveillance on me. I'm sure that I failed to notice it on dozens of other occasions. The one time was in March 1990 and I was based at the embassy in Lima, Peru. I had also been accredited as a diplomat in Argentina, which did not have its own designated liaison officer, so that I could go there to work when needed. When I made my maiden trip to Buenos Aires I was the first DLO to go there since the Falklands War. I decided to travel on a Friday and spend the weekend sightseeing in Buenos Aires before starting work on the Monday. On the Saturday I spent hours just walking around the city, taking in the atmosphere and sights, going in and out of shops. I drank a coffee in the trendy Palermo area and sat there people-watching for a while, took a walk around La Recoleta, and hopped in a taxi to see the colourful La Boca neighbourhood and the old port area.

It was late in the afternoon when I spotted the first one. As I sat with a drink in a café in La Boca, a young man in a green jacket came in and perched himself on a stool at the bar. I recognised him, and knew that I'd seen him earlier in the day. For the first time I realised that I was being followed. I hadn't thought about it properly before and had not been looking out for it. Although I had been declared to the Argentine government as a DLO, there was probably some suspicion that this might be a cover and that I was really a spy. Tensions were still very high after the Falklands. With hindsight, my perfectly innocent excursions in and out of shops and frequent doubling back after accidentally walking up dead-ends had probably fuelled their suspicions and convinced them that I was carrying out counter-surveillance.

From that point onwards, I started looking out for them. When I left the café, I walked up the street and stopped at a kiosk to buy some cigarettes, carefully glancing backwards and across the street to see if anyone stopped. I paused to light a cigarette, and then retraced my steps. I clocked a couple on the far side of the pedestrian walkway as they stopped and pretended to look in a shop window. Over the rest of the day I spotted three or four of them. On Sunday, as I continued my sightseeing, a fresh team followed me. I am probably still recorded somewhere in the archives of the Argentine intelligence service as a suspected British spy.

IN COLOMBIA, DAN and I developed our own tradecraft for use in handling our growing band of informants. It wasn't a game or training exercise in Colombia; the consequences if we got it wrong were stark. Later, when the team grew and Bernie and Steve arrived, we further expanded our methods with more complex routes.

Each confidential informant, or CI, was allocated a code-name, and after the first meeting we never ever used their real names. Before each meet we took elaborate measures to ensure that neither we nor they were followed. We then normally did a vehicle pick-up and took them to a secure place. Each CI was given several 'routines' to follow before we met, and each routine was also known by a codeword. There were short routines for quick meetings when the risk was low, and long ones when there was increased danger, such as after a seizure. Each involved the CI following a set route, during which we would observe from vantage points and confirm that he or she was not being followed. On the telephone I might say, 'Why don't we meet at your sister's place at 2pm?' or, 'Let's have a coffee at 5pm,' or, 'Meet me at the Spanish restaurant.' Each phrase would tell the CI exactly what path to follow and at what time. Dan and I spent many hours in the streets working out multiple routes along which we could check that informants were clean, and earmarking the best observation points and pick-up locations. We also had to think of the weather; it was no use asking a CI to follow a route along open streets in the middle of a torrential downpour. Accordingly, we had a series of dry routes that could be used.

The Santa Barbara Mall was my favourite dry route. It was a large shopping centre in northern Bogotá, with dozens of retail outlets on several levels, a cinema and restaurants. More importantly, it had eight different entrances from streets on all four sides, plus an underground car park with numerous lifts. We had various routines where CIs would start at a café and then follow an agreed route around the shops, moving levels up and down the escalators, while we checked if anyone was following them. They would then take an agreed exit and we'd pick them up in a car. Planning all of the counter-surveillance routes took a huge amount of time, but we knew it was necessary and might one day save an informant's life, or even our own. In later years, the DLOs would have armed back-up teams shadowing them when they met informants. In the early years, however, we met informants alone and with no back-up or protection. I used to joke that my safety lay in sharp wits, good tradecraft – and my ability to run fast.

For meetings, we rented hotel rooms or apartments for the day, wherever possible using venues that had underground parking and entrances so that we could not be watched from outside. Ideally, our meeting places would also afford good escape routes in case we needed to leave quickly. One of my preferred locations was the Condominio Plenitud, on Calle 127, opposite the Unicentro shopping centre. Plenitud was a large gated condo of several hundred apartments, set in its own enclosed grounds. It had a secure subterranean car park and security guards. Once we drove into the car park there was no way that anyone could follow us without being seen, or know which of the two hundred or more apartments we were going to. We used Plenitud when we needed somewhere extremely secure to have a long debrief with a CI.

Knowing that the Cali Cartel had such good intelligence systems, we also had to ensure that when informants contacted us they would not be detected. We gave each one very specific instructions on how to make contact. This was normally by an initial pager message to agree a time, and then a secure call or meeting. Telephone calls with informants were to a clean cellphone, in order to avoid detection by the cartel's call-monitoring systems that were scanning telephone dialling data. Using various contacts, we had purchased several mobile phones in genuine but untraceable names which we registered to the equivalent of PO Box addresses. The phones were never used except when an informant called. Incoming calls were then automatically diverted to other numbers, which in turn automatically diverted to others. In this way, our sources could telephone us without the calls being detected or traced back.

It didn't always go smoothly. I once had to pay a large amount of money to CI Mike. He had just given us a big cocaine seizure and it was a period of high risk, so Steve and I had planned one of the longer routes. I sent Mike a message to meet me for coffee at 1 p.m. Steve and I watched him from different vantage points as he approached the café exactly on time and went inside. We took note of people who went in after him, and looked hard for anyone in the street outside who might have been following and who might now look for somewhere discreet to wait until he came out again. Five minutes later Mike emerged, and we watched as he walked a short route to his car a few blocks away. It all seemed clear. Mike then drove an agreed route to a car park several miles away. I followed at a distance, looking out for any surveillance on him, and Steve followed further behind, looking out for any surveillance on me.

Mike knew that he must park in the underground car park at Santa Barbara, then walk through the basement to the far exit, and I would pick him up as he came out into a side street. As we approached Santa Barbara, everything seemed fine. Then Steve's voice came over the radio.

'You have company behind.'

I had seen the green car behind me, but it had only joined us a few minutes earlier and I couldn't think why Steve might be worried about it.

'Yeah, I see him. But he's only just joined me. What's wrong?'

'I saw the same car back at the café.'

'Are you sure?'

'One hundred per cent. I clocked his reg. I'm not happy. You should abort.'

Time was always precious. We were so busy, so stressed, and had just spent an hour preparing the meet. To abort now would mean rearranging it all for another day and wasting more time. We were getting close to Santa Barbara and I needed to decide quickly. I hesitated. The car was probably just a coincidence. I was thinking of taking a chance and carrying on.

Steve's voice came over the radio again.

'It is two-up, both males. I say definitely abort.' Then he added, very firmly, 'Abort!'

'Yes, yes,' I said. 'I'll go to the right. Can you stick with him for a while and see what he does?'

'Yes, yes.'

I took the next right turn, into a side street. The green car went straight on and no other car followed. I pulled up further down the road and sent a pager message to CI Mike: 'Sorry, can't make it for coffee. I am sick. Nothing serious I hope. I'll call tomorrow.' Mike would know what that meant, and what to do.

We never knew whether the green car and its two occupants were following me or not. Perhaps it really was just a coincidence, but unlikely. Perhaps they were traffickers following me to see who my informants were, or following Mike to see if he was an informant and who he met. Maybe it was DAS intelligence, wanting to see what I was up to; we knew that they did this from time to time, to identify diplomats who were really spies or engaged in illicit activity. There were many possibilities. But whoever they were and whatever their motive, we couldn't take the risk of letting them see us meet with Mike.

Despite the considerable effort that we dedicated to

avoiding detection and protecting our sources, we always knew that these counter-measures were only superficial and would not give us complete cover. If the Cartel ever applied its full resources against us, we would be in big trouble. Our main protection was always therefore to keep a low profile, never to take the credit for any seizures and never to allow ourselves to be linked to any successful investigations.

OUR ELABORATE TRADECRAFT was designed to protect us and our informants from being detected, even if the cartels put us under surveillance or monitored our communications. But a large part of our safety was also based on discretion and disinformation. The best-informed narcos knew who we were, and that we worked with the Colombian authorities, but they would not necessarily know if we were being successful. We therefore played down our role. We let it be known that we arranged training courses and exchanged routine data, but not much else. We never spoke of any seizures or 'results', nor of our intelligence-gathering. If we could give the impression that we were not causing them any damage, the cartels would not perceive us as a threat. For that reason, whenever we generated a seizure in Europe we never took the credit, and tried to attribute 'blame' to others wherever the seizure had taken place. Often this involved some discreet manipulation of press releases and other disinformation.

From the viewpoint of the cartels, when a consignment failed to arrive at its destination, there were various possible causes: it might have been stolen by people at the Colombian end, or at the port of arrival, or by the customers themselves, who could then avoid paying for it. Alternatively, it might have been found by the authorities. After every big seizure, the drug cartels would carry out an internal inquiry. Those arranging the shipment had to explain their part in the transport and confirm that it went correctly, and identify any possible problems or informants. But criminal groups also relied upon newspapers and press reports in the destination country to find out what had happened, and to learn how it had come about. Knowing this, we endeavoured to use publicity to our advantage.

Firstly, it was most important that any news release about a seizure should never mention the DLO, nor that information had been received from Colombia. Secondly, we ensured if possible that any reporting would attribute the seizure to someone else. The most common ruse was to say that it had been found by a drugs dog during a routine search. Alternatively we would occasionally say that it was 'following a lengthy investigation in the UK', implying that the intended recipients in the UK might be under investigation. We sometimes went to great lengths to ensure press coverage that would throw the cartel off the scent, and thereby protect the informant in Colombia and the DLOs.

A good example of our disinformation followed the seizure of 180 kg of cocaine at Heathrow on 9 September 1996. It had been smuggled inside secret compartments in the roofs of two 'igloos' used for cargo on the British Airways flight from Bogotá. An igloo is the colloquial term for an aluminium container into which airlines put suitcases and checked-in baggage. The seizure was the result of intelligence from one of our Colombian informants over a period of several weeks. The following day, however, the

British newspapers widely reported that the drugs had been discovered by Jasper, a customs drugs dog, during a routine search. This was the largest cocaine seizure ever at Heathrow at that time, valued at £27 million, and made Jasper a hero. Photographs of both dog and drugs appeared in the national papers, and a few days later he joined his dog-handler for an interview on breakfast TV. The dog became a celebrity, and successfully took all attention away from the informant in Colombia – and me.

Jasper wasn't the first of our canine decoys. Seven months earlier, 40 kg of cocaine had been found at Heathrow in the nose-cone of a BA flight from Bogotá. Again, this was the result of intel from one of my informants. *The Times* reported the case by saying that a customs dog had uncovered the drugs 'during a routine search of a Boeing 747 carrying holidaymakers and business travellers'.

In another case, in April 1997, 200 kg of cocaine, with a street valued of £30 million, were found on a cargo ship called the *MARGO L* at Avonmouth. The drugs had been carefully concealed beneath the ship's hull by scuba divers in Santa Marta and were destined for a criminal group in the north of England. The seizure was directly attributable to CI Marta, one of our informants in Colombia, and an intelligence operation in Santa Marta over many weeks. But we ensured that the *Times*, the *Independent* and others all reported that it was the result of a routine search of the ship's hull at Avonmouth. The ship's next port of call was Estonia, so we also suggested that the drugs were probably destined for an Estonian crime group. This completely shifted any suspicion away from the informant, and also made the criminal group in England believe that they were safe and not under suspicion, which was far from the truth.

Sometimes, however, our disinformation had unfortunate consequences. In December 1995, CI Fidel gave me information about a container that had been sent from Cartagena. It was due to be offloaded in Bremen, Germany, and then taken by road to Poland. We told German Customs, who searched the container upon arrival in Bremen, and they found 270 kg of cocaine hidden inside. We had also passed details to the Polish authorities, who said that the intended recipients were known criminals. The Germans and Poles coordinated their actions and twenty arrests were made in the two countries. To protect our source in Colombia and throw the traffickers off the scent, the Germans issued a press release saying that the seizure was a result of a 'joint investigation by the German and Polish authorities'. This wasn't strictly untrue, and it worked. The Colombian traffickers believed that the organisation in Poland had been compromised. We heard later that they were furious with the Poles and blamed them for the seizure.

Months later, I heard that four people had been murdered in Poland because of this. Whilst our press release had been successful in removing any suspicion from CI Fidel, it had the knock-on effect of putting the blame on the criminals in Poland – and led to their deaths. I did feel uncomfortable about this. People had died because of our seizure and possibly, in part, because of our disinformation. On the other hand, the traffickers knew the risks of their trade, and were always killing each other over disputes anyway. But my London management were concerned. We always took care not to tell specific lies to the press, but by choosing words carefully and making subtle suggestions, we could often get them to run with the story we wanted. However, this kind of 'collateral damage' would eventually cause Customs NIS managers to stop our use of press disinformation.

For the time being, though, our careful management of information and press releases played an important role in ensuring the safety of me, my fellow DLOs, and our agents in Colombia.

IN EARLY 1997, a week or so after the large rip-on seizures in Holland and Miami, I received an urgent call from London. They told me they had learned from highly reliable sources that Colombian traffickers had investigated the cause of the recent drug seizures from Cartagena, and believed that the British liaison officer was responsible. The Cartel had concluded that I had someone in the port who was informing, and who had told me about their rip-on shipments. More worryingly, they were now discussing what action they should take to eliminate the problem. My earlier approach of spreading the word widely amongst contacts in the port, asking for information, was probably now coming back to bite me. I was well-known to the authorities in Cartagena, and the cartel knew that I had been trying to recruit informants. Now they attributed their losses to me. The question was, what were they going to do about it?

London believed that I was at serious risk. They instructed me to suspend all travel to Cartagena and have no further contact with the informants there. I was also told to take increased security measures for myself and my family. The children of British diplomats were already closely protected and were taken to school each day by armed guards in a bullet-proof jeep. There was not much more we could do to increase their security short of sending them back to the UK, something that Luisa and I were firmly against. Our wives, however, were vulnerable. I spoke with trusted friends in DAS and they immediately provided additional security for my wife Luisa, and for the families of Steve and Bernie.

The instruction to stop going to Cartagena was really bad news. It was scary to think that the cartels were angry with me and were thinking of taking action to eliminate their problem. On the other hand, it had taken me an enormous amount of time and hard work to build up a network in the port. If I stopped talking to my sources when the chips were down and things were getting hot, they would be disillusioned and I would lose them. Some of them could meet me in other places, such as Barranquilla, a hundred miles up the coast, but others could not get away without raising suspicion. I needed to see them in Cartagena. I stopped going to there for a few weeks, but then tried to persuade London that I should continue. Peter, my boss, was not happy about the idea at first and it took some hard talking to convince him. I had known Peter for years and we had previously worked together in Birmingham and London, so he knew I wasn't likely to do anything foolish. I suggested that I could fly to Barranquilla or Santa Marta and then secretly drive to Cartagena and meet my informants without anyone knowing. Eventually he agreed that I could go, but only once a month and only if I took extra precautions, covered my tracks, and never flew there directly. Game on again. What I hadn't told him was that the drive from Santa Marta to Cartagena was probably just as dangerous as the other threat!

The following months involved a huge amount of extra work and time-consuming precautions. Meetings were made only after lengthy counter-surveillance, following long, pre-arranged routes triggered by codewords. At the end of each period of surveillance, and only when I felt confident that neither of us was being followed, I would pick up my informant and take them to an apartment. In Bogotá the pick-ups were done in an armoured jeep. For meetings in Cartagena, I would fly as promised to Santa Marta or Barranquilla and hire a car. The drive from Barranquilla to Cartagena took over two hours, from Santa Marta it took four, and the road was not safe. Frequently FARC guerrillas or criminal groups would set up random roadblocks to stop vehicles and rob the passengers of valuables. If they identified someone of worth, such as a western businessman, they might take them as hostages for ransom. Any military or police personnel stopped would most likely be killed. I would drive for hours along this risky route, there and back to Cartagena, just to meet an informant.

The increased security measures took a great deal of additional time but meant that I could continue to meet informants and receive intelligence about cocaine shipments. Despite all the precautions, anti-surveillance and tradecraft, there was always the possibility that a meeting might go wrong, that we had been followed, or that it was a trap. There were many occasions when I sat in a rented apartment or hotel room debriefing an informant and wondering whether at any moment the door might come crashing in and we would both be in deep trouble. I was often nervous, even scared, on these trips, especially when I was meeting informants on my own away from Bogotá. After many meetings I went back to my hotel and slept uneasily, not knowing if we had been seen and followed, and always conscious that during the night some heavies might burst into my room and that would be it.

From their extensive intelligence checks and contacts, the cartel did succeed in identifying possible culprits for the rip-on seizures. During the following weeks, we heard that several people working in Cartagena port were killed. These unlucky people may have been informants for the Colombian DAS, or DEA, or they may have been completely innocent workers who were identified incorrectly or simply suspected. We will never know. Whoever they were, whilst it was sad to hear that people had been killed, I was relieved to know that none of them were my informants.

I HAD RECRUITED the early informants in the ports personally, and by the end of my first year had established a small team, including Pacho, Fidel, Barry, Lech, Marta, Maribel and Mike. Because of my official liaison work and the training courses, I could speak openly with certain people, such as managers of the port authorities, port security, local police, customs and shipping companies without drawing undue attention. But I could not easily speak with those at the lower working levels, such as dock workers, cargo handlers, crane operators, security guards and night watchmen – the very people I really wanted to reach out to. I knew that it was these workers who were most hands-on and who would be able to give me the most accurate account of what was going on.

I decided that the only way forward would be to recruit others to do this for me. I gave Pacho and the other informants guidance, explained various trafficking methods and the people to look for, and proposed that they should try to recruit sub-sources. I also approached some trusted contacts in law enforcement, suggesting that if they recruited sources for me they could share the rewards. Over the following year this turned out to be a huge success. Pacho recruited three sub-sources, and Barry had four. Mike recruited and developed a network of contacts who answered to him, and Marta found a cluster of sub-sources strategically placed in various occupations in Santa Marta port, who supplied a wealth of information.

This system of working had some tremendous benefits. By using agents and sub-sources, we could connect with the kind of people that I could never meet myself but who had inside access: low-paid dockers, labourers, thieves, beggars, even the prostitutes who went on board the ships to offer their services to the crew when in port. We had on our payroll the whole rich tapestry of the lower levels of society that work in a third-world port. By using such sub-sources, I was also able to extend our reach into Santa Marta, Buenaventura, Turbo and the other banana and coal ports. This system was far safer for everyone, because I didn't have to meet the sub-sources personally, thereby avoiding risk for them as well as myself.

By the end of my second year in Colombia, we had a network of sources and sub-sources in the seaports who were passing information almost every day, and I was struggling to cope with the volume.

6

CI MIKE AND THE GO-FASTS

CI MIKE WAS one of the most professional informants that I worked with. I didn't even recruit him, he approached us, and became probably the most successful walk-in we ever had. Mike lived in Cartagena but had many friends and contacts in Medellin. He was of mixed race, with a light-brown skin from his combined Spanish and *costeño* heritage. He was thirty-five years old when I met him, but had lived his life at the sharp end and had the wisdom and worldly experience of a much older man. He had an impressive network of contacts in the ports and fishing communities on the north coast, and within the police and Customs.

In previous years Mike had done work for Pablo Escobar, Jorge Ochoa and other big traffickers from the highest echelon of the Medellin Cartel. Whenever these powerful narcos came to the north coast and wanted cars, chauffeurs, young prostitutes or indeed anything else, Mike had arranged it. Later on, when they wanted reliable speedboat crews, or sailors to carry drugs onto ships, Mike would find the right people for them. He could get just about anything done in Cartagena, or if he couldn't, he knew a man who could. He had never trafficked himself, or so he said, but was a masterful fixer, acting as the middleman between the narcos and the transportation groups. After the fall of the Medellin Cartel, he worked for the powerful Don Berna and the North Valley Cartel, again as a broker to arrange boat crews and introduce transport connections.

Mike had started working as an informant because he was sickened by the bloodlust of the Medellin traffickers, who had tortured and murdered one of his close friends. He continued to act as their middleman, but started to inform against them. At first he had worked for the DEA, who had a small sub-office in Barranquilla. He passed them several cases but became disillusioned by the way they handled his information and their scant regard for his safety. In one case the DEA allowed his name, along with the information he had given, to be released in court proceedings in the USA, something which would put his life at risk several years later. So he stopped working with the DEA and came to us instead.

Through his extensive contacts, Mike skilfully gathered information about drug trafficking in Cartagena, Santa Marta and Turbo, the banana port in the Gulf of Urabá. He built up a network of sub-sources, and gave us a constant flow of intelligence that resulted in dozens of drug seizures. When we first worked together, he had infiltrated a group based in Medellin and Cartagena that was sending large amounts of cocaine to Jamaica by go-fast.

Go-fasts were modified fishing boats with powerful outboard engines that were used to carry loads of cocaine at great speed. They were a common method of transporting coke from South America to Caribbean islands such as Jamaica and Haiti, and to Central America. Go-fasts were also used to load motherships as they sailed by the north coast of Colombia. Being small and very fast, they were difficult to detect and even more difficult to catch. Unless they had a mechanical failure, they were virtually impossible to intercept, as they could out-run just about any law enforcement vessel. They normally left the coast at night, especially at weekends when the Coast Guard were off duty. They would thus make a large part of their journey under cover of darkness. Even if detected in daylight, there was little that anyone could do to stop them as they sped northward.

The US Coast Guard regularly patrolled this part of the Western Caribbean, occasionally supported by American, British and French warships. When they spotted a go-fast, the ship's helicopter would pursue it and order it to stop. They would fire warning shots across its bows to compel it to stop. The drivers normally ignored this futile action and kept going at full speed, sometimes even waving or making rude gestures to the helicopter above. The crews knew that the Coast Guard and navy ships were too slow to catch them, and that whilst the helicopter might follow them for a while there was nothing it could do to stop them. They would soon take the chopper beyond its permissible range from the parent ship, and it would need to abandon the chase and return. Worst case, the helicopter would run out of fuel long before the go-fast did. The launches always carried numerous plastic drums of fuel so that they could do the entire run without stopping. Consequently they were virtually unstoppable at sea.

We were already familiar with the growing use of go-fasts to take coke from Colombia to Jamaica. We did a case with DAS when I first arrived against an organisation based in San Andrés, which was running drugs from Cartagena to San Andrés in go-fasts, and then on to Jamaica. This route was important to us because Jamaica was a transit route to the UK. Tonnes of cocaine were being stashed in Jamaica and then sent onward to the UK in smaller quantities, carried by couriers on regular commercial flights. Jamaican gangs were supplying the highly addictive crack cocaine market that was growing in our inner cities, and generating a surge in gun crime, thefts and violence. It was a UK priority to disrupt this route.

In October 1994 Mike told me he had infiltrated an important group supplying Jamaica. I met him in a room I rented at the Hotel Hilton on Boca Grande, Cartagena, and over several hours he gave me a detailed briefing. He told me that the main transport organiser was a man from Cartagena called Faride, who used a launch called the *Midnight Moon*, a sleek, thirty-foot fishing boat with powerful outboard motors. The *Midnight Moon* would figure in many of our operations over the next three years. Faride was in contact with another man called Sergio, who came from Medellin. Mike warned me that Sergio was dangerous. A trafficker in his own right, he also represented other powerful narcos from Medellin and had contacts with the AUC paramilitaries. He was not to be crossed.

Sergio wanted Faride to take large quantities of cocaine to Jamaica. Mike gave me precise details of Faride's drug runs and the routes that they took. He explained that they exploited the chain of Colombian-owned islands that runs northwards through the entire length of the Western Caribbean, in a long curving arc stretching to within a few hundred miles of Jamaica. The go-fasts departed from remote beaches near Cartagena and took a course that followed this chain, as the islands offered safety in the case of bad weather or mechanical breakdown. There was a shorter route, sailing directly north in a straight line, but it was still a long journey across open sea and was more dangerous.

Mike laid it all out for me. The go-fasts first headed for San Andrés and Providencia, two Colombian islands that lie about a hundred miles off the coast of Nicaragua and about five hundred miles north-west of Cartagena. They next went north-east towards Roncador Cay, a sandy, uninhabited atoll, then north to Bajo Nuevo Bank. Bajo Nuevo consisted of two deserted atolls with a cluster of smaller sandbanks, altogether about fifteen miles long and in the middle of the Caribbean Sea, 175 miles south of Jamaica. Finally, they went on to Pedro Bank Cay, a small island fifty miles south of Jamaica inhabited only by fishermen. There they handed over the cocaine to Jamaicans and received fuel for the journey home. The entire run took a brutal twenty-four to thirty hours non-stop, depending on the sea and weather. Go-fasts normally carried loads of 250 to 800 kg at a time and were doing runs every week.

Mike said that Sergio was currently arranging a large run on behalf of a Medellin client, using Faride's go-fast. He could get full details of when it would leave Cartagena, and when and where the drugs would be delivered in Jamaica, but he would need to participate himself. When traffickers arranged a large shipment, they would often invite trusted associates to take part, and would put together a consolidated load. In this way they could share the transport costs and also the risk. Consolidated loads were very common in maritime shipments and were one of the reasons why traffickers marked their cocaine with different logos and specific packaging, so that the various recipients could distinguish which packets belonged to which organisation.

Mike said that if he could participate in the next consolidated load he would be able to infiltrate the transport organisation further and get full details. Those were the rules of the game: if you weren't investing in the deal you didn't get the details. He had already asked Sergio, who had agreed that Mike could send four kilos of cocaine in the shipment. Mike asked me for permission to go ahead. This seemed to me like a good plan, but very risky. I told him I'd have to check with London to get their agreement to go ahead, and would let him know.

After consulting with London, I told Mike that he could go ahead and send his four kilos, but that I could not authorise him to send real drugs. He would have to make it four kilos of something similar instead. A few days later Mike duly gave Sergio four kilo-weight packages. They contained cornflour instead of cocaine.

THE *MIDNIGHT MOON* powered out of Cartagena on the night of Saturday, October 22. Just as he had promised, Mike supplied full details of the run. He told me that it had a crew of four Colombians on board and that it carried a large consignment that would be handed over to a man called Leonidas, at Pedro Bank Cay. Leonidas would then take the drugs in a Jamaican speedboat to Montego Bay, and hand over to another group of Colombians. Mike was confident that with such accurate information, we could not fail to seize the drugs at Pedro Bank.

Unfortunately, his confidence in Caribbean law enforcement was misplaced. A Jamaican Defence Force Coast Guard vessel lay in wait for the *Midnight Moon* at Pedro Bank, ready to spring the trap when it arrived, but at the critical last minute it had a mechanical problem and broke down. The captain of the *Midnight Moon*, called Miguel, was then warned off by local fishermen as he approached Pedro Bank, saw the Coast Guard vessel and took evasive action. He took off for mainland Jamaica and went to Black River, where he knew a contact called Larry who ran a small hotel near the beach. Black River was a small village set in a bay on the south-west coast, with an inlet and a mangrove swamp where the Black River flows into the sea. It was a place where small boats could easily be hidden. Miguel stashed the drugs with Larry, and a few days later they were collected by Leonidas.

When I told Mike that the Jamaicans had failed to intercept the boat at Pedro Bank, and that the drugs had been successfully delivered to Jamaica, he was horrified.

'Oh my god,' he gasped. 'We have to get my four kilos back quickly or Sergio will kill me. I told him that I had a contact in Jamaica who would buy them, but I don't. I never imagined that the Jamaicans wouldn't seize it. If no one comes to collect them then Leonidas will sell them to someone else, and they will find out that it's only cornflour.'

Mike was terrified as he thought through what might happen next. 'When Sergio hears that my four kilos are flour, he'll know for certain that I've tried to betray him. He'll know that I'm an informant, and he'll guess that's why the Coast Guard were waiting for Miguel at Pedro Bank. He'll have me killed for certain.'

This was bad. I told him not to worry, but to lie low and avoid any calls or contact from Sergio or Miguel. I would try to sort it. There was not much more I could say. I quickly called my colleague Alan, the DLO in Kingston, and we talked it though. He knew how local law enforcement worked and how best to approach such a thorny problem. Over the next few days, we arranged for a Jamaican undercover officer to contact Leonidas, posing as Mike's customer, and ask for a handover of the 'drugs' sent by Mike. The undercover had to pay Leonidas $1,000 per kilo for transportation costs, but during the ensuing operation we were able to gather even more intelligence about the Colombian operation. The Jamaicans fully identified Leonidas, the phone numbers he used, and a house inland where he stashed the drugs. A few days after buying back the four kilos, the Jamaican authorities seized twenty-five kilos from Leonidas's stash, along with a large sum of money. It was only a small fraction of the coke that had been delivered, but at least it was something.

From the viewpoint of Sergio and the Medellin suppliers, the run to Black River had gone well, and the cocaine had been delivered. They decided to use it again for another, much bigger drug run. Back in London however, my Investigation Division managers were not so happy. We had gathered a lot of intel but had failed to seize most of the drugs. On top of that, we'd had to pay $4,000 to a Jamaican druglord to recover $10 worth of cornflour.

On a positive note, Mike was now established within the organisation, and was trusted by both Sergio and Faride. They planned several runs in January and February 1995 that we were told about, but all were cancelled at the last minute because the *Midnight Moon* had been damaged. A new boat was purchased, and the runs were re-scheduled.

In early March, Mike told me that Sergio and his captain, Miguel, would soon travel to Montego Bay for a week of important meetings with Leonidas and the Colombian group who would receive the drugs in Jamaica. We decided to put Sergio and Miguel under surveillance, to find out who they met in Jamaica and hopefully discover their future plans. When Sergio arrived at Bogotá Airport in March 1995 to catch his flight to Montego Bay, I was there to watch him check in. He was about thirty-five years old, with dark brown hair, clean-shaven, of medium build, wearing a light blue polo shirt and beige chinos. He had a small red suitcase and carried a black briefcase. I passed his description to Alan in Kingston to make it easier for the Jamaican surveillance team to pick him up when he landed. When he boarded the plane, I boarded after him, looking out to see if he associated with any other passengers. And when he arrived and was tailed to the Holiday Inn at Montego Bay, I booked in to the hotel shortly after him. Miguel had travelled separately and rented an apartment nearby.

Sergio stayed at the hotel all week. The Jamaican surveillance team kept him under surveillance when he left each day, to see who he met, and I covered any meetings he had inside. I also translated the recordings and paperwork in Spanish that the surveillance team obtained. The week was an intelligence bonanza. Sergio was seen meeting Clara, a middle-aged woman from Medellin who lived in Jamaica with her partner, Tito. They were a scary-looking couple and were responsible for most of the Colombian cocaine coming into Jamaica at that time. Sergio and Miguel also went to Black River and met Larry, so that Miguel could see the area himself and agree the exact landing point on the river, along with escape routes and a back-up plan should anything go wrong.

We now knew that they were planning two go-fast runs in the coming weeks, and knew where the boats would come ashore at the beach and where they would take the cocaine to be stashed, which was to be Leonidas's house, a two-hour drive from Montego Bay. All we needed was for Mike to tell us the date and time of the run.

As usual, Mike's information was spot-on. On the night of Saturday, March 25, he called me. 'Señor, it left Cartagena a few hours ago. It is a white, thirty-three-foot go-fast called *Intrepid*, with Miguel as captain and three crew on board. They are carrying several hundred kilos of cocaine.'

Mike said they would arrive at the beach at Black River between 2 and 3 a.m. on Monday 27, and would hand over the drugs to Larry and Leonidas, who would be waiting with trucks on the beach. Clara, the scary boss from Medellin, would also be there to see that things went smoothly.

Alan coordinated action by the Jamaican Defence Force. The JDF deployed several CROPS – covert rural operations – officers, who dug in and concealed themselves at the edges of the beach. The main JDF strike force hid in a wooded area a short distance away, ready to react when called in by the CROPS team. The plan was for the concealed surveillance officers to watch Leonidas and his associates arrive at the beach, report their numbers and vehicles, then wait and observe the go-fast arrive and see the drugs being unloaded before ordering the 'strike'.

The back-up teams would then rush to the beach to arrest them all, while other units sealed off the roads to prevent any escape. A Coast Guard pursuit vessel waiting further along the coast would speed in to cut off any attempted escape by sea.

The timing of the strike was critical. If the CROPS officers called it too soon, before the drugs were offloaded onto the beach, then the go-fast would speed off and all would be lost. If they called it too late, after the drugs had been loaded onto the waiting vehicles and everyone was leaving, it could result in a car chase along unlit country lanes and could get very messy. It was therefore agreed that they must wait until the whole consignment was off the boat and on the beach before calling the strike.

Events unfolded exactly as CI Mike had told us they would. At 2.30 a.m. on Monday, the gurgling hum of the *Intrepid*'s outboard engines could be heard approaching in the darkness. A light was seen to flash several times as Miguel signalled to shore with a torch. Leonidas, Larry and Clara, waiting on the beach with vehicles, signalled back to the boat. Within minutes, the sound of the powerful engines grew to a throaty grumble as the speedboat eased in and ran its nose gently up onto the beach. Miguel and the crew jumped off and quickly spoke with the waiting group, who had come to the water's edge. It was a clear night and the CROPS officers were watching patiently through binoculars from their concealed positions. They radioed a rolling commentary back to the strike force, warning them to stand by.

'Go-fast now on the beach,' a voice whispered over the radio.

'Engines off …'

'Four males out of boat and talking to three targets on the beach …'

'Two vehicles now being reversed up closer to the water's edge …'

The listening strike force began to tense up.

'They have dropped the tailgate of pick-up truck, ready to load …'

'The crew are starting to get bags from go-fast …'

The commentary from the CROPS observer continued. But then, perhaps overcome with the excitement of it all, he called it over the radio – far too early.

'Strike! Strike! Strike!'

Within a minute the headlight beams of several 4x4 jeeps lit up the beach as they roared towards the group, and chaos erupted as people ran in all directions. Miguel, the captain, quickly leapt back onto the *Intrepid* and fired up the engines.

'Push out! Push out!' he shouted, and two of the crew ran forward and shoved the boat backwards into the water. As they did so, Miguel swirled the boat around and, with outboards screaming, disappeared into the night. The strike force arrived to catch five Colombians and one Jamaican on the beach, but no drugs.

When Alan telephoned to tell me, I was gutted. This was the second time that we had given the Jamaicans a big go-fast shipment on a plate, and they had messed it up again.

Miguel hugged the coast for a while and then pulled in to a secluded inlet hidden by mangroves, where he lay low for the rest of the night and all the next day. He knew that the JDF would be out searching for him with aircraft as well as boats. Two days later he took the drugs to a trafficker called Raymond who he knew in Ocho Rios, on the north side of Jamaica, and coordinated a handover to the Colombian organisers. And a week after that the second go-fast delivered another load, but this time it avoided Black River and reverted to the previous practice of handing over at Pedro Bank Cays.

CI Mike had worked hard and spent months infiltrating this organisation. Yet despite him passing detailed and accurate information, they had completed three successful runs to Jamaica and we had not been able to seize the drugs or arrest the traffickers. This was extremely frustrating. But things were about to get even worse. Mike told us that Sergio and the Medellin suppliers were concerned that on two of the recent runs the JDF were clearly waiting for them. They asked the Colombian group there to pay corrupt Jamaican police to find out if they were being investigated. A few days later the reply came back: the Jamaican police had spoken with the DEA in Kingston, and the DEA agents told them that the British had an informant in Cartagena who was passing information about the go-fast runs!

It was normal practice to inform the DEA in overseas posts of our ongoing operations, and they informed us likewise of theirs. This was to avoid blue-on-blue situations where we could be working on the same case, or investigating each other's informants. But these mutual briefings were obviously highly confidential and for internal use only. It was against all the rules, not to mention highly dangerous, for the DEA to tell local cops about our sources. To make matter worse, they had told corrupt ones.

This leak put Mike in considerable danger. The organisation was now looking for a *soplón*, a snitch in their midst, so he kept his head down and discreetly withdrew for a while.

A year later, Mike rang one morning to say that a go-fast called *Maku II* had left Rosario, an island near Cartagena, at 10 p.m. the previous night. Miguel and two crew had 350 kg of coke on board for Jamaica. They would follow the route past San Andrés, Providencia, Bajo Nuevo Bank and Pedro Bank Cay, then take the drugs to Raymond in Ocho Rios.

I called Martin in Miami, and he coordinated with the Americans at JIATF. This time we were in luck. There was a US Coast Guard vessel with a helicopter patrolling off the coast of Nicaragua, so it positioned itself just north of Providencia, right in the go-fast's path. On 29 November 1996, the US Coast Guard intercepted the *Maku II* and gave chase. The go-fast headed at full speed towards the safety of Nicaraguan waters, with the Coast Guard in pursuit and a helicopter overhead. The crew threw the bundles of drugs overboard into the sea to slow down their pursuers, and the Coast Guard vessel stopped to collect the drugs whilst its helicopter continued the chase and coordinated by radio with Nicaraguan navy vessels, who joined the hunt. The go-fast crew ultimately abandoned their boat on a remote Nicaraguan beach and fled. A total of 350kg of cocaine were recovered from the sea, and the boat was found and seized.

At last Mike had a successful go-fast seizure. It had taken two years, during which he had told us of about eight different runs, and we had intercepted only one.

Throughout all of that period, CI Pacho had also been telling me about go-fast runs to Jamaica, but with equally little success. He had named Faride and many of the same people identified by Mike.

At the end of the day, the go-fasts were a nightmare to deal with. Even when we had very detailed and specific intelligence, they were extremely difficult to interdict. It would take a few more years before we finally got our act together and started to have success. British Nimrods began to fly from US airbases in Florida to spot the boats and track them as they headed north. US Coast Guard ships with helicopters would then intercept them. The US, and later the French, started putting specialist snipers on their helicopters, who would fire large rounds into the outboard engines to disable them, stopping the go-fasts in their tracks. The flood of cocaine into Jamaica by go-fasts was eventually stopped, although it remained the main method of sending drugs to Honduras and other Central American countries, for onward shipment to the USA. Fortunately, Mike had much better success reporting on other methods of transport, in particular, the banana ships that sailed from Turbo and Santa Marta.

7

PACHO AND THE MOTHERSHIPS

P ACHO WAS A young Afro-Caribbean in his early twenties, from one of the poorer *barrios* of Cartagena. His forefathers would have arrived on the north coast from West Africa several hundred years earlier, along with the thousands of other black slaves brought by English and Spanish traders to build the 'New World'. Because of this historical legacy, even today many of the communities in the poorer coastal areas of Colombia are predominantly of African descent. Pacho had a thin, wiry build, all sinew and muscle with no surplus fat. His friendly personality was immediately apparent from the cheeky twinkle in his eyes and a dazzling beam of a smile, speckled with splashes of gold filling, that spread the width of his face. I guessed that he'd probably never had steady employment but would do informal work, and a bit of thieving, here and there. Nonetheless he was a very likeable lad.

Pacho was introduced to me by a police contact in the early days, when I was keen to talk to anyone who knew about Cartagena port. He had contacts among dock workers, fishermen and boat people in both Cartagena and Barranquilla, and acquaintances in the various fishing villages that lie between the two. He could blend in and mix in these communities, chatting with people and listening out for gossip and snippets of information about drugs.

Pacho had previously been involved with groups that stole from shipping containers. Like most South American ports, Cartagena docks were plagued with robberies and thefts of imported goods. Containers arrived daily from Panama and the USA full of high-value cargos such as cigarettes, computers and electronic goods, but when they reached their final destinations a few days later the owners would often find that a large number of items had gone missing. The Cartagena port mafia would identify the high-value imports, break open the containers, remove some of the contents and then re-seal the containers; a sort of reverse rip-on. Their booty was then spirited out of the port, past the twenty-four-hour security and CCTV, and sold on the back market. It was a well organised and highly profitable criminal enterprise. Pacho had worked with these gangs, and was well in with the bad boys of the port.

The first useful tip he gave me was about a small freighter carrying cocaine to Cuba. It was completely accurate and led to the seizure of 176 kg in Havana in February 1996, and the arrest of seven people. For the next six months, he gave me regular updates on large amounts of coke being sent to Jamaica by go-fasts, but we were never able to intercept them: they were too fast, too manoeuvrable and almost impossible to find on the high seas. After a while I told Pacho to stop telling me about them. I didn't doubt his word but we were just not catching them, so it was point-less for both of us. I told him that instead he should focus his efforts on shipments on larger and slower ships, ones that we actually stood some chance of catching. He would have to spend more time in the port, talking to crewmen and dockers to find out what was going on. I never imagined how successful this change of direction would prove to be.

Pacho did as instructed. Within a few months he was telling me about a series of so-called motherships that were delivering loads of cocaine to Europe for the Cali and North Valley cartels. A mothership was the term we gave to a vessel that transported a multi-tonne consignment. The drugs were often loaded at sea off the Colombian coast by go-fasts, and then handed over to smaller craft such as speedboats or fishing boats at the receiver destination. Shipments by this method were often enormous, certainly the biggest we knew about. Some we would seize, others we would miss. One of them would cause a huge amount of publicity and the sacking of a senior customs manager in Spain. Another would one day cause Pacho's downfall.

PACHO HAD REPORTED that a trafficking group in Barranquilla was planning to send two bulk consignments on cargo ships. The coke was owned by the Cali Cartel, but the transport arrangements were coordinated by a group in Barranquilla. The first shipment was on the *Limerick*, the ship that famously ran aground in Cuban waters. He got its name wrong at first, and I wasted a lot of time searching maritime intelligence sources trying to locate a ship that didn't exist. I later realised that he and most of his pals in the fishing hamlets along the coast had difficulty reading and writing, and in his small community of contacts, information was never written down but was passed verbally. Hence, and not helped by their strong accents and bad pronunciation, the *Limerick* was reported to me as the *Lee Merick*. Apart from that initial misunderstanding, what he gave me was detailed and accurate. He not only knew when the vessel sailed from Barranquilla but also described in great detail where the drugs were concealed. His precise information led the Cuban and US authorities to 6.6 tonnes of cocaine, a record-breaking seizure.

The other ship was a freighter called the *Gold Star*. He had heard that this would be used to transport one tonne. However, after the seizure of the *Limerick*, I told Pacho to keep his head down and go about his business as usual. The owners of the cocaine in Colombia would be trying to identify who was responsible, and it was important that Pacho kept a low profile. He should certainly not try to get any further information about drugs for a while. I told him to keep quiet and stay at home with his family for the approaching Christmas period.

But he could not stay quiet, and within a week he reported that the *Gold Star* was moored in the Palermo jetty of Barranquilla. Furthermore, he told me it was being made ready to transport a large quantity of cocaine to the USA, and that special concealments had been built inside. At the same time, he said that another vessel, the *Marshall*, was also in Palermo, moored near to the *Gold Star*, and was connected with the same people. It would also be used to send drugs.

I told Pacho, even more firmly, to remain at home, and flew to Barranquilla in early November 1996 to see the two ships for myself, and I took some discreet photographs. The *Marshall* and *Gold Star* were anchored within a few hundred yards of each other in the Magdalena river, at a remote and unused spot occupied only by a couple of wrecks. There was nothing there – no jetty and no sensible reason for legitimate cargo ships to be moored there. Pacho was right, they were no doubt killing time waiting for something.

Throughout November, Pacho and I monitored both ships. The *Marshall* left Barranquilla and sailed to Cartagena, where it had some 'repairs' done to its propeller. This was a good sign, as repairs were often used as a cover so that a ship could go into a workshop to make concealments. It then returned to Barranquilla, where it anchored in Boca de Cenizas, at the mouth of the Magdalena river. On 15 November it sailed to Cartagena again, loaded a cargo of fertilisers and departed. Port records showed that the *Marshall* declared it was taking the fertilisers to Tumaco, on the Pacific coast of Colombia. In the event, it never arrived there, and was last seen on 28 November sailing in the opposite direction, eastwards towards Europe. We would not hear anything of it for another four months.

All was quiet over Christmas. Then in late January 1997, Pacho made contact and reported that the *Gold Star* had just left Barranquilla and was heading for the USA. He had heard it was hiding approximately 1.2 tonnes of cocaine. With very little time to spare, I passed the information via our Miami DLO to the maritime intelligence centre at JIATF. Once again, they came up trumps. The *Gold Star* was located by a US surveillance aircraft, tracked, and intercepted as it approached the Florida coast. It was escorted into Miami, where US Customs found 550 kg in a deep concealment, and arrested the ten crew. Pacho had insisted that there were two concealments on board; one in the rear and another, with 700 kg, beneath the water tanks in the front of the ship. Unfortunately US Customs found only the one in the rear. Perhaps Pacho was wrong about the other one, or perhaps the rummagers didn't look hard enough. We will never know, but I think the latter is more likely. By then the *Marshall* had been missing for almost three months and we could only assume that it had carried out a successful run to Europe. It certainly never turned up in Tumaco, where it was said to be going.

I learnt from experience that there were several key indicators that help identify motherships. The main ones were:

a. Inactivity. Genuine cargo ships are kept busy. They are expensive assets to own and run, so legitimate ship owners have agents who ensure that they are always carrying cargo and earning fees. Ships owned or chartered by the cartels, however, often hang around, inactive and waiting for the drugs to be brought and hidden. Traffickers are not as punctual or well-organised as regular traders, and often suffer long delays.

b. Repairs. Concealments and secret compartments are often built into ships to hide the drugs. This entails a ship going into a small, lesser-known workshop or boatyard.

c. Erratic and unnecessary movements. The cartels are aware that vessels may be known to the authorities and might be under observation or on watch lists. Before they load drugs, they often get the ship to make a few journeys as test runs, so they can see whether law enforcement agencies follow or intercept.

d. Change of appearance, colour and name. If a ship has been previously used, they often have it re-painted in different colours and sometimes re-name the ship to confuse any law enforcement vessels looking out for it.

e. Inexpensive cover cargo. The most important and expensive cargo that the ship must deliver is the drugs. However, for the sake of credibility and appearance, they must take on a cover cargo. The traffickers often use something cheap, such as waste products, scrap metal or fertiliser.

The *Marshall* had fulfilled four of the above five indicators. Added to the information from Pacho, and the fact that it didn't deliver its cargo to Tumaco but instead disappeared, it seemed likely that it had made a successful run. By April 1997 it was back in Cartagena, moored alongside another vessel, the *Zeeland*. The *Zeeland* also fitted the criteria, and was added to the list for separate action. The *Marshall* would be kept under surveillance over the next two years, and would eventually be seized with cocaine, although we would encounter a few problems along the way before then.

WITH THE LARGE seizures on the *Limerick* and *Gold Star*, plus the *Marshall* run we had missed, it was clear to me that Pacho had hit a rich seam of intelligence. He had managed to infiltrate a transport group shipping multi-tonne loads on freighter vessels for the Cali and North Valley cartels. Two of these had been intercepted, losing the cartels more than seven tonnes of cocaine in less than three months. Their bosses would be furious. But despite their losses, Pacho said that more ships were already being prepared to take massive loads to Europe.

Pacho was due to be paid rewards for the *Limerick* and *Gold Star*, but when it came to money, tradecraft and security, he turned out to be a nightmare. Steve and I met him in Cartagena in early December 1996. Steve had arrived in Colombia the previous June and was a seasoned investigator, having served in the Alpha intelligence team, a posting that tended to go to only the best officers, and the Romeos cocaine team, which could boast of taking down some of London's most notorious gangsters. He worked hard to quickly become fluent in Spanish, and because of that I decided that he should start to co-handle many of the informants. This was a good opportunity for him to meet Pacho.

We discussed payment of the seizure rewards. Pacho would receive many thousands of dollars, but it was important that he did not show any sudden signs of wealth. He lived with his wife in a rented house in one of the poorer districts, had never owned a car and always wore cheap clothing. If he started splashing the cash, he would come under immediate suspicion, so I gave him some basic financial advice.

'Listen, Pacho, you need to open several savings and current accounts with different banks,' I told him. 'You can do this in your own name, but even better would be in the names of your wife and any other family members that you really trust. We can split your reward money and pay it into the various accounts in smaller amounts. That way, you'll have access to the money anytime you like, but there'll be no single account large enough to attract attention.'

I also suggested that he could invest the money in buying a property or house, and rent it out for future income. 'But above all,' I stressed, 'you should not touch the money for several months. The organisation will be trying to identify possible informers and they have contacts in banks and other businesses. It is absolutely vital for your safety that you don't flash lots of cash or let your friends, neighbours or other people see that you have suddenly come into money.'

'*Sí*, señor,' said Pacho, listening attentively, his big smile gleaming bright as ever. He then promptly declined our best advice and asked to be paid the whole amount in cash.

'I do not have a bank account,' he said. 'Sorry, I don't trust banks. I prefer cash, please, señor. But I promise I will hide it in safe places in my house, that only I will know. And I will not spend it.'

I could not dissuade him, so in the end I arranged to meet him again the week before Christmas to pay the reward in notes. I stressed that we needed to take great precautions and meet under the most secure conditions. It was important that we took great care to ensure that neither he nor we were followed, not only because the cartel was looking for an informant but because we would be handing over a very large sum.

Back in Bogotá I arranged to withdraw the money from the British embassy bank account. Several days later, I had sixty-nine million Colombian pesos spread in wads all over my desk, and realised that I would need to buy a very large holdall to put it in. Steve and I carefully counted and re-counted the bundles of notes. Then, six days before Christmas, we caught a flight to Cartagena. I carried a flight bag with a change of clothes on top; beneath them it was packed full of money. At the controls at Bogotá airport I flashed my diplomatic passport and walked swiftly through without putting the bag through X-ray. No one said anything.

We booked into the Cartagena Hilton and Steve went off to collect a hire car. We had pre-booked a four-door saloon to use, first for counter-surveillance and then to pick up Pacho and go to the hotel. A four-door was important so that Pacho could jump quickly into the back seat and we could drive off without delay; a fast pick-up would make it harder for anyone to follow. In Bogotá we had armour-plated, bullet-proof jeeps to collect informants, and in years to come the DLOs would have the same in Cartagena, plus back-up security, but for now, it was just me and Steve and we had to make do with a hire car. Unfortunately, it wasn't our lucky day. Despite having asked specifically for a four-door saloon, the only car available was a tiny, two-door Nissan Micra. It meant that Steve would have to sit in the back seat when we did the pick-up so that Pacho could jump into the front. Its one-litre engine wasn't exactly going to give us a speedy getaway if anything went wrong.

After conducting counter-surveillance on ourselves around Cartagena for fifteen minutes, we approached the agreed pick-up point. Pacho should be ready to come out of a record shop as we drove by, then a quick stop, in and away at speed. I pulled up and saw him walk out of the shop towards the car, as per the plan. But as I threw open the passenger door, a group of people appeared behind him. Danger signs flashed in my mind and the adrenalin surged. I recognised one of Pacho's sub-sources, who I had met before, and there was another man and a girl with a baby, all coming to the car. By all the rules of tradecraft, I should have hit the accelerator and gone. But I hesitated.

'Who the fuck are all these people?' I asked him as he got to the car.

'Its OK, they are with me. They are friends, and they helped me do the case. I said they could come because they wanted to see you and …'

I cut him off.

'Bloody hell. Get into the car quick. The lot of you.'

It was like a scene from a comedy sketch – although I wasn't laughing – with Steve, Pacho and two unknown Colombian men crammed into the back seat, and the young lady and her baby, complete with changing bag and nappies, in the front passenger seat next to me. I floored the accelerator and the Micra did its pathetic best to speed off.

After a bit of anti-surveillance, we drove into the car park of the Hilton Hotel and went up to the room. Once safely inside, Pacho explained.

'Señor, I'm very sorry. These people helped me get the information about the *Limerick*. I got the tip-off about it from two friends who worked on the river near where the ship was anchored. They heard from other workers that the ship was going to take drugs. After that I was able to infiltrate the organisation and find out more myself, but without their help I would never have known about the *Limerick*.'

He paused for my reaction, and because there wasn't any he continued. 'I promised to share part of the reward with them. But they insisted on coming to my meeting with you to hear the actual amount, in case I cheated on them and paid them less than a fair share.'

'But who on earth is the young lady with a baby?' I asked.

'Oh, one of them, José, couldn't make it so he sent his

wife along instead. But she had no one to leave the baby with.'

I was furious, but I had to keep a grip and get the job done.

'Look, Pacho, this is ridiculous. You can't have a whole group of people turn up for a reward payment. This must never, ever, happen again.' I looked pointedly around the whole group to make sure they were all listening. They were. 'You must trust each other. But more important, you have to take your security seriously or you will all end up dead. Our lives depend in it. Do you understand?'

What should have been a discreet mobile pick-up had turned into a fiasco. We'd made so much noise and fuss trying to fit everyone into the car that anyone watching could not have failed to find it suspicious. If anyone working for the drug traffickers had seen all of them standing together on the open street and getting picked up by the DLOs from the British embassy we would all be in deep trouble.

Steve and I got the bundles of notes out onto the small hotel room coffee table and carefully counted the money before Pacho, so that he could agree the exact amount. It took a good ten minutes, with three additional pairs of bulging eyes watching on attentively. Once the notes had been counted and signed for, we put the bundles inside a holdall bought for the occasion and gave it to Pacho. We reminded him and the others that they should be sensible with the money, not talk about it to others, and take care not to show any signs of unexpected income. Then they all left together. Steve and I went to the bar for a well-deserved rum and coke.

The nightmare over Pacho's reward was only just starting, however. When Steve and I met him again six weeks later he was a man transformed. Pacho swaggered into the hotel foyer wearing a Lacoste polo shirt, expensive designer shoes and a pair of Ray-Ban sunglasses. Were it not for his usual beaming smile (and I was sure that I noticed a few more gold fillings in there), he was barely recognisable. Around his neck hung the thickest gold chain that I had ever seen, and on his wrist a matching chunky bracelet and gold Rolex watch, although no doubt the latter was fake. My jaw dropped. *Oh my God*, I thought, *he's going to get us all killed*.

It was a cultural trait amongst the poor communities of Colombia's coastal region that the young men tried to be flashy. They loved gold and bling, particularly the young criminals and up-and-coming narcos. Whenever they made a score, instead of investing in property or savings they bought sports cars, fat gold chains and watches. Young traffickers might live in a slum and have barely enough to feed their families, but they would wear showy jewellery to make a statement about their importance and power. There was something about a gold chain that told everyone how successful you were, and the fatter the chain the more important the man. Well, Pacho was definitely trying to make a statement and had gone for the thickest chain he could find. I could only imagine that in the run-down *barrio* where he lived everyone must now know beyond any doubt that he was either a very successful drug trafficker or a successful informant.

'Pacho,' I said, not even trying to conceal my annoyance, 'what are you doing? You have completely ignored my advice. This is stupid! If you continue to act this irresponsibly, then we will stop working with you. You're putting yourself at risk, and if you carry on like this you will get yourself in big trouble. If the traffickers put surveillance on you, you might be followed to a meeting with me, and then could get both of us killed. Listen to me very carefully. You must take your security much, much more seriously, or you can no longer work for me or any of the British officers. Do you understand?'

That seemed to do the trick. Pacho subsequently reverted to his former self, wearing scruffy T-shirts and jeans. Or at least that's what he wore on the days that he met me. I suspect that he probably carried on as usual with his flash clothes and bling, and just dressed down for the days when we had meetings. For future rewards, he accepted our advice and opened savings accounts into which the money was discreetly deposited and invested for the future. None of us knew it at the time, but for Pacho the future would be relatively short anyway.

8

THE BEACON TEAM

IN APRIL 1997, a few months after the *Gold Star* seizure, Pacho reported that a ship called the *Zeeland* was anchored at Albornoz, in the bay of Cartagena. He had spotted it because it was near the *Marshall*, which we were still watching. It was an old fishing trawler with two cranes, a single hold and a rust-coloured outer hull. Its name, which should have been clearly visible on the sides of its hull, had been covered over with brown paint and was barely discernible. It was moored a short distance offshore from a breaker's yard where decommissioned ships were cut into scrap metal. The area was a graveyard of rusting hulks at various stages of being stripped of re-useable machine parts and then broken apart and sliced into scrap. It was an isolated, industrial part of the bay, well away from the main shipping routes, and a very strange place for a fishing trawler to anchor, unless it was trying to hide from attention.

'I'll ask around about it, señor, to see if anybody knows,' said Pacho.

He managed to find out fairly quickly that the *Zeeland* was going to be used for drugs, and over the following months he kept an eye on it. He found a place where he could see it from land and passed by there every few days to watch for movement. Meanwhile I ran checks and discovered that it was registered in Belize but had dubious ownership and did not have a licence to fish in Colombian waters.

It was amazing how easily Pacho infiltrated maritime transport groups. With his look, accent and local background, he had an ability to quickly mix in with dockers, fishermen and their ilk. His roguish charm and quick wit made it easy for him to strike up a conversation with anyone he met. So I was not surprised when, a short time later, he told me that he had managed to befriend one of the crew of the *Zeeland*.

'I've found out about the crew, señor. They come from Ecuador and Peru, mainly. But they are sad and pissed-off. They have not been paid for many weeks. They have to live on the ship, and are waiting for a man to come from Medellin with their wages. They have no money.'

More importantly, Pacho said that workmen with welding equipment were on board constructing a compartment inside. And although the crew were South American, the captain was Italian and there was also a Croatian on board, so he thought that the ship would be going to Europe.

On the strength of this, I tasked Pacho to keep a regular check on the *Zeeland* and report any developments, and agreed to pay his expenses. He continued to check the vessel over the following months but nothing happened until early November, when he saw it being repainted blue over its former brown. It may have seemed a small detail, but for me the painting of the hull in a different colour was a strong indicator that the *Zeeland* was getting ready to go. I had now seen three clear key indicators: the ship had been inactive for almost seven months since we first saw it back in April; 'repairs' had been carried out on board (making concealments, according to Pacho); and it was being painted to change its appearance. I knew that the *Zeeland* was probably going to make its run soon, and I needed to make plans to have it intercepted.

A few weeks later, the ship moved out from Albornoz jetty and anchored in the bay about 500 metres from shore. Once a ship leaves port it can be extremely difficult to locate without electronic tracking devices on board. In the cases of the *Limerick* and the *Gold Star*, the US authorities at JIATF had struck lucky and their surveillance aircraft had found the ships, but it is normally almost impossible to find a vessel in the open sea unless you have precise information about its course, speed or destination. Locating a ship in the Caribbean was hard enough, but if the *Zeeland* was heading to Europe there would be little chance of finding it in the vast expanse of the Atlantic.

For that reason, when the ID had strong information that a ship was to be used for a large drugs shipment we often tried to put a covert tracking device, or 'beacon', on the vessel. Customs experts in the UK could then track its position anywhere in the world over many months. They could see when the ship left port, where it went to load fuel and cargo, and where it might collect the drugs. Knowing exactly where it was at all times, they could then arrange for it to be intercepted and the drugs seized before it reached its destination.

Now that the intelligence about the *Zeeland* looked good, I asked London to send a team to beacon the ship. The

ID, which had been re-named the National Investigation Service, or NIS, in June 1996, had its own Tactical Support Unit, or TSU, who planted tracking devices. These experts had put beacons on many vessels before, and in many different locations in the world, but had never done one in Colombia. It had always been considered too dangerous. Before deciding, they asked me to send a detailed report so that they could evaluate the scale of the job, the risks involved and whether it was feasible. They needed a full description of the *Zeeland*'s location, with precise coordinates, photographs, maps and details of the Albornoz jetty, plus information about any guards, dogs or night security. Pacho could have obtained much of this for me, but we kept our beaconing operations strictly confidential and I couldn't tell him of the plan. I would have to get all the information myself.

I borrowed a small motorboat from a contact, and over several days I sailed into the bay and took covert photographs of the *Zeeland* from various angles and got exact GPS coordinates and maps of its location. It was a little scary doing this on my own. If the bad guys spotted me taking photographs I could easily just disappear and no-one would ever know what had happened. But there was no-one I could trust in Cartagena to help me, either in the police or Customs. I managed to get what I needed, and then sent a detailed report to Customs NIS in London requesting deployment of a specialist team. I also asked if they would also beacon the *Marshall*, which had returned to Cartagena and was anchored nearby.

London agreed, and arrangements were made to immediately deploy a specialist undercover team for both ships.

A few weeks later they discreetly arrived in two separate groups. Some flew in from Panama posing as tourists on a scuba-diving holiday and brought the underwater kit. The others landed on British Airways at Bogotá and brought equipment and the tracking devices. It was a strange mixture of kit, varying from lightweight extendable ladders to scale the sides of ships to high-tech electronic trackers and frequency scanners. Bernie and I met them on arrival at the airport in case these extremely tough-looking men were questioned by Customs or DAS about the reason for their visit and the strange paraphernalia they had brought with them. We were lucky and they came through without being questioned. This was just as well, as neither Bernie nor I could think of any credible story that might explain what they were up to.

The *Marshall* was at a marine buoy in the bay of Cartagena, where large ships often anchor as they wait for a pilot to escort them into the port. It was located 1.5 kms from the entrance to the main port and only about 1,000 metres from shore at the tip of the long sand-spit of Boca Grande. I booked rooms for myself and the senior officer of the beaconing team in the luxury Hilton situated at the tip of Boca Grande. Although a little expensive, the Hilton was one of my favourite hotels in Cartagena because of its prime location. The seaward rooms on the upper floors gave an unrestricted view over the entire bay, including the entrance to the port, and you could watch ships come and go. It was a perfect obs point. I specifically paid extra to book two rooms on the very top floor, with a terrace facing the sea. From there we had a clear view of the *Marshall* at its anchorage. No need to deploy CROPS teams to watch from some filthy hide or mangrove swamp; we could maintain twenty-four-hour surveillance with our feet up and a cold beer in hand, from the comfort of a top-class hotel. We also had a clear line of sight across the bay, and with binoculars could just see Albornoz and the mangrove islands shielding the *Zeeland*.

Once booked in, the senior officer and I sat on my terrace in the sunshine, opened a couple of tins, and settled down to go over the plans for the beaconing. They wanted to do the *Marshall* first, because it was the easiest and least dangerous. As we pored over the surveillance photographs and charts, I glanced up at the bay. My jaw dropped. Was it my imagination or had the *Marshall* moved a little? It had been anchored at the same buoy for more than a month and there had been almost no activity on board nor any sign of impending movement.

I watched carefully for a moment, and realised that very slowly, almost imperceptibly, it seemed to be turning. I grabbed for the binoculars and could then see clearly that its anchor had been raised, its engines were churning up white water at the rear and it was turning to face the exit of the bay. It was now 18.20 and we both watched from the terrace as the *Marshall* started to move off from its anchorage towards the exit of Cartagena Bay. By 19.30 it could be seen in open sea, heading north into the Caribbean. We were bitterly disappointed. The team had flown halfway across the world, only to watch the *Marshall* leave just hours before they could put a tracker beacon on it.

Once again, we lost track of the ship. We would not hear of it again until early 1998, when Pacho reported that it was back in Cartagena, at the SIPSA boatyard, where it was undergoing 'repairs'. It would be many months more before the *Marshall* was finally intercepted.

That left the *Zeeland*, which was moored at an industrial breaker's yard back at Albornoz, on the far side of Cartagena bay. The shoreline was industrial land littered with washed up refuse, waste and scrap metal, and was deemed inaccessible. The team would only by able to approach from the shore side via the Albornoz jetty, but security guards and guard dogs controlled it by night. About a hundred metres offshore, however, was a string of small islands, really just clumps of mangrove swamp that stuck out above the water. The *Zeeland* was moored about a hundred metres from one of these islands, at the start of the open water that then stretched out into the shipping lanes and across to the far side of the bay. We assessed that the only way to approach the ship without being seen would be to swim. Fortunately the beaconing team included trained divers and had come prepared with scuba equipment.

The team got to work. We knew the ship could leave at any time, and didn't want another disappointment like the *Marshall*. Several of the team were tasked with twenty-four-hour observations to identify how many people were on board, whether they were armed, their daily routines and their patterns for going to sleep. It was particularly important to know whether any guards patrolled the vessel at night. Over the following forty-eight hours the observations team watched the *Zeeland* from the small, stagnant mangrove island. They reported back that there appeared to be seven crew on board at all times.

The team were confident that they could do the job, but they had to consider every angle. There were numerous pitfalls. If they were stopped and questioned by a police patrol launch whilst on their way to deploy the beacon, they would need someone in authority to get them out of trouble. If the Marine Police stumbled across a bunch of foreigners in diving gear, blacked up like commandos in the middle of the night, they could be taken for terrorists and arrested. Worse still, they might come under fire. And if the crew of the *Zeeland* caught them trying to place the beacon, they could be captured or shot at. For each of these eventualities, we would need to have a fast-response team as back-up.

Although beaconing operations are always kept confidential, we never conducted covert operations on foreign soil without the agreement of a senior official from that country. In this case, we agreed that I would approach a ranking commander of the Colombian Navy, who I knew and trusted. The vice-admiral agreed, and I obtained approval for the beaconing operation at the highest level. Aware of the need for secrecy, a small team of elite Colombian Navy submarine commandos were nominated to support the operation, and by way of cover story we agreed that the UK team would give a short training course to the commandos on covert beaconing. During the following days, using the guise of training, the deployment plan was agreed and rehearsed, and the equipment checked.

At around 3 a.m. on the night of the operation, a Colombian Navy rigid inflatable boat, or RIB, carrying a team of commandos and a British beaconing team left the naval base and sailed silently into the darkness of Cartagena Bay. The divers were dropped off quietly into the sea about fifty metres the far side of the mangrove island. The RIB took up a position a few hundred metres further down the coast, hidden in the mangroves, with armed commandos onboard ready to speed forward to effect a rescue in an emergency. An observations team hidden on the island watched for the duration of the operation, to call a warning if anything went wrong. I sat in a temporary makeshift command centre back at the naval commando base, with the senior officer of the beaconing team and a navy lieutenant, and listened to the radio silence, broken only by an occasional crackle of static, waiting for a call.

The divers disappeared into the pitch-black waters. Just a kilometre away, in open water, the sea would be crystal clear with a visibility of several metres, but near the edges of the bay it was muddy and dirty, with visibility down to less than a few feet. In the darkness of night the team was virtually blind, and could not use torches for fear of being seen by the crew as they approached. They ran the constant risk of swimming into a jagged piece of wreckage or scrap metal sticking up from the bottom, so they had to slowly feel their way through the murky waters until they reached the *Zeeland*.

Instead of the normal bulky oxygen scuba tanks, they used re-breather equipment. This advanced technology meant that the diver breathed from a closed loop, holding enough oxygen for just a few breaths, and the same air was re-used repeatedly. After each exhalation, the poisonous carbon dioxide was removed by chemical filters, the air was cleaned, and a squirt of oxygen was added from a small cylinder before the diver breathed it back in again. The benefits were that no heavy tanks had to be carried and the divers could operate with just small lightweight packs on their chests. The main benefit for covert operations though, was that they exhaled no bubbles. Anyone watching from the ship as they approached would not see the tell-tale signs of air rising to the surface that scuba divers would normally leave.

Once at the ship, the divers slowly and silently climbed on board, and got ready to fix the tracking beacon in a place where the crew would not see it in daylight. At the commando base the radio crackled and a soft voice from the observation post in the mangrove swamp reported, 'Alphas one and two on target.'

A few minutes later, just as they were getting ready to place the beacon, a more urgent message came over the air. 'Hostile on deck, port side,' the same voice whispered. A crewman had come out from below to smoke a cigarette. The team froze in the darkness as he stood just a few strides away and lit up. Two officers were crouched in the shadows by a lifeboat at the side of the ship, and the slightest movement might attract his attention. Whilst he couldn't see them, they knew that his eyes would slowly become accustomed to the darkness and he might at any time suddenly detect their outlines and raise the alarm. There was nothing they could do but to remain perfectly still, barely breathing, and hope for the best.

After a few heart-pounding minutes, he finished his cigarette, flicked the stub into the sea and returned below. It had been a close shave. Now they sought to move fast to finish the job as quickly as possible and get off the boat before anything else could go wrong. From a careful study of the ship beforehand, using blown-up images of the photos that I had supplied, they had already decided in advance exactly where to put the beacon. It was an overhang at the rear of the ship that couldn't be seen by anyone on board.

I had been surprised, and a little concerned, when I heard at the briefing how they planned to fix the tracker to the ship. The beacon itself was expensive, incorporating the latest technology, and it had also cost thousands of pounds to send the team to Colombia. Yet despite this expense and high-tech, the method used to fix the beacon to the ship was common household glue: one of those where the glue in tube A is mixed in equal portions with the hardener from tube B, and then allowed to stand for thirty seconds before applying to both surfaces, which should be spotlessly clean and free of any grease or loose particles. It seemed strange to me that a very expensive and important international covert operation should depend, at the end of the day, on a cheap tube of glue. I had imagined that they would have some kind of specialist high-impact adhesive. This would turn out to be a major issue.

Once at the rear of the *Zeeland*, they came to apply the glue to the beacon and hold it in place. Then a horrible realisation dawned upon the officers. Due to the heat and high humidity, the glue would not harden. Instead of setting in about sixty seconds, as it would in the UK, it remained a gooey mess. An officer had to try again, holding the beacon firmly in place for several minutes before it finally seemed to take hold and stick. It must have felt like an eternity as he stood there in the open, pushing the device against the stern and waiting for the glue to set, on a drugs boat with a gang of armed crewmen just a few metres away. Finally it stuck firm, and the team quietly left the ship, slipped back into the water and swam to the RIB waiting in the darkness to pick them up.

A few hours later, after a de-briefing back at the commando hangar, a call to London confirmed that the beacon was transmitting correctly. The lieutenant produced a bottle of Colombian rum, and a celebration drink was in order. Then we all went to bed, shattered.

Next morning came the bad news. After transmitting for just a few hours, the beacon had stopped working.

We considered the possibility that it had been discovered by the crew and smashed, or handed over to the cartel, but we knew that it was placed in a location where the crew could never have seen it. In any case, had it been found it would still have continued transmitting for longer and the change of location would have been noticed in London.

What had really happened was that, due to the humidity and temperature, the glue had not hardened properly. It had slowly become undone and the beacon had fallen off and plopped into the sea, sinking into the dense silt at the bottom. An operation that had cost many thousands of pounds in time, kit and airfares, had used world-leading technology, and required considerable bravery on the part of the team, had ultimately failed because of a cheap tube of British glue.

There was no time to redo the operation. The beacon team were needed on another case elsewhere and were booked on a flight to leave. After all that effort, the *Zeeland* would just have to be tracked the hard way. I tasked Pacho to keep an eye on it.

*

IN MID-NOVEMBER 1997, the *Zeeland* moved away from Albornoz to a new anchorage in the middle of the bay. The concealment and other preparations were probably now completed, and they were waiting for the cocaine to be brought from the interior. On 12 December, Pacho reported seeing lots of activity near the ship. Several vehicles had visited the jetty nearby, including an expensive Mercedes and some Jeep trucks. On 16 December, the *Zeeland* raised anchor and quietly slipped out of the bay. It disappeared at sea for several days, before returning to Cartagena. I was relieved when it came back, and assumed that this manoeuvre was a trial run to see whether the authorities stopped and searched it when it left, but it also had me worried. If this had been the real run, we would have lost it.

I decided to tell the Colombian Navy intelligence unit at Cartagena. I had never worked with them but had been introduced to them during the beaconing operation. I had always thought that the navy were in cahoots with the traffickers, but decided I had nothing to lose. The *Zeeland* eventually departed again in early January 1998 and headed along the north coast in an easterly direction towards the Atlantic. It was kept under surveillance by naval radars and then, as it sailed past Santa Marta and headed for open sea, it was intercepted by a warship. It was escorted back to Cartagena and searched, and 1.2 tonnes of cocaine was found in a specially welded concealment beneath the deck. The Italian captain and nine crew were arrested.

It had been nine months since Pacho had first spotted the *Zeeland* at Albornoz. His intelligence had proven to be good again, and another mothership had been seized, – despite the British glue.

9

THE NEIGHBOUR

HAD BEEN IN Colombia for just a few days when I saw my first corpse.

My initial impressions of Bogotá were mixed. The city looked quite picturesque from my aeroplane window as we came in to land, with its sprawling suburbs nestling against the green mountain slopes of the eastern Andes. Once I was through the arrivals hall and into a waiting embassy car, however, everything changed. The trip from the airport, as in most South American cities, was complete madness. My senses were overwhelmed by the sheer noise and swirl of activity all around, with horns incessantly beeping, and cars, lorries and motorbikes swerving in and out with manic disregard, as my driver fought his way through the traffic to the hotel.

Once settled in, it didn't take too long before I started to feel a sense of the danger. On the first weekend, we were driving out to a restaurant in Chia, to the north of Bogotá, when I saw a dead body by the roadside, just lying in the gutter as cars drove past. I asked the driver why no-one was stopping and why the police hadn't removed it.

'Oh, you'll see lots of bodies by the roadside,' he said,

nonchalantly. 'There are so many that they can't come out and remove them very quickly.'

He said that it was a big problem for some Colombian cities, especially Medellin and Bogotá. There were so many murders that the municipal councils did not have enough staff or budget to remove and deal with all the bodies. They were going bankrupt because of it.

'Don't worry, a truck picks them up during the night,' he added.

We stayed for a few weeks in a hotel apartment in a nice area of northern Bogotá, until I found long-term accommodation. It was reasonably safe there to walk outside to a restaurant or the shops, but I was struck by the presence of security everywhere. There were armed police, soldiers and private guards on almost every corner. The nicer restaurants, shops and apartment blocks all had guards outside with handguns and pump-action shotguns. After a while you stopped noticing it, but at first the constant presence of weaponry put you on edge. It was a permanent reminder that Bogotá was a very dangerous place.

The management section at the British embassy offered to help me find housing, and showed me several apartments nearby that they thought would be suitable. I rejected them all as not secure enough. This caused some frowning in the embassy, as the apartments were of the same standard offered to other diplomats, but from my viewpoint they fell far short of the kind of security that I wanted for my wife and family. They all had only one entrance, with a single guard at reception. I knew well that one security man could easily be bribed: the money or the bullet again. No poorly paid security guy would turn down a large bribe, and few would risk their lives just to protect a foreign diplomat renting a place in the block. Having a single guard was not enough.

I intended to do some dangerous work during the coming years and knew there was a possibility, if things went wrong, that *sicarios* might one day come looking for me. I would be travelling away a lot, and needed to know that my family were safe. I wanted an apartment that had several independent guards, making bribery more difficult, and I wanted not just one secure entrance but a series of doors and barriers to get through before they reached my apartment. The management officer was doubtful that I would find such a place in Bogotá, and certainly not within my accommodation budget, but I started looking myself.

Two weeks later, we found it. The urbanisation Montearroyo was in the north-eastern part of the city, in a nice residential suburb about five miles north of the embassy. It would take over an hour to get to work in the morning rush-hour traffic, but it was well worth it. The apartments were outstanding and the security was impressive. Visitors had to go through three separate, manned checkpoints before they could reach my door. At the entrance to the urbanisation was a control point with barriers across the road to stop people entering and leaving. Armed guards recorded the names and vehicle details of all visitors, who had to specify who they wished to visit before they were allowed to enter. Visitors then drove up a private road, which had a series of apartment buildings on each side. Each block sat within its own grounds, secured within high fences, and had eight floors, with one luxury apartment occupying each floor. At the entrance gate to my block, another barrier and security office blocked further progress. Visitors had to identify themselves again and this time had to hand in their ID document to the guard, who would return it when they left. They could then enter the parking area.

Entering the apartment building itself, the visitor was met by yet another guard at reception. They would again have to say who they were visiting and the reception guard would telephone me to say that I had a visitor and to confirm that I was happy for them to come up. Once that was agreed, they were invited to step into the lift and wait. The lift would only operate if a resident inserted a key or summoned it from their apartment. Having now gone through three manned control points, and then the key-controlled lift, any unwanted visitor still could not get into the apartment unless we opened a final steel-reinforced door that led from the lift to our door. This was the kind of security I wanted. About a month after arriving in Bogotá, we moved in to a fourth-floor apartment in Montearroyo, and I finally felt that we were secure.

The other residents of Montearroyo were people who also needed a high level of security. They included politicians, senior diplomats and international executives. My future colleagues Steve and Bernie would also live there when they arrived, as would the deputy head of the British embassy. The kidnapping of business people or their families was a lucrative enterprise at that time, and executives and the elite sought the security that gated communities like Montearroyo offered. Unfortunately, sometimes wealthy criminals sought the same kind of security for their families too.

MY SON SEBASTIAN was the first to tell me about our neighbours. They had a young boy of roughly the same age, called Julian, and Seb was pleased to find a friend. The two boys started to play together, often in our apartment or in theirs on the sixth floor. Later, Seb told me that Julian's father was very wealthy. According to the young boy, his father had teams of bodyguards to protect him, and dozens of cars, so many in fact that he used a different one each day. He worked in Cali and was very important, but his work kept him away and he seldom came to the family home in Bogotá. They met him when he had a day off, but always at another place, away from the apartment. Seb also told me that the family on the sixth floor had many gold statues and ornaments. In his child's mind, and as his new friend bragged, our neighbours were super-rich and very important.

I went up to our neighbour's apartment myself several times, mainly to collect Seb at meal-times, and met the woman of the house, who was young, very polite and friendly. I noticed the expensive ornaments that Seb had mentioned, and that the apartment was furnished lavishly; maybe a little too lavishly for good taste. I passed details of the family on the sixth floor to Colonel Gallego at the ANP. I suspected that my neighbour was probably a drug trafficker, and I asked Gallego to have it checked out. Then one day they all disappeared, and we never saw them again.

A few weeks later, in late June 1995, Luisa called me at work.

'Tom, can you come home, please? There are lots of police outside, some in uniform and heavily armed, and others in civilian clothes. They are trying to break in to the apartment above us on the sixth floor, Seb's friend's apartment. There's been lots of banging and I think they were using sledgehammers and cutting equipment, but security tell me they can't get in because the doors are armoured, like ours. They're now trying to get in through the windows using the fire brigade's extended ladder. They are climbing up past our windows as I speak, and I'm a bit worried. They say they are police, but who knows? Can you come home?'

I rushed home and saw a small crowd of men in uniform, most them armed. I found the senior police officer, and a *fiscal* who was overseeing the operation, and spoke with them. They said that the apartment belonged to Victor Patiño, a leading figure of the Cali Cartel, and they had authorisation to search and secure it.

Victor Patiño Fomeque was one of the most dangerous men in Colombia. A former police officer, he had started working for the Cali Cartel in 1988. He became a personal bodyguard to Gilberto and Miguel Orejuela, the bosses, and quickly gained their confidence. Patiño was promoted to head of security for their cocaine laboratories and production sites, hence his nickname of 'The Chemist'. For reasons that I can only imagine, he was also later known as 'La Fiera', meaning 'The Beast'. By early 1994, Patiño was a high-ranking member of the cartel, said to be number five in their leadership structure, and was responsible for the security of their maritime transport operations. His job was to ensure that their shipments of drugs by sea to the USA and Europe went smoothly, to identify any problems in the ports or on the routes, and to resolve them. This included hunting down anyone who might be passing information to the authorities or traitors who might be stealing drugs, and having such problems eliminated. He could call upon the cartel's teams of hit men to eliminate any turncoats, informants or opponents.

Patiño spent most of his time working away. The drug trade involved constant violence, treachery, kidnappings and internecine killings. If one mob could not get to a rival, they often went after their children or family or instead. Patiño made many enemies, and so needed a safe place for his family. It was no doubt for that reason that he chose Montearroyo as a discreet safe haven. It was away from Cali, and somewhere where his wife and children could live anonymously and securely.

The roles of Victor Patiño and myself were in direct opposition. His job was to ensure the security of the cartel's maritime drug shipments, and my job was to disrupt them and have them seized. His work included hunting out informants in the ports and eliminating them, whereas my role was to recruit them and use their information without them being detected or killed. We were opponents. It is frightening to think, therefore, that we were also neighbours in the same apartment block. In 1994 Colombia had a population of 37 million, yet of all the places to live Patiño and his family had chosen two floors above us. Our children played together and I met his wife and family. I had been inside his home, and his wife and children had been inside ours. Fortunately, neither of us was aware of the other. I was extremely lucky, as this was a situation that could have so easily gone horribly wrong.

Victor Patiño would spend most of the following fifteen years in jail. He was incarcerated for six years in Colombia, then in 2002 was extradited to the USA, where he agreed to cooperate in return for a reduced sentence and security for his immediate family. He gave the DEA a tremendous amount of information about the Cali and North Valley cartels, including the locations of production laboratories and transport routes, and testified against other cartel leaders. In return, the cartels murdered over thirty-five members of his extended family in Colombia. His wife Flor and their children, and his mother Deisy, were able to relocate to safety in the USA, but his remaining relatives were massacred in revenge for his treachery. His half-brother Luis, who had been Victor's closest associate, was dismembered and thrown into the river Cauca, near Cali.

I felt very relieved that Patiño never discovered who his neighbour was on the fourth floor.

10

COCAINE LABS AND A KIDNAPPING

I N THE SUMMER of 1996 the British embassy in Bogotá relocated to larger, purpose-built premises on the upper floors of a ten-storey building on Calle 76, about a mile nearer to the city centre than its previous location. Sir Leycester Coltman was the ambassador from 1994 to 1998. As in most embassies his diplomatic team was divided into various sections: political, defence, commercial, consular, management, and the drug liaison officers. We DLOs had our own suite of offices within the chancery, a secure, confidential area of the inner embassy on the top floor. The ambassador was extremely supportive of our work, as were our colleagues in the defence and political sections, and this helped us to obtain Foreign Office funding for our port training courses. The Foreign Office and defence section had also supported training by SAS for the ANP *Jungla* teams, the elite units that went into remote, guerrilla-held territories to destroy cocaine laboratories.

Locating and burning illicit labs was one of the main functions of the ANP. These labs varied in size and were mostly located in jungle regions. Hundreds of them were scattered throughout the coca cultivation areas and produced *base*, the first stage of making cocaine. Bigger and more sophisticated laboratories were used to produce not only base but also cocaine hydrochloride, the final product. Some of these were large complexes hidden deep in the jungle, incorporating several processing facilities and accommodation buildings for scores of workers, and sometimes even airplane landing strips. The more advanced labs were heavily protected by *sicarios* and FARC guerrillas. But whether large or small, most of them were located deep inside the Colombian jungle, normally near a river tributary used to bring in the required chemicals and supplies, in the main coca areas of the south-east, towards the borders with Brazil and Venezuela.

The ANP had a forward base about 250 miles south-east of Bogotá at San Jose, a small, isolated town on the river Guaviare. From there the brown, silt-laden river meanders slowly eastward through tropical forest for more than 350 miles before joining the Orinoco on the border with Venezuela. From their base at San Jose, the ANP coordinated the fumigation and eradication of coca plantations and launched raids against remote labs. When they received reliable intelligence about a location, their heavily-armed teams would fly out in UH-1H helicopters, the famous Hueys, in a lightning raid to destroy it.

The first time I was invited to accompany them, we took off in three Hueys, each with a six-man team on board and two gunners. The ANP officers looked more like commandos than police officers: tough, weather-beaten men in military fatigues. As we skimmed low over the tree canopy, the open side of the chopper revealed an expanse of jungle as far as the eye could see; nothing but foliage, save for the thin brown line of the Guaviare, which appeared from time to time through the trees as it twisted and looped towards Venezuela. In many places the dark green of the rainforest was broken by patches of brown, where the trees had been felled to grow coca, and by a patchwork of lighter green colours that indicated where coca plants were now being grown. As I looked closer, I could see hundreds of such patches. The scale of it was breathtaking.

After about forty-five minutes we arrived on target. The tension palpably rose as the ANP team checked their kit, tightened belts and webbing, and readied their assault rifles. The side gunners opened the lids of metal boxes containing long belts of bullets, which fed into the sides of their machine guns. The *Teniente* nudged me and pointed below.

'There, there! Can you see it?' he shouted above the noise of the Huey's engines.

Somewhere down below was a cocaine lab, but all I could see was jungle.

Our Huey went lower, tilted sharply to the right and started to bank in a wide circle. Suddenly the right-hand machine gunner opened up. The deafening noise of his gun made me jump as it rained scores of bullets into the trees below, and the whole helicopter shuddered violently with the recoils. Empty bullet casings were churned out and filled a metal box at an impressive rate.

The *Teniente* called to me on the headset.

'Don't worry, he is not shooting at any specific people. He is just trying to draw fire from any guerrilla or guards that are down there. They normally run away and hide in the jungle, but if they fire back then we know that they are up for a fight and we can try to see where they are.'

Draw fire? I started to wish that I had gone in one of

151

the other helicopters. How on earth had I got myself into this? I had once been a simple VAT inspector, aspiring to one day get a job searching ships in a British port; now I was surrounded by a team of wild-eyed Rambos, in a helicopter gunship firing a blazing trail of bullets at unseen guerrillas in the Colombian jungle, and hoping to draw fire back from them. *How did that happen?* It was surreal.

In the event there was no resistance. The laboratory workers and guards fled into the jungle as soon as they heard the three helicopters coming. The first Huey came down to a clearing about fifty metres from the laboratory and hovered off the ground for just half a minute while the six ANP leapt out. Then it left. The ANP team spread out in a circle to secure the clearing perimeter. The second Huey did the same, hovering a metre from the ground just long enough for its six officers to jump out before soaring upwards again. The second unit spread further afield, making the secure area wider. The third did the same. I was in the third drop-off with the *Teniente*, and I stuck to him like glue. Within five minutes we were all on the ground, had secured an extensive area around the clearing, and the three Hueys were flying in circles above, with guns trained on the jungle around the team to offer supporting firepower.

One team stayed behind to keep the clearing area secure for our return. The rest of us made our way quickly to the laboratory, hidden in the jungle about fifty metres from the clearing. When we got there, it was empty; everyone had fled. I saw the drums of chemicals, large vats of coca mush being processed, and the whitish product spread on a table, some in bags and some in blocks. The ANP officers hurried to carry out field drug tests, take samples, and photograph and gather evidence from the lab. They had to work quickly because this was a FARC-controlled area, and the guerrillas could come back at any time.

The process of making cocaine from coca leaves involves gasoline and other volatile chemicals, so the destruction of a laboratory was relatively easy. They put the drums of chemicals into the centre of the lab, threw petrol over the drugs, machinery and equipment, then kicked over one of the drums of fuel to soak the whole area. The *Teniente* shouted an order and everyone withdrew to a safe distance. A trail of petrol was laid and then he lit it. Within a few seconds the whole complex went up in a huge ball of flame. But there was no time to watch, as the guerrillas might regroup and attack at any time. We all rushed back to the clearing where one by one the helicopters returned to pick up their teams, the other two always circling above to give covering fire if needed.

The ANP units raided laboratories like this several times a month and were often attacked by large groups of guerrillas, and frequently had men killed during such operations. Because of this, they were extremely grateful for the specialist training given by the British Special Air Service. Colonel Gallego would later tell me that the SAS training saved many of his men's lives.

SECURITY AT OUR embassy was tight, with private guards at the main entrance of the building in addition to armed police from the diplomatic protection unit. The embassy also employed its own guards at its entrance on the ninth floor, and at the car park. Each morning when I and other staff drove in, the guards would politely stop us, check the car back seat and boot, and then search beneath with mirrors and torches for explosives, trackers or other foreign devices. It took a tedious five minutes every morning, but was a necessary to ensure the safety of the embassy and its staff.

One morning I arrived at the entrance to the underground car park and, as usual, the guard made me stop and started checking my vehicle. Then one of them tapped lightly at the thick bullet-proof glass of my car window, and spoke in a quiet voice.

'Señor, would you please leave your engine running, put the hand-brake on and then gently open the door and step out of the vehicle.'

'What's the problem, José?'

'Señor, this is serious. Please don't turn the engine off or make any sharp movements. Please just get out of the car. There is something suspicious underneath it.'

His expression betrayed his concern. I did as he asked and gently opened the door, then gingerly stepped out of the vehicle.

He indicated for me to come around to the passenger side and together we got down onto the floor and looked under the car. José held out his search mirror, which had a two-metre extended pole with a torch attached to throw light at the point where the mirror reflected. There, beneath the undercarriage of the car at the rear passenger side, was a grenade, stuck to the petrol tank with tape.

'Señor,' said José gravely, 'we must step away from the car and notify the bomb disposal unit immediately.'

I was about to agree, but something about the grenade looked familiar.

'Just a minute,' I said. I took hold of José's extended mirror and put my head back under the car to have a closer look. Then I crawled further under the car, took hold of the grenade and with a big tug I yanked it free. José looked horrified.

As I came out from beneath the car, I held out an authentic-looking toy grenade, moulded in green plastic, for him to see.

My young son Sebastian had decided to play a game to 'test' the security guards. At the time, he thought that this would be a bit of fun, not realising that he would nearly give poor José a heart attack.

PERHAPS PARTLY BECAUSE of the air of danger in which we all operated, the spirit within the embassy was fantastic. There was strong cooperation between the various sections and we all helped each other out to promote the broader British interest. The fight against drugs was a high priority for the UK, and the ambassador and the political section supported us whenever they could. They helped us in getting Special Forces training for the ANP and DAS, and in return the DLOs gave advice and support to the ambassador and his staff on drugs matters. We were an important element of the embassy team. Our value was perhaps best demonstrated during the kidnapping.

The defence section consisted of Colonel Michael Ponikowski, the defence attaché, and his support officer, Tim Cowley. Tim was a married army sergeant, thirty-two years old, tall, fit and energetic. In his free time he enjoyed long-distance running with the Bogotá Hash

House Harriers and was an avid birdwatcher. It was his love of the latter that would disrupt the work of the whole embassy for several months. On Saturday, 12 August 1995, Tim went to the countryside in Tolima, about sixty miles west of Bogotá, with a Colombian birdwatcher friend. They hoped to see the Tolima dove, a unique and endangered bird that is only found in a very small area on the eastern slopes of the Colombian Andes, between Tolima and Huila. While looking for this creature, or *Leptotila conoveri*, as it is apparently known, they were stopped by a band of FARC guerrillas and taken hostage.

Tim's Colombian colleague was later released to take word of his capture back to the British embassy. A crisis meeting took place in the secure chancery on Monday morning. We were instructed that no one outside chancery staff must know about the kidnapping; it would be kept absolutely secret so that negotiations for Tim's recovery could have the best chance of success. We were all pretty shocked, and extremely worried for Tim. The FARC had kidnapped hundreds of people during previous years. Some had been released without harm after the payment of sizeable rewards by their employers, families or governments; others had been held for years. Many had been killed. Just two weeks before Tim's capture, the guerrillas had executed Trevor Catton, a twenty-two-year-old British student. He had been a hostage for two months and the ransom FARC demanded had not been paid within their specified deadline. Three years earlier, another British hostage had been killed. Peter Kessler, a sixty-five-year old businessman, was shot by FARC when a Colombian army patrol approached their camp. (In July 2008 the

Colombian authorities would rescue Ingrid Betancourt, a well-known politician, after FARC had held her captive for over six years. At the same time they also rescued eleven Colombian police and military staff, some of whom had been captured in 1998 and held for over a decade. It was said at the time that FARC still had over 700 hostages.)

In Tim's case, the situation was complicated because he was a diplomat and would be seen as a representative of the British Government. FARC might decide to use him as a political tool. If his captors realised that he was a serving sergeant in the British army, the situation could become even more dangerous. The British military had given training and equipment to the Colombian authorities. The SAS had even trained the ANP's *Jungla* units, who often fought against FARC when they went to remote areas to destroy cocaine laboratories. The FARC guerrillas protected cocaine labs in jungle regions, and the SAS training was specifically aimed at helping the ANP to thwart any counter-attacks during their antinarcotics work. If Tim's captors thought he had played a part in this, he would be in deep trouble. They might decide to kill him outright, or hand him to the drug cartels or criminal groups. His situation was grave.

Nothing was heard for two days, and then a telephone call was received at the embassy instructing us to get an HF radio and to be listening on a specified frequency on Friday at 11 a.m. Mike and Lorne, two hostage negotiators from the Metropolitan Police, arrived within days. They would later be joined by two more negotiators, Andy and Laurie, and rotated so that there were always two negotiators *in situ*. Although the British Government would never pay a reward to get Tim back, it was extremely important to open negotiations with his captors as soon as possible. The negotiators did not speak Spanish, and the matter was so confidential that we could not employ translators, so Mike and Lorne looked to the DLOs for assistance.

Mike explained to me that the first thing they needed was a safe base from where they could negotiate. It had to be secure, ultra discreet, and have no links whatsoever to the embassy. We needed to keep all negotiations confidential, and it was critical that the press and others should not become aware. They also needed a place that had a roof-top terrace or large area where they could extend an HF antenna several metres long. Through our contacts we rented a top-floor apartment in Plenitud, with access to the roof. I took an open-ended rental, knowing that this might take just a few weeks or perhaps many months.

The next thing Mike wanted was a small team of trustworthy Colombians to work with. They would need to develop any information that could be obtained during the negotiations, and carry out an intelligence operation to identify Tim's captors and, hopefully, their location. We explained to Mike that DAS were the best agency for this role. They had a lot of experience in dealing with high-level kidnap cases and had a good success rate, although mostly in urban areas. More importantly, DAS believed in an intelligence-focused approach, with their priority being the safe recovery of the hostage. The Army and police also dealt with hostage cases but their primary focus sometimes appeared to be killing the guerrillas rather than the safety of the prisoner. I spoke with the Director of DAS and he allocated a small team of experienced agents to work with us. DAS also offered an English-speaking negotiator who had experience in dealing with FARC on hostage cases to advise the Met Police team.

Mike and his team were amazing people and incredible mediators. I discovered during the following weeks that it takes a unique kind of person to be a hostage negotiator. With someone's life depending on what you say, on how you react to sudden demands, and upon your very next words, it requires a huge amount of confidence, positive attitude, quick-thinking and calm. Add to that bucketfuls of patience, an ability to play chess and spin plates at the same time, and a calm voice and nature that will charm a snake into giving up its prey – and you are getting close. It must be an extremely daunting and challenging task to barter for someone's life. Mistakes are fatal and there is no second chance. In this case, Mike and his team had another burden – they were strictly forbidden from offering any payment. The Government stuck firmly to its policy of never paying ransoms. Consequently, Mike and his team had absolutely nothing to offer.

Despite this, they patiently negotiated for Tim's release for the next four months. Almost every day, the police officers would talk to representatives of the captors by HF radio. I went there every day too at the start, to act as a link officer for the negotiators and agree plans of action with DAS. Later, DAS brought in an English-speaking liaison officer so that I could be released to do my other work. The DAS team gave us advice about negotiating with FARC and explored the intelligence leads that came from the conversations. The smallest leads, the tiniest pieces of information, were all followed up, developed and exploited, to add to the jigsaw picture that the DAS team was building up to locate the guerrilla unit.

Initially the guerrillas demanded $2 million for Tim. After a time, this was reduced to $1 million, and then $500,000. Mike had to repeatedly ask for proof that Tim was still alive, and then continuously explain, calmly and patiently, that the British would not pay a single dollar or penny.

A few weeks into the kidnapping, an SAS team arrived. Their guys also didn't speak much Spanish, so they turned to the DLOs for support. We gave them half of our office to use as their base, and shared desks. Our room soon filled up with a clutter of communications and other equipment. It had been agreed by the Colombian authorities at the highest level that the SAS could deploy in Colombia to help rescue Tim. It was political dynamite for the Colombian President and Minister of Defence to allow foreign military forces to take actions on Colombian soil. They asked us to keep it an absolute secret.

Our first dilemma therefore was how to get an armed military unit and all their equipment into the country without the press and public becoming aware. Colonel Ponikowski came up with a great idea: just a few days earlier, Hurricane Luis had hit the Eastern Caribbean and caused catastrophic damage to Antigua, Barbuda and Anguilla. A Royal Navy frigate was providing assistance, and a Hercules military cargo aircraft was about to fly from the UK to take medical and other supplies. Colonel Ponikowski suggested that the SAS equipment could be loaded onto the Hercules and, after it had dropped off in to

Antigua, it could fly to Bogotá. We would tell the Colombian airport authorities that it was delivering surplus medicines to the British embassy, for donation to Colombian charities.

Colonel Ponikowski made the appropriate arrangements with the Colombian Ministry of Defence, and I arranged things with Customs, DAS and airport security. In the very early hours one morning in September 1995, an RAF Hercules landed at the military area of Bogotá airport. Embassy staff drove a minibus and a large truck on to the tarmac and right up to the aircraft cargo doors. We quickly offloaded SAS personnel and their military equipment into the bus and truck, along with some token boxes of medical supplies, and left the airport. The drug cartels were very good at smuggling drugs out of the airport, but I felt rather proud that we had just done a huge smuggle in the opposite direction, of an SAS team and several tonnes of munitions and equipment, without Customs, DAS or anyone else at the airport knowing about it.

The Colombian government also insisted that the SAS must not try to rescue Tim or engage in military action against FARC by themselves, but could act only in support of a Colombian force. It was agreed again that DAS would be the best agency to work with. They were already with us on the negotiation and intelligence development aspects, and it made sense to stick with the same agency. The SAS commanding officer agreed, but was concerned about his team going into action with another group who were not trained to the same standard nor familiar with their methods and operating procedures. He said they would need to train the DAS agents to a higher standard so that they could work effectively together. DAS selected some of their best operatives and allocated a small team to work with us. Over the following two months, the SAS gave them intensive training at a DAS school in northern Bogotá, so that the joint force could work together cohesively as a rescue team.

Then the day arrived when they deployed for real. We had received intelligence from reliable sources that Tim and his captors might be hiding in a particular remote area. To try to corroborate the intelligence, we tasked a military surveillance aircraft to carry out a reconnaissance flight during the night, and its forward-looking infra-red cameras detected a group of heat sources. The sensitive infra-red systems found heat images that appeared to be a group of between fifteen and twenty people camped closely together. The area was mountainous with cloud-forest vegetation. There could be no reason for a large group of people to be camping out there, unless they were guerrillas. It also fitted with other intelligence from DAS that this was the unit holding Tim.

The SAS–DAS team were secretly flown to the region by helicopter and dropped off several miles away in the next valley. It took them a full day's hike over mountainous and difficult terrain to reach the location where Tim and his captors were believed to be. They moved stealthily towards the spot, ready to put into effect their well-rehearsed rescue plan. Unfortunately, instead of a group of FARC guerrillas and a hostage, there they found a goatherd and his flock of rather large goats. They withdrew as quietly and stealthily as they had arrived, but were extremely disappointed. The goatherd will never know how lucky he was.

By that time, in September 1995, I had built-up a network

of more than a dozen informants, and was in the process of recruiting several more. They were passing me intelligence almost daily and each meeting with an informant took time: the counter-surveillance, the meeting itself, writing up notebooks, checking and verifying facts, sending intelligence reports to London and planning operations. On top of that, we were running several cases with DAS and ANP, with scores of telephone intercepts that were generating a constant flow of information about British criminals and Colombians sending drugs to the UK. It was a busy time and we were working long hours.

Then Tim got kidnapped, and suddenly everyone needed our help. The ambassador and FCO needed us to get agreements and permissions from the Colombian authorities, the Met Police negotiators needed our help, and then the SAS team arrived and brought a whole new wave of extra work. Naturally, the work to help get Tim free was the most important and took top priority, but it took a huge amount of our time and we still had to somehow carry on with our normal DLO work.

Throughout the kidnapping, the DLOs played an important supporting role in the efforts to get Tim released. During the days I would be helping Mike and the Met Police negotiators, listening in on their radio communications with FARC and then coordinating action with DAS who were carrying out intelligence ops to identify the guerrilla cell holding Tim. Then for the SAS team, we acted as their link with the Colombian authorities and arranged whatever they needed to do their job. This varied from smuggling their equipment into the country when they arrived and acting as translators when they trained the DAS strike team, to arranging helicopters to fly them, plus back-up evacuation and medical teams when they deployed – and all using our discreet contacts to keep it under wraps from the media.

In whatever small gaps of time I had left, mostly in the evenings, I would meet informants and send intelligence logs to the UK to develop our cases. Throughout all this time, CI Marta was telling me about shipments of cocaine on banana ships, CI Mike was telling me about go-fast runs and rip-ons, Fidel gave me seizures in containers, and CIs Sonya and Alberto were reporting in daily with details of cocaine consignments by air from Bogotá airport. During the kidnapping, and apart from everything else going on, we generated fifteen seizures in Europe, totalling over twenty-three tonnes of drugs. I worked horrendously long hours, hardly saw Luisa for days on end, and didn't have a day off in three months. I was trying to keep dozens of plates spinning at the same time but didn't have enough hands or enough time. This was probably one of the most stressful periods of my life.

It is testament to the negotiating skills of Mike and his colleagues that, after three months of communication, the guerrillas said they would be happy to release Tim if they could recover their costs. Day after day, the Met Police negotiators had convinced the FARC that they must not harm Tim. If they did, they would be hunted down until they were either killed or put in jail for life. The Colombian press had finally found out about the SAS and published articles saying that elite British SAS units were combing the mountains for the kidnappers and, despite our fears about publicity, this actually worked in our favour. FARC were having to move camp in the mountains every two days to avoid detection. They were under pressure and realised that it would be better to give up Tim, as there was no hope of getting any money for him.

Finally, the FARC negotiators explained that for almost four months they had been feeding Tim and those guarding him, and that this had cost them a considerable amount of money. They accepted that the British Government would not pay a ransom for him, but asked if we would at least reimburse them for the cost of his food and accommodation during his stay.

On Friday, 8 December 1995, exactly one hundred and nineteen days after his capture, Tim was recovered by the Colombian army. Following an anonymous telephone call telling them where to go, he was found alone, tied to a tree. His FARC captors had left him there and fled. The incident had caused huge disruption to the work of the British embassy and the DLOs over a period of four months but everyone was delighted that Tim had been recovered. During his four months in captivity Tim had been able to improve his Spanish by talking to his captors and had been treated reasonably well. He was in good health and had even put on weight. To cap it all, he also got to see a Tolima dove. It was said that, for a joke, the guerrillas had one day served him one on a plate for lunch.

11

GUNS FOR DRUGS

NTELLIGENCE FROM TELEPHONE intercept is extremely valuable but can sometimes mislead. Listening to calls between criminals can give a fascinating insight into what they and their associates are planning, and in many countries – including Colombia, but not the UK – can be used in evidence against them. But crooks frequently lie to each other, so what you hear in a conversation is not necessarily the truth, and what one says he will do is not always what he then does. Informants are also very useful but, likewise, cannot always be relied upon. They often lie, exaggerate or tell half-truths, omitting details of their own complicity in crime or facts that may not suit them. Information from both intercept and informants, known respectively as sigint and humint – signals intelligence and human intelligence – must always be carefully evaluated and tested before its content can be relied upon. Sometimes we were in the fortunate position of receiving intel from both sources, and when intercept and informant came together and corroborated each other, we could at last feel confident that we had a reliable picture.

We had been working with the DAS and the ANP for several years on intercept cases and had given them extra

Top: The suspect freighter
Limerick as a US Coast Guard
boarding team approaches in a
rigid inflatable boat near Cuba.

Right: Cocaine bales found on
board. The ship was carrying
6.6 tonnes, one of the biggest
seizures ever in the Caribbean.

Below: Fidel Castro with Alan
(left), a UK drug liaison officer,
at the British ambassador's
residence in Havana. Alan
helped to negotiate a sensitive
deal between Cuba and the US.

Above: The city of Cartagena, Colombia, with Boca Grande and the Hilton Hotel in the foreground and the dockyards of the port area on the far side of the bay. *(Photograph courtesy of Jaime Borda)*

Below: A surveillance photograph of a fishing trawler anchored off Albornoz, close to mangrove islands, with its name obscured. It was to be given a paint job to change its appearance in preparation for smuggling narcotics.

Right: The author with the same vessel, the freshly-painted *Zeeland,* at the Colombian naval base in Cartagena, following its seizure with 1.2 tonnes of cocaine.

Powerful go-fast speedboats carrying cocaine across the Caribbean Sea, with a map showing their regular route from Cartagena to Jamaica, hopping between the atolls and small islands of San Andrés, Providencia and Quita Sueño Bank on the way. From Jamaica the drugs were often sent to Europe.

Montego Bay
Black River ●
JAMAICA Kingston
Port-au-Prince ⊛
● Pedro Bank

Seranilla Bank ●   ● Bajo Nuevo Bank

La Cieba

Carribean Sea

● Quita Sueño Bank

Puerto
Cabezas ● Providencia

NICARAGUA

● San Andres

Barranquilla

COSTA Puerto
RICA Límon

Cartagena

Colón Panama City

PANAMA

Daily Mail, Tuesday, September 10, 1996

Coming up roses: Jasper the springer spaniel found Heathrow's biggest drugs haul yet

A drugbuster's £30m cold nose

Daily Mail Reporter

A DOG sniffed out £30million worth of smuggled cocaine hidden in flowers yesterday.

Jasper, a springer spaniel, discovered the 28-stone haul during a routine Customs search in the hold of a passenger jet which arrived at Heathrow from South America.

It was the biggest drugs find in the country this year and the largest yet at the airport.

Left: Press reporting on the exploits of Jasper the sniffer dog, who 'found' cocaine worth £30 million inside igloo containers on a British Airways flight from Colombia.

Right: The Cali Cartel's deadly security chief, Victor Patiño Fomeque, after his arrest. He had been living in the same apartment complex as the author. *(Getty Images)*

The powerful Juan Carlos Ramírez Abadía, alias 'Chupeta', one of the leaders of the North Valley Cartel, escorted by DEA agents during his extradition from Brazil in 2008.

Santa Marta port, with coal boats loading on the right and containers in the centre. One of the best Customs informants was a young prostitute, Marta, who worked on the boats and picked up vital gossip from crew members. *(La Sociedad Portuaria Regional de Santa Marta S.A.)*

The Drummond coal port near Santa Marta, a regular platform for the cartels to send drugs to Europe and a difficult place for law enforcement. *(Courtesy Drummond Ltd)*

A HM Customs surveillance photo of the *Gold Star* (left) and *Marshall* at Palermo, Barranquilla, part of a fleet assembled by one of the biggest maritime trafficking groups. A seizure on the *Gold Star* would lead indirectly to the tragic murder of a key informant.

One that got away: the *Orto-I* in early 1997, when registered as the *Corto*. It underwent a series of name changes to disguise its role as a narcotics transport vessel. *(Fotolite)*

A Colombian Antinarcotics Police officer in a field of coca plants, with a makeshift processing laboratory ablaze behind him. These areas were often controlled by the left-wing guerillas of FARC. *(Dirección Antinarcóticos de la Policía Nacional de Colombia)*

Antinarcotics Police inside a cocaine laboratory. Hundreds of such labs were scattered across the cultivation zones. *(Dirección Antinarcóticos de la Policía Nacional de Colombia)*

The author outside a burning cocaine lab during a police raid in the Colombian jungle. Shootouts on such raids were not unknown, hence the flak jacket.

equipment and training. Both agencies tapped phones and pagers legally, authorised by a Colombian *fiscal*, and when they were listening to calls with English-speaking traffickers, would often ask us to translate for them. Even when the calls were between two Colombians in Spanish, the junior police listeners would sometimes not really understand what was going on, and we would help them to interpret. Traffickers spoke in code, or what we called 'rocker', and it was important to know how they worked in order to understand what they were really saying.

'No, they are not really buying twenty chickens,' we would explain to Holguin, the ANP listener. 'That means twenty kilos of cocaine.'

'No, they are not really delivering the drugs to someone at a cheese factory, they are sending it to Holland. Holland is where cheese is made.'

'No, his dog is not really sick, he is telling his accomplice that he thinks his telephone is being intercepted.'

We coordinated many joint investigations with the ANP and DAS, and at the busiest times might have several cases running at once, with scores of targets being eavesdropped, all talking about sending drugs to Europe.

In 1995 the arrival of encrypted digital cellphones in Colombia made our work far more complicated. The mobiles before then had been analogue, and could easily be accessed using radio frequency scanners. However, the telephone companies knew that there was a huge potential market for secure, encrypted handsets, and when Comcel, Celumovil and others started selling digital cellphones in Colombia their advertisements deliberately promoted them as being 'secure'. They boasted openly in their marketing campaigns that these new phones could not be intercepted due to their advanced encryption. Every narco worth his salt rushed out to buy one, – or several.

With the bad guys adopting these new digital phones, law enforcement raced against time to find ways to defeat them. Two British companies were among the first to crack the encryption algorithms, and they developed portable units that could intercept the new Colombian mobiles. The DEA also had some units but these were less effective. We invited the British companies to send us prototypes so that we could test them on live cases. The equipment had advanced IT software and various analytical capabilities. We could programme in large lists of target numbers and it would record and analyse all dialling data involving those numbers. It also had some hidden features for our own security: we put in our own phone numbers so that they could not be intercepted, and had a system to check which numbers had been intercepted in the previous weeks. There was also a fail-safe 'kill' facility: if a unit were stolen or fell into the wrong hands, we could dial in and delete the hard-drive to render it unusable. At the time, this was world-leading technology.

Operation Papagayo was an excellent example of how humint and sigint could complement each other to deliver a successful result. The case started in mid-1995, when an informant told us that a powerful trafficking group in Cali was negotiating a deal with the Russian mafia to exchange arms for cocaine. The Cali group planned to send 500 kg by sea to Bulgaria. The consignment would then be sent onward to customers in the UK and Holland, on behalf of the Russians. In return, the Russians would send an ex-military Antonov cargo plane loaded with firearms, including modern assault rifles and RPG grenade launchers. It was believed that the guns were destined for the right-wing AUC paramilitaries, who were fighting the left-wing FARC guerrillas and expanding their control over large areas of rural Colombia.

As so often in large trafficking deals, neither side wanted to send their goods without first having a large pre-payment or cast-iron guarantee that the other side would deliver on their half of the deal. After preliminary negotiations, it had been agreed that the Colombians would first send a smaller amount of cocaine as a test. It would also include a consignment of fifteen tonnes of marijuana, which would be sent to Spain but was ultimately destined for the UK. The proceeds of this initial shipment would be used as a down payment on the firearms.

The main organisers in Colombia were said to be two brothers, Gustavo and Tico. They were new-generation narcos, both in their early thirties, with expensive lifestyles. They represented even more powerful men from Cali, who would supply the drugs, but it was Tico and Gustavo who had brought everyone together. From their luxury apartment near the beach in the Boca Grande area of Cartagena, they had managed to broker a deal between the mafias in Cali and Russia, the customers in Spain and the UK, and the transport providers in Cartagena.

A cocaine-for-firearms swap was of great interest to DAS, who were mad keen to start an investigation. However, Tico and Gustavo were using the latest encrypted digital mobiles, and DAS did not yet have the technology to crack them. I arranged for the newly developed prototype units to be sent from London to use on the case. Their one drawback was that they had a limited range and would need to be close to the target. In October 1995, I went to Boca Grande and rented a small apartment to use as a listening post, just one block from Gustavo's pad. Within a few weeks we had installed the intercept equipment. A small team of DAS intelligence agents were allocated to the case, and we spent a large part of the next nine months working with them in Cartagena, gathering intelligence about Tico and Gustavo's plans.

Tico and Gustavo were in regular contact with the suppliers in Cali, and with the organisation in Spain and Bulgaria. From the intercepts, DAS were able to identify the Cali end and other associates involved. They also identified their contacts in Spain, and we passed details to the Spanish Police, who started their own investigation. By January 1996 a joint operation was ongoing in Spain, UK and Colombia, with a constant exchange of intelligence. Tico made several trips to Europe to coordinate with the organisation's representatives in the UK, Spain and Holland, whilst Gustavo made the arrangements in Colombia. Jimmy and Alex were the principals in Spain who would receive the drugs on arrival and ensure their safe passage through customs controls. Jimmy would then stash the drugs and arrange their onward transport in smaller loads to the UK. The British customer, called 'Tony', was also identified. At the Colombian end, Tico, Gustavo, William, Fernando and others got everything ready.

By early June, 1996, it was all prepared. Telephone intercepts in Cartagena and Spain had revealed all of the participants in both continents. We knew that they would send a container, that it would contain 480 boxes of 'denim jeans', and that inside the box they would hide drugs with a few pairs of jeans on top. They were actually getting three containers ready, and once the first consignment was successfully received, a second would be sent immediately to the same consignee. Then a third would go to Varna, in Bulgaria.

We were still missing the key pieces of information, however. We did not know when it would happen, which ship, the container number, the exporter or the importer. Without this, it would be virtually impossible to find the right container. At one point in early June we thought we had missed it. William was heard telling the Spanish that it was safely on its way. I frantically searched manifests and lists of exports but could not find any jeans that had been shipped to Spain. Maybe they had changed plans and described it as something else. I was sure we had lost it. It was a blessed relief, then, when we heard that due to a problem with paperwork it had been delayed. But it was now imminent.

By the end of June, Gustavo had sent all details of the container to Spain by courier. The British customer, Tony, was waiting in Spain with Jimmy, and Tico and William booked tickets to fly there too, to be present when it arrived. It was unlikely that we would get any more information from the intercepts, and we still did not have any details of the container. I was pulling out my hair in frustration. Having worked on the case for many months we knew all of the players but could still not identify the bloody container. Despite all our hard work, we could well miss it.

Then, completely out of the blue, CI Fidel telephoned. It was June 28.

'Good morning, señor. How are you? I have some good information for you. A container of jeans has just left Santa Marta on the ship *Autor*, destined for Valencia, Spain. I believe it contains a large quantity of drugs.'

Ah, sweet music. We had been working this case for over nine months, had dozens of telephones intercepted and knew the exact method of transport, but couldn't discover which container. Now Fidel was handing it to me on a plate. I could have hugged him.

'Fantastic news, my friend. Fantastic. Can you get details of the container?'

'But of course, señor. When can we meet?'

We met later that day. Fidel told me that the exporter was a Cali company called Fabuz SL, and he handed me a sheet of paper with full details of the importer in Spain and container number. I quickly passed them to the Spanish. They were delighted.

The ship arrived in Valencia on 19 July and was put under blanket surveillance as it offloaded. In the subsequent Spanish Police operation, thirteen tonnes of marijuana were seized and thirty-nine people were arrested, including Colombians, Brits, Bulgarians and Spanish. An entire criminal network was taken down.

An informant had started the case, by telling us about Tico and Gustavo and the drugs-for-guns enterprise. Intercepts, in both Colombia and Spain, had identified the people involved and provided evidence that would be used to convict them in court. And a second informant had identified the container and made the seizure possible. The three sources, both sigint and humint, had dovetailed to bring a resounding 'win'. Papagayo was the first successful investigation in Colombia that involved the interception of the new secure digital cellphones.

12

TRAINING COURSES

A FTER MY INITIAL success in recruiting agents during 1994 and early 1995, I had the idea of offering training courses for staff in the ports of Cartagena, Santa Marta, Barranquilla and Buenaventura. I hoped to use these to make contacts among the people working at ground level in all four ports. A colleague from Customs ID in London, Bob, agreed to help me coordinate a series of two-week courses during 1996, one in every port. Each course would be attended by between eighteen and twenty-one Colombians, selected from port security, the customs export inspectors, and antinarcotics police. We specified that they must all be operatives who physically worked in the port itself, and who would remain in those duties for at least the following two years. The training was delivered by Bob and other British officers with expertise in maritime trafficking, and focused on the identification, selection and search of suspect containers, cargo and vessels. We also donated practical search tools so that they had effective equipment.

The first course took place in Cartagena in January 1996 and was immediately followed by another in Santa Marta. The courses in Buenaventura and Barranquilla took place in May and June. For two weeks, our trainers showed the selected staff how to work together as a team to analyse customs and shipping documentation and to identify suspect or high-risk containers and cargo ships. They then had practical exercises over several days to search the highest-risk containers to find illicit items, such as drugs and firearms. The heads of security for Santa Marta and Cartagena ports, along with directors of the port authorities, were supportive and provided suitable facilities and access to port areas.

The training successfully raised the capabilities of the enforcement staff. During the Santa Marta course, they made two seizures, of 24 kg and 18 kg of cocaine respectively, from banana ships bound for Europe. Immediately after the Cartagena course, the newly trained team seized 200 kg of coke from a container. In Buenaventura, they seized twenty tonnes of marijuana and a container of precursor chemicals. The students themselves were motivated by the training and equipment, as well as the spirit of interagency collaboration that we promoted.

More importantly, the courses enabled me to establish contacts with a large group of key workers in each port. The customs staff responsible for inspecting export containers were there, and I knew that these would be ideal material to recruit from. Likewise the security supervisors, who I knew would be able to identify rip-ons, dodgy crewmen and other criminal activity, if only I could persuade them to work with me. From each course, I earmarked several students as possible recruitment targets, and made efforts to befriend them. During the months after the courses, I slowly built upon these relationships, developing friendship and trust before pitching them to work with me.

During the course in Santa Marta, however, an incident took place that would remind us of the high levels of corruption and put into perspective the limited value of the training. It concerned a shipment identified by CI Nancy.

I HAD MET Nancy in September 1995. She was involved with two men in Bogotá called Agosto and Hugo, who were sending large amounts of drugs to Europe. Nancy told me that Agosto worked with a big Medellin trafficker called Diego, and that they were shipping loads of cocaine and marijuana to customers in the UK and the Netherlands. She even gave me the names and contact details of the principal customers. The main Dutchman, Hans, was based in Amsterdam and the British customers were based in Merseyside. Nancy said that they were planning to send two shipments of marijuana to the UK in the coming month, inside two containers of cotton T-shirts. The first would be five tonnes, the second another five tonnes and an unknown quantity of cocaine.

Over the following months I met Nancy numerous times, normally in restaurants and apartments in downtown Bogotá, and she provided me with updates on the planned shipments. Agosto had wanted to send the first container in November, but it was delayed because of a disagreement with the Scousers over payment. It was rescheduled for December, but was again delayed at the last minute. Finally, after months of wrangling between the Colombian suppliers, Dutch intermediaries and Liverpool buyers, it was arranged to ship the first container from Santa Marta in January 1996.

On 26 January, I met Nancy in the north of Bogotá. After watching her follow the normal counter-surveillance route, I picked her up and we had a meeting in a budget hamburger restaurant on Calle 140. We sat in the far corner at a dirty plastic table, with cigarette butts and pieces of discarded food littering the floor, as she gave me the lowdown on the first shipment, in between mouthfuls of greasy cheese-burger. She was very precise. A consignment of 452 boxes of cotton T-Shirts, with a weight of 7,000 kg, had been loaded inside a twenty-foot container. The exporter was a company called Importex SA, based in Bogotá. The container was being shipped to a company called Entara in the UK. Nancy said that each of the 452 boxes had a few T-shirts on top, but apart from that were completely filled with drugs. Instead of 7,000 kg of T-shirts, the container had about 1,500kg of T-shirts and the other 5.5 tonnes was marijuana.

'What about the cocaine?' I asked.

'I don't know,' she said. 'I am not sure if any has also been sent. But I know the container will be loaded onto a ship called *Sierra Express*. And it will leave Santa Marta on January 31.'

I didn't say anything, but I had a horrible feeling in my stomach. This was the worst possible date to send a container from Santa Marta.

I rushed back to the office and hurriedly checked through my papers to find our training course programme. Sure enough, there it was: the departure of the *Sierra Express* would be slap in the middle of our planned course in Santa Marta. The programme for the 30th indicated that the trainers would be having a practical exercise to show the students how to identify the most high-risk containers. On the 31st they had a practical exercise in the port to search suspect containers. This meant that twenty-one students and two British customs experts would be examining all of the bills of lading for the *Sierra Express*, and then searching containers before they were loaded. They would almost certainly identify the container of jeans from Importex SA and select it for search.

Having spent months on this, we really wanted it to be shipped to the UK so that we could investigate and arrest the criminal group back home. All that hard work would be lost if the course students chose to search it. I thought of rearranging the course, but it was too late for that.

On Monday, 29 January, I flew from Bogotá to Santa Marta and joined Bob and Mark, the HM Customs trainers, as they delivered their course. I said that I had come to observe. I quietly briefed the two trainers that evening, and explained that if at all possible they should try to steer the attendees away from the suspect container from Importex SA. I prayed that there might be other more suspicious containers worthy of their attention. The trainers had previously obtained the schedule of vessels loading in the port and the *Sierra Express* was the only container ship that would be carrying cargo to Europe. Bob had arranged that on the 30th the customs attendees would retrieve the bills of lading and shipping documents for all the containers that were about to be loaded on to the *Sierra Express*. Then he would analyse the documents in detail with the students, showing them how to carry out basic checks and how to identify the most suspicious.

The next day, I watched nervously as the course students went through the documents, checking indicators and discussing which ones looked suspect. I waited for them to come across the one from Importex SA, a company which I knew had only just been formed and operated from a tiny office in Bogotá, and hence should immediately arouse their suspicion. But it did not appear. I later went through all of the paperwork myself, and the papers for the container of T-shirts from Importex were definitely not there.

I should have known that the mafia would sort out the problem. Once traffickers have paid off the port mafia to ensure safe passage of a consignment, it is guaranteed. The mafia would not allow the presence of HMCE and a training course to impede their shipment. At first, I imagined that the traffickers might have postponed the shipment to another date. However, a few days later our freight intelligence team in London confirmed that the suspect container from Importex SA was indeed on board the *Sierra Express*. We realised that the port mafia had removed the bill of lading and other documents from customs records, and also from the port authority loading database, so that the container 'disappeared'. Once the training course had finished and the ship departed, the documents were put back.

Two weeks later, the container arrived in Felixstowe. HM Customs discovered 5.5 tonnes of marijuana inside the boxes, just as Nancy had said. An operation followed to arrest the criminal organisation in the UK.

The incident brought home to me the power of the corrupt mafias in the port, and the possible futility of delivering training. The port mafias controlled safe passage for the cartels. Even if we tried to find honest staff and then trained them to profile containers, the mafia could simply make the documentation disappear so that certain containers were invisible. Drugs could easily be shipped right beneath our noses.

ANOTHER INCIDENT THAT ensued from the Santa Marta training course related to a customs inspector. It gave me a strong reminder of how dangerous it was to try to recruit informants in ports. The Customs Service, DIAN, had inspectors in each port whose function was to search containers before departure for contraband and prohibited exports. The port mafia would pay the inspectors and their senior managers to ensure that containers with drugs inside were never searched. I assumed that most of the customs inspectors on export duties must *de facto* be corrupt. Even in the unlikely event that one of them was not, and wanted to do the job properly, they would soon be offered the bribe or bullet and obliged to either cooperate or leave.

Against this backdrop, I decided that I would try to recruit some of the inspectors. We had a dozen or so attending our Santa Marta and Cartagena courses, and of these I selected two to approach. One of them, who I shall call Rafael, had the perfect profile. He had graduated from university with a degree in business administration, was intelligent, sharp, friendly and very sociable. When out of uniform, he dressed smartly and clearly had a reasonable income. Given the low salaries paid to customs inspectors, my suspicions were further heightened when I found out that he also had an expensive car and a nice apartment.

During the Cartagena course I spoke with him a lot, and we went for drinks afterwards with the trainers and others. Over the following months I visited Cartagena once or twice a month, and on each trip I made time to have a coffee or go out for a meal or drinks with him. I also raised the possibility of getting him a place on training courses in the UK or an exchange visit to HMCE in London, something in which he was very interested. We slowly became friends, and I learnt more about him and about how the inspectors operated in Cartagena. He let me know that he owned an apartment in Fort Lauderdale, Florida, although he quickly backtracked and said that he had inherited it from grandparents. Either way, he clearly had a lifestyle way beyond what his salary could justify.

Eventually, several months later and over drinks one evening, I suggested to him that many customs inspectors must be taking bribes to smooth the safe passage of certain containers. I was encouraged when he did not deny it. Whilst taking great care to avoid any accusation that he might himself be corrupt, I proposed that if he ever overheard anything from his colleagues about such containers, I could pay good rewards for information. Rafael listened calmly, and seemed keen, so I went on to explain that we worked very discreetly, that HM Customs would handle any information so carefully that he would never be put at risk, and that we would pay well for the right information.

When I finished, he paused for a moment and then calmly said that he was very interested in what I had said but needed to explain something to me.

'Tom, you are a nice guy. It is really fantastic that you

have tried to help us in customs by giving us training courses and equipment. We really appreciate that. What you and the customs trainers have done is tremendous.'

He paused for a moment, seeming to choose his words carefully before continuing.

'There is nothing that you've said that isn't true. You know how it is, and how the mafia operates to get drugs out. Yes, customs inspectors take money to turn a blind eye. That is how it works. The pay is shit, and that is how we feed our families and get on. And even if I wanted to change that, I couldn't. It is far too dangerous.'

I was getting a good feeling. He seemed relaxed and I felt sure that he was about to accept the offer. Instead, he hit me with a bombshell.

'But let's be clear about this. You need to understand that what you have just said is very dangerous. If you repeat what you have said to me to anyone else around here, it will get you killed. Now I like you, you are a nice guy. So I'm going to forget what you said and pretend that I never heard it. But I warn you that if you say it to any of the other customs guys, they will report it back, and it will put you in big danger.'

He then told me that he did not want to be associated with me any more, and not to bother calling him next time I came to Cartagena. As he left, his parting works were, 'You're a nice guy, Tom, and you mean well. But I think you're going to get yourself killed.'

Back in my hotel room, I took stock. I was bitterly disappointed that I had spent months trying to recruit Rafael and had failed. On the other hand, by investing a lot of time befriending him before making a pitch, at least I hoped that he wasn't going to tell anyone. But I was a shaken by his warnings. I had met another informant earlier that day and afterwards thought that I might have been followed; I saw the same two young guys several times. All in all it had been a bad day. I lay on my hotel bed that night feeling very uneasy, and didn't sleep much. The next morning, I decided to check out and catch an early flight back to Bogotá, just in case.

SEVERAL MONTHS LATER I tried to recruit another customs inspector from a different port. I had marked her out during one of the training courses. Raquel was single and lived with her parents, was intelligent and seemed a nice person. I followed the same lengthy and time-consuming process that I had used for Rafael, befriending her over several months before pitching her. This time I felt certain that I had cracked it. Raquel accepted that some of her colleagues worked for the traffickers. Whilst not admitting to being involved herself, she acknowledged that she did sometimes see things and overhear colleagues talking about suspicious containers. More importantly, she agreed to work with me and to pass me information. I was chuffed to bits. I knew that Raquel could open the floodgates and give me a flow of rich intelligence.

About a month later, Raquel passed me details of a container heading to Spain which was suspicious. She said that a shipping agent had offered colleagues money not to inspect it. I told Poddy, who arranged to have the container searched when it arrived. I was gutted when they told us that it didn't appear to contain anything other than the declared cargo. I assumed that the Spanish hadn't looked properly.

A few months later, she phoned with details of three containers that had been shipped to Spain on the vessel *Dinamarca*. She said they were all highly suspicious and almost certainly contained drugs. We passed the information to the Spanish and the containers were searched when they arrived in Cadiz, but again were all negative.

After that, Raquel would periodically pass me details of containers. She would say that she had overheard from colleagues that they contained drugs, or had seen strange activity at the container, or had other reasons to suspect that they contained drugs. They were always clean when searched. I came to realise that Raquel was wasting my time. I suspect that she had probably reported my approach to her corrupt managers, or to the mafia in the port, and had been instructed to go along with it and pass me false information. During the following year she succeeded in wasting my time, and the time of numerous officers in Spain and Holland when they made pointless searches of containers acting on her false information. I have no doubt that there would have been real shipments of drugs on each of those ships, and Raquel was just distracting our attention.

DESPITE SEVERAL ATTEMPTS, I was never able to break into the tightly knit groups of customs inspectors and recruit any of them. Nonetheless, the training exercises did enable me to make valuable contacts and to recruit several sources amongst port security, police and other port workers. The recruitment of CIs Roberto, Andy, Jairo and Oso were all made possible by the port courses.

The training also genuinely raised the capabilities of the police and customs in detecting maritime shipments, and earned us considerable goodwill. I attended the last two or three days of each of the courses myself, and delivered a session on intelligence. A key component of this session was informants. I sought to emphasise to attendees on each course that they themselves could pass information in complete confidence and safety, and could receive significant recompense. I also suggested that they could receive information from others and pass it to us on their behalf, again in absolute secrecy. I left a large pile of my business cards with a mobile number on it, and said they could call me any time, day or night, and did not even have to give their real names. They all took a card, and some of them took several, clearly intending to pass them to others. In the months following each course I received several calls. Perhaps the one that best demonstrated the long-term benefit of the training courses was CI Roy.

On 5 February 1998, I took a telephone call from an unknown male. I could see that he was calling from a number in Cartagena. He asked for me by name, but would not give his own name. He said that he worked in Cartagena docks and could give me information about a drug shipment that was on its way to Europe. He needed to speak urgently as it would arrive soon. I invited him to fly to Bogotá and said that I'd pay for his ticket. He agreed, and said he would come the very next morning.

At 9.30 a.m. the next day, Steve and I met with CI Roy for the first time. He said he had been given my name and number by a friend who had attended one of our courses two years earlier, in Cartagena. His friend had showed Roy my business card, and told him that he could pass me information in confidence. Roy said that the banana ship *Ivory Bay* had departed Turbo approximately eight days previously and that 45 kg of cocaine were being transported by crewmen. It was hidden inside four vests, and when they arrived in Antwerp dock workers would come on board to collect. The dockers would put the vests on, cover them with their own clothes, and walk off the ship. The *Ivory Bay* was due to arrive in Antwerp on 10 February. Furthermore, Roy said that if this first piece of information went well, he would be able to tell us much more in future. He also said he knew others in the port interested in working with us. The Belgian authorities carried out surveillance on the *Ivory Bay* when it berthed in Antwerp. They saw two dock workers go on board and disembark a short time later. They were followed and searched at a routine security checkpoint. They were carrying 31 kg of cocaine inside specially adapted vests, and were arrested.

CI Roy continued working for the British DLOs for several years. He produced a regular stream of valuable intelligence about trafficking from Turbo, and generated numerous seizures in Europe. It was remarkable to think that we had recruited Roy because of a training course that took place two years earlier, in January 1996.

13

PROSTITUTES, BANANAS AND STOWAWAYS

COLOMBIA WAS THE third largest exporter of bananas in the world during the 1990s, after Ecuador and Costa Rica. The crop was cultivated in the Urabá and Magdalena regions in the north-east and north-west respectively, and was exported from the two main ports there, Turbo and Santa Marta. Banana ships for the Chiquita company and the Star Line plied the route to Europe on a weekly basis and the cartels used them as a convenient and reliable way to transport cocaine.

Turbo is in the Gulf of Urabá, less than 50 km from the border with Panama and 340 km north of Medellin. Constant conflict and power struggles between the FARC guerrillas, AUC paramilitaries and drug cartels rendered it unsafe for outsiders. Such was the violence that banana producing companies paid the AUC paramilitaries large sums to protect their employees and installations. It was far too dangerous for me to go there and try to recruit informants myself.

During my first two years in Colombia, CI Gerardo gave me a lot of information about coke on the banana ships from Turbo and Santa Marta. It included details of several large shipments to Belgium on the vessels *Chiquita Rostock*,

Ariake Star and *Avila Star*. Gerardo also described the various concealment methods being used. Consignments of up to 50 kg were frequently hidden in the refrigerated cargo holds. The floors of the hold were not solid but made of metal grates with hollow spaces beneath, to allow air to flow around the cargo and help maintain it at the correct temperature during the voyage. The narcos in Santa Marta and Turbo would conceal bags of cocaine beneath the floor grates, and once the fruit was loaded into the hold the consignment was safe. When the bananas were unloaded in Europe, the drugs could be recovered from beneath the floor grates and carried off the ship. Gerardo said much larger amounts, of 100–200 kg, were being hidden in the propeller shaft or rudder housing and were recovered by scuba divers on arrival in Belgium.

CI Mike passed me similar information, but despite the details that they both gave, the Belgians were unable to intercept any coke. Antwerp port was completely overwhelmed at that time by the huge flow of drugs from South America, and customs and the police had only small teams to deal with the scores of ships arriving daily. Unless we could give them very specific information, they did not have the resources to respond.

In mid-1995, our London desk officer went over to Antwerp and spoke with the police team there. He explained that when we gave them information about the banana ships, it had come from a very reliable source in Santa Marta. Whilst he couldn't officially tell them about that source, they needed to understand that the intel was one hundred per cent reliable. Following this visit, the Belgians started to take us more seriously. Seizures began to follow.

At around the same time, CI Mike infiltrated the organisation of Lucho M in Santa Marta and started getting access to information about his banana boat shipments. Lucho was a well-known trafficker on the north coast. He lived in Cartagena and ran a ships' provisions company, which gave him access to the ports. He used this to provide transport services for the Cali Cartel and arrange their shipments through both Cartagena and Santa Marta. He had access to rip-on facilities in Cartagena and regularly sent cocaine inside containers. He also had an efficient transport route with crewmen on the Santa Marta banana ships. The quantities on the latter were much smaller, normally 20–40 kg per shipment, but ran regularly several times a month.

CI Mike recruited a sub-source close to Lucho's contacts in Santa Marta port. This new informant was able to tell us when cocaine was being sent on a particular ship, and could say which grate it was under in which floor area. This was the precise information that we knew the Belgians needed. In May 1995, Mike told me that Lucho had sent 20 kg with two Filipino crewmen on the *Ariake Star*. They had been given the drugs in Santa Marta, and at Antwerp would carry them off the ship and hand them to two men who would arrive by car from Amsterdam. Mike was even able to give descriptions of the crewmen, and when the *Ariake Star* docked in Antwerp, the Belgian police were able to identify and follow them as they left the ship. They went to a café near the port, where they met three men in a car. All five people were arrested as the crewmen handed over 20 kg of coke to three Colombians in the car.

A few months later, CI Marta gave me information about a consignment that Lucho had sent on the *Fuji Star* beneath the grates of the floor in hold two. Acting on our information, the Belgians seized 35 kg from the ship in Antwerp on October 31. A few days later, CI Mike passed information about another shipment by Lucho on the *Ariake Star* and the Belgians took out another 20 kg.

Lucho was furious about the seizure of three of his consignments, particularly the last two, which had been lost within a week. He blamed his contacts in Antwerp, accusing them of carelessness, and summoned them to a meeting to find out what had gone wrong. At the end of November, Lucho's main contact in Antwerp flew to Colombia to meet him and make future plans. Anton worked in security at the port, was married to a Colombian and spoke Spanish. Thanks to CI Mike we were aware of his imminent arrival, the hotel where he would stay in Santa Marta, and his itinerary. We coordinated an intelligence operation to find out as much as possible about the plans Anton would make with Lucho for their future shipments. His hotel room was bugged, the telephones tapped, and surveillance teams followed his every movement.

Antwerp was an open port without physical security controls at the entrance, and people could go in and out easily. This was one of the main reasons why it was so attractive to criminals and had become the port of choice for the Colombians. Anton brought with him a map of Antwerp port and showed it to Lucho to agree places where their crewmen, stowaways and dockers could meet and hand over drugs. It was important that Lucho gave clear instructions to his people in Santa Marta so that Anton could recover the drugs smoothly, without problems. Anton explained that from jetty number 188 his people could observe the banana ships when they arrived. Colombian banana ships always berthed at jetties 111 to 127. From there, the stowaways or crewmen carrying off drugs should walk to a café at Luchtbal, on the corner of Noordlaan, near jetty 188, where they would hand over the drugs to Anton's crew. Anton would also have people watching out for any surveillance by the police or anything suspicious. As a fall-back plan in case of problems, a second meeting place would be the Novotel hotel, 500 metres up the road from the café. A second fall-back would be the Stella Maris Seaman's club. Anton and Lucho were happy with these new arrangements and did not expect any further problems.

Unfortunately for Lucho and Anton, not only did we now know about their plans but also Mike and CI Marta had recruited new sub-sources within their transport organisation in Santa Marta.

SHORTLY AFTER ANTON'S visit to Colombia, Marta told me that she had recruited a sub-source who worked as a prostitute in Santa Marta docks and spent time with crewmen on the banana ships. I was a little concerned to hear this. I wasn't bothered about the moral aspect, and prostitution is legal in Colombia, but I wondered how London might react. I could imagine the headlines if the press ever found out:

British diplomat gives public funds to Colombian prostitute

Or perhaps

Customs officer paid hooker to go undercover

Or even

Customs and Sex-cise

I could see the potential for acute embarrassment. Normally I insisted on meeting all sub-sources personally at least once when they first started. I had to ensure that they clearly understood our rules of engagement; for example, that they must not participate in smuggling or other criminal activities themselves, must never incite or entice others to crime, and must be truthful and tell us everything. Once I had confirmed that they knew our rules, I could step back and let the lead informant handle them. In the case of Marta's prostitute, however, I decided that it was probably better for all concerned if I didn't meet her personally. I left it for Marta to explain the rules of the game, as it were.

Marta (P), as the sub-source became known, frequented the banana and coal boats while they were loaded in Santa Marta. She would often spend several days on board whilst a ship was in port, and in the process could gather a valuable stream of information about which crewmen were transporting drugs, and where they were hidden. It was remarkable how freely they spoke in front of her, but no doubts their minds were on other matters at the time.

With Marta (P) into the transport crewmen, and CI Mike having infiltrated the organiser, Lucho, I was able to combine intel from different perspectives, an ideal situation. The first seizure came in January 1996 when Marta (P), through fraternising on the ships, told us that two crew members of the *Nedlloyd Neerlandia* had taken a large quantity of drugs on board and would hand it over in Antwerp. Again it was hidden beneath the floor grates in the second hold, between levels B and C. The Belgian authorities were waiting when the ship berthed, and seized 75 kg of cocaine from the two men as they disembarked.

Marta (P) also said that a sailor on the *Akebono Star* was transporting 15 kg, which he would carry off in a jacket. Belgian police followed him when he left the ship in Antwerp and arrested him at a nearby café as he handed the jacket, which actually contained 16 kg of coke, to a receiver.

Just a few weeks later, Marta told us that the cook and others on the *Swan Stream* were involved. Observations on the ship when it arrived in Antwerp on 20 February 1996 led to the arrest of four people as they handed over 70 kg of cocaine.

These three seizures within less than a month caused huge problems for Lucho. He had lost 161 kg of cocaine in a month and six people had been arrested in Antwerp. He knew that there must be an informant somewhere but had no way of telling whether it was in Santa Marta, Antwerp or somewhere else.

During the following twelve months, we supplied the authorities in Antwerp with a constant stream of intelligence about shipments, often telling them precisely where the drugs had been concealed, which crewmen were involved, and the people who would collect or receive it. They started giving our intelligence priority, and a flurry of seizures followed in quick succession:

50 kg from the vessel *La Pampa* in Amsterdam,
30 kg from the *Chiquita Elke* in Antwerp
40 kg from the *Ivory Cape* in Antwerp

40 kg from the *Ivory Ace* in Antwerp
40 kg from the *Polar Argentina* in Antwerp

In addition to the drugs seized, at least twenty-one people were arrested in Antwerp, causing significant disruption to the criminal organisation there. Lucho's transport route was effectively dismantled. He had lost narcotics worth several million dollars and the traffickers in Colombia and Europe had lost confidence in him. More importantly, he was held responsible by his clients for their losses, faced financial ruin and lived in fear of assassination.

Yet the flow of cocaine on the banana ships continued. In addition to Lucho M, several other organisations were using the banana ships. Perhaps the biggest of them was the Bogotá Cartel.

'LA ROLA' WAS a woman in her mid-fifties from Bogotá. She was professional, well-organised, and controlled the flow of cocaine from Santa Marta to Holland, via Antwerp, on banana ships for the Bogotá Cartel. La Rola had developed a very effective system. Her team in Holland was led by her brother, nicknamed 'El Enano' – 'The Dwarf' – and another Colombian female called Luz Marina, known as 'La Mona', or 'Cutie'. El Enano and Luz Marina controlled a group of corrupt Antwerp port workers, mainly Surinamese dockers, cleaners and sanitation staff, and had useful contacts in Belgian Customs. The port workers in Antwerp wore bright yellow high-visibility vests so that they could be easily identified. Marina stole several of these and sent them to La Rola in Colombia, who had dozens of vests made of the same design, shape, fabric and colour. They were identical to the original except for one important detail: the Colombian ones had secret pockets on the inside. These could contain 15 kg of powder per vest, concealed in thin blocks that could not be seen when worn.

La Rola arranged for vests packed with drugs to be given to crewmen on the banana ships when they loaded in Santa Marta. Alternatively, the vests were hidden in the holds or in other pre-agreed places. Often five or six vests, each with 15 kg inside, would be sent on each ship. On arrival in Antwerp, workers would recover the vests and put them on over their own vest. It was then easy to carry the drugs off the ship and out of the port. El Enano and Luz Marina would drive down from Holland and meet the workers in a café close to the port to receive the drugs and pay them. On average this well-organised group had a ninety per cent success rate, losing just one or two of every twenty vests that were sent. Hundreds of kilos got through each month.

At the start of 1997, the Star Line ships changed their route and started going to Marin and Vigo in Spain, before going on to Antwerp. The trafficking groups welcomed this, and made arrangements for drugs to be received in Spain as well as Antwerp. Cocaine was still concealed in the cargo holds, but different hiding places had to be used if the drugs were to be offloaded in Marin, because the holds were still full of bananas bound for Antwerp and the floor grates could not be lifted. Mike and Marta provided a wealth of information about drugs on the banana ships that left from Santa Marta, but the authorities in Antwerp were so overwhelmed by the flow of drugs that only about a third of the consignments that we identified were seized.

Although we had developed good sources in Santa Marta, I was increasingly frustrated by the fact that I could still not get reliable information about shipments from Turbo. Our breakthrough there came in the shapely form of Angelina. She was a very pretty young *mulata* who, had she been born in a different time and place, could have been a model, gracing the covers of glossy magazines. Fate had dealt her a much weaker hand, and instead she was a prostitute in the port of Turbo.

The ships there did not load bananas from a quayside or conventional dock. Instead, they anchored in the estuary and cargo was brought out to them on large commercial barges, known to the locals as *bongos*. Tugs would tow out a train of *bongos* all linked together, and the bananas and other cargo would be loaded from them by crane. When a ship first arrived, prostitutes would also be taken out on the barges, along with supplies. The girls would remain on board for several days, entertaining the crew whilst the ship was at anchor and being loaded. Sometimes they were also paid by traffickers to carry drugs out to the crewmen.

In addition to her other skills, Angelina had an entrepreneurial flair and realised that she could tap into multiple income streams from this murky business: she could get paid to perform her habitual services, get paid to carry drugs out to the ship, and get paid for telling us about it afterwards. Mike recruited her as a sub-source. I warned him that we could not agree to her carrying drugs out to the ships herself. However there was no problem in her telling us about what she saw, heard and learnt from her other friends in the trade and from her clients.

Angelina became our eyes and ears in Turbo. We had little control over what she got up to once she went out to the ships, or what methods she used to obtain her information, but she sent us a regular stream of reports about which ships were loading, when they departed, and which crewmen were carrying drugs to Antwerp and other European ports. Over the following year she told us about dozens of shipments on the banana boats, revealing where the drugs were stashed and which crewmen were responsible, and we were able to organise numerous seizures on their arrival in Belgium and Spain.

For obvious reasons I didn't want to pay Angelina reward money myself, and I never got to meet her personally, leaving CI Mike to deal with her. She was, however, a superb source.

IT TOOK A long time before I could get any quality intelligence about ship stowaways from Turbo. Early in 1997 CI Mike told me that two of them were on the *Trojan Star*, carrying 50 kg of coke to Marin, Spain. They were hiding inside the refrigerated hold. Once the vessel had docked and was unloaded, they would get the drugs and sneak off the ship at night. Their instructions were to climb through a hole in the perimeter fence out onto the public walkway, and follow a map they had been given showing where to find a public telephone. They were to call a local number, the drugs would be taken from them and they would be paid. They were then free to start a new life in Spain.

Just a few weeks later, another stowaway was said to be on the *Afric Star* to Marin with 30 kg of coke, using the same system. Unfortunately on both these occasions we told the Spanish police but they were not able to spot the stowaways or seize the drugs. These were the lucky ones.

On 4 May 1997, CI Pacho telephoned me and said that the *Afric Star* had left Turbo the previous week and was due to arrive in Marin in two days' time. He explained that a stowaway had sneaked on board in Turbo and was minding a consignment of more than 70 kg hidden in the rudder housing. His hiding place was at the rear of the ship, in a space above the steering rudder known as the rudder trunk. He wore a wetsuit to keep warm and had life vests with him. When the ship berthed in Marin, he was to put on the vests and jump into the sea with the drugs, which were in two large waterproof holdalls with flotation devices. He would be picked up by a small fishing boat that would be waiting for him.

Pacho's information was extremely detailed; he even gave me the name, age and description of the stowaway. I immediately informed our DLO in Spain, who coordinated with the local authorities. The Spanish did a great job and were watching the ship as it approached Marin and docked. In the event, the stowaway did not jump into the sea as instructed, as he feared being hit by the propellers, or drowned. That was probably a wise decision, because he couldn't swim and there was no fishing boat waiting to pick him up as promised. Instead he waited until nightfall, then quietly crept off the ship and out of the port. He made a call to a Spanish mobile number that he had been given in case of emergency. The Spanish police had him under surveillance, and when a car with three Colombians inside arrived to collect him, they were all arrested. A search of the ship's rudder trunk revealed 91 kg of cocaine, plus the remnants of food and drink from his eleven-day journey.

This was our first successful arrest of a stowaway from Turbo, and confirmed the information that CI Mike and Gerardo had been feeding me during the previous two years. Both of them had told me about the use of desperate young men prepared to take appalling risks to hide in the ships. The Urabá region was one of the poorest in Colombia. It had suffered years of internal civil war and conflicts between the guerrilla and right-wing paramilitaries, with both sides carrying out massacres of the local population if they were considered sympathetic to the other side. Young people faced a harsh life of poverty, crime, violence and little prospect of a good job or stable future. Against this backdrop it was not difficult for traffickers to find young men who would be willing to stow away in return for the opportunity of a better life in Spain.

Sometimes drugs were hidden in the holds of the ships and stowaways were promised several thousand dollars to hide with them and mind the drugs, then carry them off upon arrival. However, the cargo holds of banana ships were refrigerated, so they would have to stay hidden in dark, damp and very cold conditions for ten to twelve days. Coming from Turbo, with its hot and humid climate, the men were not accustomed to cold, and didn't have any warm clothing to protect themselves from freezing during the journey.

At other times, they would hide in the anchor chain space at the front or rear of ships. They would have a holdall containing maybe 30kg of cocaine, and would be instructed to carry it off and hand it over to people waiting in Marin or Antwerp. The anchor spaces were large enough to rig up a reasonably comfortable sleeping space for the journey. However, they were very dangerous places. Some stowaways would fall out during rough weather, or be dragged out by the chain if taken unawares on arrival.

On other occasions, people hid in the rudder housing, as the one arrested in Marin had done. The lucky ones were provided with wetsuits to keep warm, and sometimes life jackets, and would sit in the cold and wet space in complete darkness for up to twelve days.

In August 1997, CI Mike told me about a stowaway run that was almost identical to the method used for the earlier 91 kg that Pacho had described, except that it was going to the Netherlands and not Spain. He said that the ship *Autor* had just left from Santa Marta with an undeclared passenger hiding in the rudder space at the rear. He was wearing a wetsuit beneath his clothes and had a life vest, and had been given 40 kg of coke inside a large, waterproof holdall with foam inside so that it would float. He had been instructed that on arrival in Rotterdam he should wait until the propellers stopped turning, then climb down the steering column into the sea and swim away from the ship carrying the holdall. He would be picked up by a small fishing boat. We told the Dutch, but unfortunately they did not see him, and we heard later that the run went through.

It is difficult to imagine how horrible it must be to sit cramped up in a small, freezing, wet rudder trunk, in complete darkness, in a moving ship rolling side to side on the high seas, with the waves just a few feet below, and the nonstop pounding of the engine and propellers. Then, after nearly two weeks in such horrific conditions, to jump into the cold sea with bags of drugs, hoping not to drown but to be picked up by a fishing boat that may, or may not, be waiting. Yet these desperate young men from Urabá did just that. Some were lucky and earned their new life in Europe. Others were caught and spent several years in jail. Many others disappeared, probably having fallen into the sea.

The use of stowaways from Turbo and Santa Marta continued right up until I left Colombia, and is still a successful method today.

14

UNDER THE WATER

THE CONCEALMENT OF drugs underwater, beneath the hulls of ships, was virtually unheard of until the mid-1990s. Prior to that, the smugglers used a range of traditional methods: inside containers, in bulk cargo, and hidden inside different types of produce. They were highly imaginative and devised ingenious concealments such as inside fresh fruit, inside carved handicrafts, within tinned products, impregnated into clothing, and even making false 'coal' and other objects from modified and painted cocaine hydrochloride. Drugs were also hidden onboard ships, for example in the engine room, the paint store, the anchor chain housing, and a plethora of other concealment places that are well-known to experienced smugglers, sailors and customs men.

But when drugs are hidden in cargo or onboard a ship, there is always a risk that they might be detected and seized during searches at their destination. The cartels started using under-the-hull concealments in the mid-1990s because it would avoid normal customs controls, and would therefore be almost impossible to detect. They used three main locations under the waterline: the sea chest, the rudder housing, and parasitic attachments, or 'torpedoes', as they became known.

The sea chest is a recess in the side of a ship, located near the bottom of the hull and typically adjacent to the engine room. It is a water inlet system, through which seawater is drawn in to cool the engine and for ballast. The recesses vary in size and are always covered by a metal grate to prevent foreign objects being sucked in and fouling the cooling systems. On larger vessels, sea chests can be several square metres in size and large enough to accommodate several hundred kilos of cocaine.

The rudder housing, also known as the rudder trunk, is the area where the steering mechanism comes out from the stern of a ship. In large cargo vessels, this can be several metres wide. The area is dry when ships are empty of cargo and sitting high in the water, but becomes submerged or semi-submerged when they are loaded. The space is often large enough to accommodate several hundred kilos of drugs and also human stowaways, and can be accessed from underwater and sometimes via hatches from inside.

Parasitic attachments are extraneous items such as metal tubes that are welded to the hull, beneath the waterline. They were often long and torpedo-like, hence the name.

All three of these underwater concealment methods had the advantage that there was no need for any involvement by crew members, nor any need to pay corrupt port security and customs staff. Scuba divers were employed to put the drugs in place, and to recover them at the port of destination. It was therefore a very secure method.

However, the under-the-hull method could not be used in every port, nor for every destination. To secure a consignment beneath the hull, divers needed clear water with good visibility and for the ship to be stationary, with all engines off, for a reasonable period of time. Busy commercial ports such as Cartagena were dangerous for divers as there were unpredictable currents caused by the constant movement of ships, toxic and dangerous materials in the water, and high risks of being injured by propellers and moving ships. Likewise, ports such as Barranquilla, sitting on the dirty river Magdalena full of debris and silt, were unsuitable. The ideal ports for this method were those that were less busy, where the water visibility was good and where ships would stay for several days to load. That made Turbo and Santa Marta the perfect locations.

Turbo is on the Gulf of Urabá, on the Caribbean Sea, in the north-east of Colombia, and was the closest and most accessible port for traffickers in Medellin. Banana ships and smaller container ships continuously plied the route from Turbo to Europe. They would often sit at anchor for several days in the calmer waters of the gulf whilst being loaded from barges, and were easy targets for divers wishing to conceal drugs. However, Urubá was a dangerous and unstable region at the time, often under the control of FARC guerrillas or the AUC paramilitaries, and was difficult terrain in which to recruit informants.

Santa Marta is on the north-western Caribbean coast, and has a natural deep-water anchorage with docks for container and bulk cargo ships. In addition to its main port, it had three coal ports that were well-suited to this method of shipping drugs and which soon became the preferred locations for under-the-hull jobs. Large coal boats were loaded by conveyor belt or crane, a slow process that normally took several days. That meant that the ships sat immobile in clear water for lengthy periods, which gave the diving teams plenty of time to do their work.

Carboandes was a coal production business that had been linked to the Medellin Cartel. The company president, Gustavo Tapias Ospina, alias 'Techo', was rumoured to have managed maritime transport routes for the cartel, and was later convicted of drug trafficking in the USA. Carboandes loaded its coal boats from its private jetty within the main port area. Prodeco was another large Colombian coal exporter and had its own port a few miles outside of Santa Marta.

Drummond was the largest coal port. It had its own private port facility 16 km south of Santa Marta with two very long piers, each over a mile in length, that went out into the deeper waters of the Caribbean. Large coal boats anchored at the piers and were loaded by conveyor belts that were themselves over a mile long and brought the coal from the stockpiles to the end of the pier. Again, this was ideal for the traffickers. Large coal boats destined for Europe sat at anchor in clear open waters for up to a week while the coal was loaded. The Drummond boats became regular platforms for the cartels to send drugs to Europe.

THE PROBLEM WITH under-the-hull concealments was that the only people who knew about them were the traffickers and the scuba divers. The owners and operators of the coal ships did not know, nor did the captain and crew. There were no shipping agents, customs or dock workers involved who I might try to recruit. This considerably narrowed my possibilities.

By 1995 we knew that underwater shipments were taking place regularly to Europe. I had received information from several contacts in the ports and there had been seizures in Spain. I tasked CIs Mike, Marta, Barry and Pacho to try to recruit sub-sources who could get us specific information. Marta was the first to get results. In early February 1996, she contacted me and said that the coal ship *Cape Ray* had left Santa Marta bound for Rotterdam. Marta had never heard of a sea chest but her description was clear, and I knew exactly what she meant. She explained that on the side of the hull of the ship, beneath the water line, there was some kind of hole or large recess, and that divers had put four dark-blue canvas bags, known as *tulas*, inside. The divers tied the *tulas* to a metal grille with rope so that they were secure. She said they contained between 100 and 160 kg of cocaine, and that as soon as the vessel arrived in Rotterdam, Dutch divers would go and recover it.

I told the ever-reliable Poddy, who coordinated action with the Dutch authorities. On 19 February, the *Cape Ray* arrived at Rotterdam, and as soon as it had berthed and stopped engines, navy divers went down and searched beneath the hull. They unscrewed the steel grate cover of the sea chest and found four waterproof canvas bags tied to the grating inside. Once ashore, they found that the bags contained 125 kg of cocaine.

For the rest of the year I received an increasing amount of information about ships from Turbo and Santa Marta with drugs beneath the hull. They were nearly always going to Antwerp, but despite my passing precise details, the Belgian authorities could never find anything. Then in February 1997, CI Mike gained access to a new sub-source who gave us more detail about the traffic to Belgium and Spain, and I realised what was going wrong. He explained that about every two weeks, divers in Turbo were putting cocaine inside the water intake vents of Star Line banana ships. These first went to Marin in Spain, and then on to Antwerp. Larger amounts up to 200 kg were put into the sea chests of coal ships that left from the Drummond jetty in Santa Marta. When the ships arrived in Antwerp, divers went to recover the drugs as soon as the ship berthed. The traffickers knew that Belgian Gendarmerie divers didn't normally check the vessels until the day after arrival, which was always too late.

My informants told me that in Santa Marta the traffickers paid Colombian Navy scuba divers to put the drugs under the ships. The Colombia Navy had a small team in Santa Marta who were used by the police and coal companies to inspect beneath the coal boats before they departed. The coal companies thought that these inspections would be a deterrent. Unfortunately the traffickers paid the very same divers to put the drugs under the hull after they had inspected it. The divers were being paid by both sides. I decided to try to recruit some of the same divers to tell me about it afterwards.

By early 1997 I had established a good network of agents in Santa Marta and was receiving a constant flow of intelligence. Whether drugs were being sent by container, banana ship or coal boat, we had sources covering each method. Such was my confidence in my team of sources that I jokingly bragged to London that no-one could send a large shipment of drugs to Europe from Santa Marta without me hearing about it. My confidence would soon be tested.

In February 1997, Customs NIS in London told me that they had an ongoing investigation into a group in the Manchester area who were planning for a consignment of 200 kg cocaine. According to London, two British divers were already in Santa Marta and were going to put the drugs beneath the hull of a coal boat going to Avonmouth. I told London that I didn't think this was true. I was confident that if there were British divers in Santa Marta our informants would have told me. I was equally confident that if 200 kg of cocaine was being shipped to the UK on a coal boat from Santa Marta I would have heard about it. I heard nothing more from London about it.

Some six weeks later, CI Mike contacted me and said that he had heard that a coal boat would leave Santa Marta the next day destined for Bristol, and that it would carry a sizeable quantity of drugs. Mike said he would go to Santa Marta to get more details in person. That very same morning, CI Marta contacted me about the same subject. She said that the vessel *Margo L* was in the Carboandes port, had finished loading coal, and during the night Colombian Navy divers had 'inspected' the hull and had put about 200 kg of coke beneath it. Medellin traffickers were behind the shipment and would travel to the UK to collect payment from the customers after the ship arrived.

I passed the information back to London, where the investigation team were delighted, and said they would mount an operation when the ship arrived. Three weeks later, on 12 April, the *Margo L* docked at Avonmouth to discharge part of its cargo of coal. Surveillance by HMCE investigators detected two divers trying and failing to recover the drugs; they made several attempts but each time were carried away from the vessel by the strong river currents on the Avon. This was a great shame, as it would have been a tremendous result to have caught the divers handing over the drugs to the crime gang responsible. In the end, they gave up and our own divers had to go down to recover the bags concealed in the water intake vents, or sea chest. A total of 200 kg of cocaine was seized.

Throughout 1997 and 1998, I received regular information from CIs Marta, Barry, Walter and Mike about the coal boats and the Star Line banana ships from Santa Marta. Sources told me that a trafficker called Manjarres was one of the most powerful traffickers there, and was sending 200 kg every two weeks to Europe under the hulls of vessels. Unfortunately, it seemed that law enforcement divers at the European end were always too slow and missed the majority of them. Marta told us that the same organisation behind the *Margo L* had later sent another 200 kg from the Carboandes jetty on the vessel *Bona Foam* to Ijmuiden in Holland. This was missed also.

In late January 1998, CI Barry telephoned and told me about yet another shipment: 250 kg had been put under hull of a banana ship called *Alameda Star*, which had left Santa Marta the previous week, destined for Antwerp. I was frustrated that the Belgians kept missing these under-water shipments so this time, instead of just passing the information via London, I also spoke directly to Frank Jennes, a senior Belgian Gendarmerie colonel who I knew.

Frank promised me that something would be done. Sure enough, thanks to his insistence, the Belgians pulled out all the stops. When the *Alameda Star* arrived in Zeebrugge, Gendarmerie divers were waiting for it, along with a surveillance team on land. They saw divers go to the boat and recover the drugs from the sea chest, then take them ashore. They were all arrested while loading up a vehicle, and 290 kg of cocaine was seized.

Despite our best efforts, a large number of cocaine shipments were successfully sent to Europe beneath the hulls of ships from Santa Marta. Whilst we were able to identify dozens of them, the authorities in Europe failed to seize the majority. To this day, this method continues to be highly successful, and almost impossible to stop without inside information.

CI MIKE HAD seen first-hand what the cartels did to informants. He told me that he was once forced to watch while Medellin traffickers tortured someone he knew, a suspected informant. He had not been able to walk away nor oppose their actions without putting himself at great risk. He simply had to watch, but felt sick inside. Mike was acutely aware that this might one day happen to him. He was determined that if he was ever found out, he would not allow himself to be captured. He carried a 9 mm pistol inside his trouser belt, and in his car he kept a hand grenade that he had obtained from an army friend. He vowed that if they tried to take him he would pull the pin and blow himself up with his captors, rather than let himself be taken alive and tortured.

During the four years that I worked with him, Mike had several scares and close shaves from the work that he did with us, and even more from cases that he had previously done with the DEA. He was an incredibly calm and courageous man, and took the pressure in his stride. In January 1997, he told me that one of his sub-sources in Cartagena had been killed. Some heavies had come to his home and taken him away, leaving his wife and children distraught. He had then been tortured and murdered. They telephoned his wife a few days later and told her where to find the body. Mike didn't think that it was related to any of our cases, but he couldn't be sure whether his sub-source might have identified him.

Several months later, Mike told me that Cali traffickers had taken Lucho M from his home. The cartel was angry about the string of seizures from Lucho's transport route from Santa Marta. Lucho didn't have enough money to repay them for the seized drugs, so they killed him. A reliable contact also told Mike that the Cali group had worked out who the informant was and had sent a team to kill him. That could only mean Mike himself.

'Señor, I think this may be a serious problem for us,' he said.

'What are you going to do?' I asked. 'You really need to leave and go into hiding immediately.'

Mike stayed calm. He was always calm. 'No, señor, that is exactly what they will expect. If they believe I am the informant they will expect me to run. As soon as I disappear I am confirming that I am guilty, and sooner or later they will find me and kill me. No, I'll take precautions and hire a team to watch my back, but I will stay and call their bluff. I will let it be known that I am angry about Lucho's death, but I am not an informant and have nothing to fear.'

We discovered several weeks later that Lucho had not been killed. They had deliberately fed Mike false information to see how he reacted. If he had panicked and fled, he would have signed his own death warrant. Nonetheless, it indicated that he was under some suspicion.

Just a week or so after the Lucho incident, Mike was summoned to a meeting at a *finca* in the countryside several miles from Cartagena. Some Medellin traffickers were there, and they accused Mike of being an informant and causing several seizures in which they had lost money. Mike fronted it out and deflected the blame, accusing another person who was present at the meeting of being the informant. The argument lasted well into the night, and at one point guns were drawn. His sheer bravado defused the situation, and by the time he left the meeting, in the early hours of the following day, another person had become the prime suspect. But it was cause for grave concern that these security incidents were becoming too frequent.

In late 1997, Mike rang me and said that he had a big problem and needed to go away. I agreed to meet him, and Steve came with me. Knowing that there was a problem, we were particularly careful to check that he was not being followed. We watched Mike as he followed his pre-planned route through the Santa Barbara shopping mall, then outside around the streets of Usaquen, before picking him up and taking him to one of the Plenitud apartments near the Fontana Hotel. Once securely inside the apartment, we could talk calmly.

'Do you remember that I told you about the case I did

for the DEA a few years back, and they burnt me?' he asked. 'When they told the court that I was an informant, and caused me a huge problem?'

Steve and I nodded, we both remembered it well.

'I always knew that it was a ticking timebomb, and that one day it would catch me up. Well, now it has come back to haunt me, and I have a very serious problem.'

'OK, run me through it,' I said. 'What's happened?'

'I've heard from friends that Jorge, the trafficker I got arrested and locked up in Florida, has been released from jail in the States and is back in Colombia. He has been trying to find me and has contracted a team of *sicarios* to kill me. But this time the situation is very bad. The people he has contracted are a professional team of well-trained, former military men from Pereira. They will find me sooner or later.'

'So are you going to hide or go away until the heat dies down a bit?' I asked. 'How can I help?'

'These guys won't stop until they have found me and killed me. Or until Jorge withdraws his contract or is himself killed. I'm going to go away for a while, maybe to the States, until it is sorted. I am owed a couple of rewards from the last seizures. Can you advance me some money for my travel costs?'

Mike fled the country, but before he left he paid contacts to spread word that Jorge had been released early from prison because he had been flipped and was now working for the DEA. Mike returned a month later and told me that the trafficker had been killed by other Medellin narcos. His disinformation had worked, and the security problem was resolved. Such was the brutal reality of the Colombian drug trade.

*

IN ANOTHER INCIDENT, corrupt officials in Spain caused a serious security problem for both Mike and the British DLOs. We had given several seizures to the Spanish, one of which was on a ship called *Cielo de Livorno* in January 1998. The Spanish had seized 20 kg of cocaine and arrested five people in Barcelona based on our information. Whilst it wasn't a huge quantity, the Medellin traffickers who owned this consignment asked their Spanish customers to investigate how it had been found, and in turn the trafficking group in Spain paid a member of the Guardia Civil for information. He told them that the seizure, and several others including one of 500 kg in Valencia, had come from information provided by the British DLOs, who had informants in Turbo and Cartagena.

Mike's contacts told him that the Medellin narcos had now contracted a group of paramilitaries in Turbo to find out who the informants were, and to kill them. The paramilitary group were professionals from the police and naval intelligence, and were people to be extremely concerned about. He said that this was a serious risk to us both, and that we must be very careful when we met or communicated. He also suggested that we should take great care about what we told the Spanish.

In late March 1999, about a year after the scare over the *Cielo de Livorno* and the leaks by the Guardia Civil, Mike received a telephone call from one of his contacts in the port, who asked to speak with him urgently to pass some information. They arranged to meet. Mike left his home in the Chiquinquira district of Cartagena and had walked only two blocks when a motorcycle came up from behind and slowed alongside him. Mike was very good at his tradecraft, but on this day for some reason he was distracted. By the time he noticed and looked to his side, it was already too late. Two *sicarios* on the bike drew weapons and fired six shots into him. He died on the spot, in a pool of blood and filth on the pavement.

I had left Colombia the previous year and was back working in the UK. It is hard to describe how I felt when Steve told me the news. We are not supposed to get close to informants, but when you have worked closely with someone for four years, doing dangerous cases together and sharing some very stressful and scary situations, it is hard to avoid. I liked Mike. He was professional and worked well with me. He was also a nice guy, an honest person with good values who had found himself mixed up with some of the world's most ruthless criminals. He had tried to work for the right side and had paid the price. I was deeply saddened by his death.

15

ALBERTO AND THE PASSPORT FACTORY

ALBERTO HAD ALREADY been working for the DLOs for about a year when I arrived in Bogotá, although he hadn't generated any significant results. I met him during my first week and found him a friendly character. He was forty-eight years old, always wore a jacket and tie, claimed to have a degree in engineering, and was a family man, frequently talking about his wife and daughters in Bogotá. He was a sort of Colombian 'Del-Boy', mixing with the fringes of the criminal underworld and constantly on the lookout for a scheme to make some money. He was also always broke, and forever having to pay some pressing debt. I don't think he had ever trafficked drugs or committed any serious crime himself, but he acted as a go-between and provided ancillary services to the criminal fraternity, ducking and diving around the edges of a violent and ruthless world to make a living. But he was a gentleman, and a likeable rogue.

Alberto would contact me almost weekly during my first few months to tell me about couriers travelling from Bogotá to Spain, Zurich, Germany and the UK. He spent a lot of time with people at the airport, doing odd jobs such as minding couriers, driving or acting as a look-out, and was always picking up snippets of information. He also introduced me to a man who worked as a baggage handler at the airport, who would later become an informant codenamed 'Saddam'. None of his early information generated any results, but in November he gave me the name and description of a courier travelling to Paris, and said he would have 2.5 kg cocaine concealed in the sides of his black, hard-sided briefcase. Sure enough, when he was stopped at Paris airport French Customs found the cocaine within false sides of his case.

Over the next two years, Alberto regularly passed details of couriers going to Europe. In many cases the information proved negative, but that did not necessarily mean it was untrue. With hundreds of passengers flooding through the controls, it was difficult to locate and intercept couriers even when given a description or a name. And on six or seven occasions Alberto's information did result in seizures and the arrest of couriers and meeters.

Alberto's real benefit to us, however, was not just the information he gave about couriers, but his facilitation services in providing 'clean' passports and mobile telephones to the criminal fraternity. Alberto had discovered a niche business model for himself by providing false passports for use by crooks and couriers. It was not unusual for serious criminals to want a spare passport in a different name, in case of emergency. If the authorities were looking for them, or perhaps other criminals were after them because of some dispute, it was always handy to be able to leave the country under a false identity and elude detection. Traffickers also frequently wanted fake passports for their drug couriers. A single Colombian female travelling alone to Europe would normally be considered as high-profile, and would probably receive attention from customs on arrival. Traffickers therefore often supplied their couriers with false Spanish passports so that the risk of being searched was lower. EU passports also had the advantage of enabling the courier to travel to other EU countries without a visa.

Alberto had contacts who ran an underground 'passport factory' in downtown Bogotá. They could supply a document for any nationality, in a variety of formats: stolen, forged, even authentic, for a range of prices depending upon the quality. The client would provide a photo and within a few days Alberto would hand them with a passport in a false name and nationality of their choice, bearing that photo. They were top quality and guaranteed to pass inspection. For couriers, Alberto realised that he could also pass me the details and hopefully make money from both sides. The trafficker would pay him for the passport, but before handling it over Alberto would secretly take a photocopy and give it to me. If we managed to locate and intercept the courier with drugs, Alberto would also get a reward. He was onto a nice little double-earner.

The Colombians were renowned as top-class professionals at counterfeiting. But the idea of a passport factory in Bogotá providing top-quality, bespoke travel documents was something I found fascinating. I realised that this would be of some interest and potential use to other UK departments and agencies, and notified them. One asked if I could obtain a Colombian passport, purely to see the quality. I got one from Alberto that cost about £100. They were impressed, and asked if I could get a Spanish passport and accompanying ID document for a female of a certain age, again purely out of interest, to see the quality. Two days later, Alberto handed me a quality original Spanish passport and matching ID.

Over the following months, we obtained passports to order for a variety of specified nationalities, genders and ages: Ecuadorian ones, Argentinian, Peruvian, Spanish and British. The efficiency of the passport factory was truly impressive. They could provide absolutely anything within a few days of receiving the order; it was just a question of price.

The ultimate test came when the agency asked me to obtain a Lebanese passport for a male of specific age and height, but with a valid US visa. *This one sounds a bit tricky*, I thought, and was not overly optimistic when I passed the requirement to Alberto.

A few days later, a chirpy Alberto rang me to offer a choice of options.

'Señor, do you want a genuine original Lebanese passport, or would you prefer a quality forged one? They tell me that a genuine one will take a few weeks longer but will be one hundred per cent guaranteed and is not stolen or on any databases. The forged one is top quality and can be available in just a few days and costs a little less.' Almost as an afterthought, he asked, 'Oh, and what kind of US visa do you want, and how long must it be valid for?'

It was an insight into a different world. Criminals could buy a new identity, in any name and nationality, for just a few hundred dollars. We did have a small dispute though. A certain UK agency placed an order for something quite specific. I can't recall the exact details, but it was something like a Swedish passport for a twenty-five-year-old male with blue eyes and blond hair. Alberto got it from the factory. I paid for it and handed it over. Two weeks later, having submitted it for detailed examination, the UK agency said they weren't happy with it and wanted Alberto to take it back and ask for a refund.

'F***ing hell,' I said in disbelief. I don't often swear. 'We didn't buy it from Argos, and it doesn't come with a no-quibble refund!'

Then just to make it clear: 'This place is run by heavy gangsters who have serious criminals, cut-throats and assassins as their clients. I can't send Alberto back and tell him to say that after an in-depth forensic examination he'd like his money back. They'll smell a rat and kill him.'

Alberto's access to the passport factory gave us several drug seizures, and a unique insight into how easy it was to obtain false identity documents. But we had an obligation to notify the Colombian authorities and eventually get the place shut down. I passed details to our trusted contacts in the security service, DAS, and told Alberto to stop going there for a while. He was gutted to be losing his lucrative little earner. Within a few weeks the factory had been raided by DAS, the principals arrested, and thousands of passports seized. From seized documents they also identified corrupt employees in several embassies and consulates.

AS PART OF our tradecraft in handling informants, we had a regular need for new, 'clean' mobile telephones. We would always give each informant a mobile number to call when they wanted to speak, but it had to be a one that was not in any way associated with the British DLOs or the embassy. I also needed to give a different phone number to each informant, so that if ever one went bad, he would not impact on others. The calls to clean numbers were then routed through a diverted-call system so that they eventually came to me. In short, we needed numerous mobile phones over the period I was there.

However, in an effort to make life more difficult for criminals the Colombian government had legislated so that you had to show an identity document and proof of residence in order to buy a mobile phone. This made it difficult for us, as well as for the criminals. Given his expertise in this area, I tasked Alberto to buy cellphones for us in different Colombian names and addresses. He was a Mr Fixit who could arrange these things easily. With his help, we were able to have dozens of clean mobiles, all registered to different names and a selection of PO Box addresses. Without him, this might have been hugely time-consuming, if not altogether impossible.

One day during my first year, I met with Alberto and saw immediately that something was wrong. He was terribly upset.

'What's up, Alberto? What's happened?'

'Señor, I have just heard that my mother died yesterday. She lived on her own in a small town near Cali, and a neighbour just called to tell me. It happened so suddenly.' Tears welled up in his eyes as he continued. 'I need to go there to sort things and arrange the funeral, but I have no money. Unless I can find some, she will be buried in a municipal pauper's grave. I feel so ashamed that I can't even give a proper burial to my mother. I don't even have the money to get there.'

'How much do you need, Alberto?'

'Señor, if you could just lend me a few hundred dollars, and I will repay you from the next work I do.'

There is no section in the HM Customs rule book that covers giving money to informants so that they may bury their mothers. I gave him £200 worth of pesos, which he said would be enough to go to Cali and give her a decent send-off. We both knew that I would probably never see the money again.

Over the following eighteen months, Alberto worked well and gave us several seizures and a huge amount of intelligence about the airport mafia. Then, one day when we met, he was agitated and upset. At first he would not say why, but after a bit of coaxing he told me what the problem was.

'Señor, I have just heard that my mother died yesterday. She lived on her own in a small pueblo near Cali. I need to go there to sort out things and arrange her funeral.' His voice trembled, and I could see tears in his eyes. 'But I have no money and can't afford to go there and bury her. She has no one else. If I don't pay for the burial, she will be put in a common pauper's grave with no headstone.'

In the back of my mind I had a distant, vague recollection; had his mother not died about two years ago? Had I not lent him money previously to bury her? But I was not completely sure, and I didn't want to offend him or be so disrespectful as to challenge the very death of his mother. So I commiserated with him and said of course I would help. We agreed that we'd meet later, and I would give him some money.

I went back to the office and started going through my notebooks for the last two years. Every contact with an informant, every telephone call, text, message or meeting was recorded there in detail. I had dozens of notebooks covering the past two years, and it took me considerable time to skim through them all, until I found it. There it was, eighteen months earlier: *'Mother suddenly dead...'* I read, *'a town near Cali ... no money to bury her.'*

When we met later, I calmly asked Alberto about his poor mother, how old she had been, whether she lived alone, what caused her sudden demise – and how it could be that she had previously died eighteen months ago? The poor guy was mortified. He hesitated, and then with his head lowered in shame, he explained.

'I am very sorry, señor. I had forgotten about the previous time I told you that she died. Back then my mother was still very much alive. But I had a debt to pay, I owed money to some very bad people, ruthless criminals, and unless I paid it immediately they were going to do horrific things to me and then probably kill me. I was desperate for money and thought the only way out was to tell you that my mother had died. I am so sorry and ashamed that I lied to you. It will never happen again.'

After a short pause, he continued, 'But my mother has indeed just died. And I don't have any money to bury her, or even to get there. I am telling you the truth now.'

I gave him another £200, this time from my own pocket, to bury his poor mother a second time, or rather the first time for real.

In addition to giving us five courier jobs, introducing informant Saddam at the airport, and providing clean passports and mobile phones, Alberto gave me a deep insight into the criminal underworld of traffickers, couriers and how the Bogotá Airport Mafia worked. He was a tremendously useful, and likeable, informant.

In October 1997 he gave me the details of a courier going to Germany and I then did not see him until April 1998. It was not unusual for him to drop off the radar for long periods. Over the previous years he had often lost contact for several months, only to reappear with some new information, saying that he had been in Buenaventura or Cali and for safety had not wanted to make contact. On this last meeting he did not have anything specific to report, but we had a good chat and parted on good terms.

Two months later, I left Colombia to return to the UK. I had not seen him again and was a little disappointed that I did not get the chance to say goodbye properly.

We never heard from Alberto again. Several months later, Steve told me that he had been officially reported as missing. His family had posted a report and photograph in the local newspaper entitled, 'Help us find him', pleading for information of his whereabouts. It said that he was last seen on 25 July heading to a business meeting with two women in northern Bogotá. All three had disappeared.

Given that Alberto did not have any legitimate business occupation, I assumed that the meeting must have been drug-related, and that the two young ladies with him were probably couriers. Perhaps they had stolen or lost the drugs, which sometimes happened, and had been summoned to a meeting with the owners to discuss the problem. Perhaps something else had gone wrong, or the traffickers suspected them of being informants. Or perhaps Alberto had got himself way out of his depth in some illicit scheme, or had failed to pay an outstanding debt.

For whatever reason, Alberto joined the list of many thousands of people who simply disappeared each year in Colombia, their bodies never to be found.

16

FALSE INFORMANTS

I
N ADDITION TO the many good informants that we
recruited, there were several bad ones. The worst not
only wasted time and drained our resources but were
dangerous. The best were always those we sought out and
recruited ourselves. We identified them, knew who they
were, where they worked and what might motivate them.
If anything went wrong, we knew where to find them. But
we also had frequent walk-ins, who contacted us out of the
blue to offer information. They would either come into the
embassy to ask for the person dealing with drugs, or would
telephone and claim to know something. I hated walk-ins.
In all my years in South America I never had a single
decent one; all the good sources were those I recruited
myself. Walk-ins were perilous because it was impossible
to know for sure who they were or what their real motive
might be.

Whenever I recruited an informant, I considered them
to be potentially hostile, or at least untrustworthy, until
they had given us a first sizeable seizure. Once they had
brought in a result, and received a reward, they were committed beyond the point of return. The traffickers would
kill them if they found out what they had done. I could only

be sure that they were genuine when they had produced a seizure. Even then, it was important to never completely trust them. Informants might turn at any time and betray their handler. A small number tried to play for both sides at the same time. Sometimes they facilitated shipments for the narcos, sometimes they informed. They gained benefit from both sides but also faced the risk of retribution from both. These were the most dangerous ones, requiring careful handling and fraught with risk.

I'd had my first experience of a treacherous source several years earlier, when I worked in Peru. It was October 1989 and I was new to DLO work. The receptionist at the embassy in Lima took a call from an unidentified man who wanted to speak to someone urgently about drug trafficking. She put him through to me. He offered to give me valuable information about cocaine going from Peru to the UK, but would not give any details by phone. He wanted us to meet somewhere secure, but away from the embassy.

This scenario was always a dilemma for a DLO working alone. On the one hand I wanted information, on the other hand it was dangerous to meet unknown cold-callers away from the security of the embassy. Lima was unsafe at the best of times, with constant shootings, kidnappings and murders being committed by Sendero Luminoso terrorists and other criminal groups. There was also the risk that a trafficker whose drugs had been seized might bear a grudge and seek revenge. For some DLOs, the thirst for intelligence can overcome commonsense caution. On this particular day I fell into that bracket. I cast my reservations aside and arranged to meet the stranger at Vivaldi's café at

2 p.m. He would only give his name as 'Jorge' and said that he would be wearing a dark blue suit and a red tie.

Vivaldi's was one of the nicer cafes in the centre of Miraflores, the tourist area of Lima. Its prices were well beyond the means of the ordinary Peruvian, whose average wage was less than $90 per month, and was frequented by businessmen and the wealthier middle-class. I chose to meet there because it had good security, in the form of a team with pump-action shotguns at the entrance to both the restaurant and its car park. I arrived at 1.40 p.m., ahead of the agreed time, so that I could look out for anyone suspicious. I took a seat at the far end with my back to the wall, facing the entrance, so that I had no-one behind me and a clear view of the premises. I sipped my coffee and studied the people already there. Two older men at a table halfway up the room were drinking coffee and immersed in deep conversation. In the opposite corner, three tables away from me, a well-dressed, middle-aged, balding man was at a table with a younger lady in her late twenties; probably some businessman and his secretary, or daughter. A group of three middle-aged ladies were near the window, chatting animatedly over their cappuccinos. All clear.

I spotted Jorge as soon as he walked in. He was about forty-five years old, tall, slim, dressed in a sharp blue suit and red tie, with well-polished shoes and carrying a leather document folder. He was elegant and had the look of a wealthy businessman. He introduced himself as Jorge Altamoreno, president of the Cámara Ibero Americana de Industria y Comercio, an organisation that promoted trade between Peru and external partners. I later found that it was a complete sham, set up to provide him with some

business cover. He said that his role was to assist companies wishing to import goods from Peru and to facilitate
the export procedures.

We sat and talked for an hour, and he dropped names
like confetti, claiming to know the ambassadors of various
countries as well as being a personal friend of certain
Peruvian ministers and well-known business leaders. He
would no doubt now add my name and the British embassy
to his list of acquaintances. He was a very charming,
impressive and believable character who would no doubt
have done extremely well if he had followed a career in
legitimate business, flogged timeshares or sold luxury cars.

Jorge told me that he had been approached by some
Chilean businessmen who wanted his help to send 500 kg
of cocaine to the UK by air cargo, concealed in Peruvian
handicrafts. They had offered him a considerable sum. He
asked me if I wanted him to accept their proposal so that
he could get more information. Warning bells were already
ringing in my head. They always rang when something
sounded too good, too easy. I told Jorge that he could go
ahead and speak with these people purely to obtain more
details, but that he should not do anything illegal.

I met Jorge again at Vivaldi's a week later, and this time
he had more. He said that the organisers of the enterprise
in the UK were a Peruvian called Santivanez, who was
currently serving a jail sentence in the UK for drugs trafficking, a man from Merseyside called Tony, and another
man called Hector. They were planning to send two tonnes
of cocaine over the coming year, starting with the initial
consignment of 500 kg. That would have been the biggest
amount of cocaine identified going to the UK at that time.

Jorge asked me if these people were already known to us. Alarm bells rang again; he was fishing for information. After checking with London the following day, I kept Jorge sweet by telling him that we were aware of the names but that they were not under investigation. I also told him that my Investigation Division were extremely interested in his information, and that he should carry on speaking with the Chileans but not participate in any way without consulting me first.

It was several weeks before he phoned again. He said that he was in the Cayman Islands and asked me to call him back. When I did, he claimed he had been instructed by Tony to travel there for a meeting at the last minute, had not had time to contact me, and promised to give me the full story on his return.

Once he was back in Lima, Jorge explained that in the Cayman Islands he had met with a British man called George Atkinson, who was a financial representative of the trafficking organisation in the UK. He had also spoken by telephone with a man called Peter, who was the principal in the UK and was working with Santivanez. George had taken Altamoreno to Barclays Bank in Cayman, where he was shown proof that an account had been set up in his name and six million US dollars had been deposited into it, although the funds could not be released until authorised by George. Jorge said that once the 500 kg of cocaine arrived in the UK, the money would be freed, and his role was to then launder it back to Peru, for which he would receive ten per cent. What Jorge Altamoreno did not know was that the ID had been aware of his trip to the Cayman Islands before he told us about it, and that an investigation was already in progress involving Peter, George, and the South American organisers. The ID had actually been working on the case for months before Jorge first came to the embassy.

From our first meeting, I had been suspicious that he had given the details of the British people involved, and asked whether we knew them, but did not give the names of the South American end. It was clear that he was only giving me part of the picture, and I suspected that he was fishing to find out whether we already had an investigation underway. We did indeed, but I told him that we hadn't.

Having consulted with London, we agreed that Altamoreno was probably trying to work both sides and use me as some kind of insurance policy. He was giving me enough to keep me interested in the case and to establish his credentials as an HMCE informant, but not enough to enable us to grab the drugs or arrest the principals in Peru. If the shipment was successful, he would receive a large amount of money from the traffickers. If by bad luck the drugs were seized, he would claim a reward from us. And if he was arrested, he would claim to be an informant working for HM Customs and ask us to facilitate his release.

Normally in such circumstances, when an informant is not telling the full truth, we would end the relationship and stop working with him immediately. In this case, it was agreed that I would carry on and try to make best use of him. On 7 December 1989, I had a meeting with Altamoreno in my office at the embassy. I had the conversation covertly tape-recorded and witnessed by a colleague, the assistant defence attaché, in an adjacent room. I knew that one day I might need evidence to rebut a claim from Altamoreno if he was arrested. He gave me some details of Peter and a company in Merseyside that would receive the drugs, and he repeated the financial arrangements and his own role. Partly for the benefit of the tape, I explained our rules very clearly to him, in particular that he must not participate in this drugs enterprise or any other criminality without seeking my prior agreement and must not withhold any information from me. If he did not tell me the whole truth he would cease to be considered as an informant, and we would treat him as hostile. He said that he fully understood.

For the next six months, Altamoreno continued to pass me information about the case, but I knew from other sources that what he told me was often incomplete or untruthful. Although I knew that he was stringing me along, I continue to give him the impression that I believed him. Meanwhile I also asked some trusted colleagues in the Peruvian Drugs Police, DINTID, to find out what he was really up to. They tapped his telephones.

In May 1990, Altamoreno told me that the first consignment would be 300 kg and would be sent to the UK in the following weeks by KLM or Lufthansa air cargo. A Peruvian called Jairo Gutierrez would go to the UK to be with Peter when it arrived. However, the Peruvian police intelligence officers told me that Altamoreno was also involved in several other drug activities. One of these involved the imminent shipment of 120 kg to Portugal.

I met with Altamoreno on May 29 near the Lima Cricket Club and we spoke in my car. I taped the conversation. He said the 300 kg to would happen soon, but that he had now been cut out of the arrangements and would not be able to give me any further details. He did not mention Portugal or his other dealings. I repeated the need for him to be completely truthful. He repeated that he understood.

From their wiretaps, my friends in the Peruvian Police told me that Altamoreno had purchased tickets to travel to Portugal the following week to coordinate a delivery of 120 kg. I decided to give him a final chance to tell me about it. On 8 June, I phoned and asked if he had any updates or anything to tell me. He said no. I recorded the call. Well, he couldn't say I didn't give him a fair crack of the whip.

]I never spoke with Jorge Altamoreno again. A few days later, he flew from Lima to Lisbon in Portugal. He had not told me of his travel, nor about his involvement in coordinating a shipment there. We therefore told the Portuguese Judicial Police about him, along with details of his flight and the purpose of his visit. When he landed in Lisbon, a surveillance team was waiting for him, and he was followed when he picked up a hire car and drove north to the city of Porto. The next day he met with another South American man and they both went to an industrial estate. A short time later another car arrived, and two men got out and spoke with Altamoreno. The surveillance team watched them start removing bags from the boot of one car and putting them into the boot of the other. At that point the police moved in and arrested them all. The bags contained 120 kg of pure Peruvian cocaine.

As I expected, on arrival at the police station Altamoreno told the Judicial Police that he was secretly working undercover for HM Customs. He produced my business card and told them to contact the British embassy in Lima, where I would confirm his story. He was sadly delusional. Apparently he was distraught when, later that day, they told him that it was HM Customs who had told them about his travel to Portugal, and that we had terminated his role as an informant because he had lied to us.

Altamoreno made formal complaints for months afterwards, and at his trial, that he had been working undercover. He had always planned that this would be his insurance policy if things went wrong, and produced itemised telephone bills to show his numerous calls to me during the previous eight months, and his hotel bill from the Cayman Islands. To counter his allegations, I produced my tape recordings and notes of our meetings and calls, and two Peruvian police offered to give evidence at his trial. He was shattered when he realised that his plan to use me as cover had failed. Jorge Altamoreno was convicted of drug trafficking and sentenced to fourteen years in prison in Portugal.

It was my first exposure to a double-dealing informant trying to play for both sides and use me as insurance. The experience served me well in dealing with equally treacherous sources during my later years in Colombia.

THE TWO MOST untrustworthy informants I ever dealt with were deliberately given codenames to suit: 'Judas' and 'Saddam'. Saddam was the trickiest.

Within a month of my arrival in Bogotá, CI Alberto told me about a cargo handler at the airport called Ismael, who was facilitating concealments in suitcases to Europe. Ismael was said to be working with corrupt members of several airlines, including British Airways, KLM and Iberia, and with bent police. Throughout 1994, I received regular updates from Alberto and another CI, Stern, about Ismael's activities.

I was somewhat surprised, then, when in February 1995 Ismael contacted me and asked to meet. I knew that he was connected to the dangerous Bogotá mafia, and I had no idea why he wanted to talk to me. I knew it could be some kind of trap, but agreed to meet him in the quiet bar of the Bogotá Royal Hotel. This was a reasonably safe venue for a first meeting because of guards on the entrance and exits. He explained who he was and offered to work as an informant. He said that he could tell me about suitcases of cocaine being sent to London, Amsterdam, Paris and Rome and wanted to know how much reward he could expect. At the end of this first meeting he said that a suitcase with 20 kg cocaine would be sent to Rome the following week, and that he would get more details and be in touch.

I had no doubt whatsoever that Ismael could provide good information; after all, according to Alberto and Stern he was actually arranging the shipments himself. I guessed that he must be considering changing sides, or at least working for both, and registered him as a source under the codename 'Jose'. However he didn't get back in touch for almost year. I assumed that he had got cold feet and changed his mind.

Throughout 1995, I continued to receive information from others at the airport that Ismael was facilitating couriers and rip-on luggage. Then, one Saturday afternoon in January 1996, he contacted me again and asked to meet urgently. I again suggested the bar of the Bogotá Royal. I would not normally meet sources in such a public place, but I didn't trust Jose at all and did not want to pick him up in my car or have him know any of our normal procedures for meetings. He turned up, and told me that an airport worker had put a box inside hold five of an Alitalia flight that had left Bogotá that very afternoon for Rome. He said that between 15 and 18 kg of cocaine were in the box, and that it would be ripped-off by cargo handlers on arrival in Rome. I quickly contacted Poddy. The next morning, the Italians arrested two airport workers as they tried to recover the box from the Alitalia flight. It contained 15 kg of coke.

He had given us his first seizure, but I still didn't trust him, and renamed him CI Saddam to remind me that I should never believe what he said. Still, we paid him a reward.

I met Saddam four or five times more that year, and each time he gave vague, unspecific information that could not be actioned. Meanwhile I was still receiving reports that he was at it himself. It was impossible to know who was telling the truth. It was most likely that Saddam was working for the traffickers while trying to use me as insurance. If a run went wrong and he was arrested, he would say that he was undercover for HMCE. His proof would be the 15 kg seizure he had given us, and he could ask me to vouch for him. He would be earning large sums from the traffickers, and in case of arrest he had his indemnity. On the other hand, he might not have been playing both sides at all. Maybe he was just pretending to be a facilitator in order to gather information? There was no way of knowing for certain, but I favoured the option that he was hedging his bets.

In February 1997, more than a year after he had given us the first seizure, Saddam contacted me and said two suitcases full of coke had been ripped-on to a Lufthansa flight to Germany. On 15 February 1997, German Customs observed the flight when it arrived at Frankfurt. They saw baggage handlers remove two cases from the igloos and try to steal them. Four handlers were arrested and 33 kg of cocaine were seized. Eight months later, in October 1997, Saddam gave me information about a passenger travelling to Paris with drugs in his suitcase, which enabled the French to arrest a courier and 3 kg cocaine.

During the rest of 1997 and 1998, Saddam occasionally provided reports of mules and rip-on suitcases being sent to European capitals on Avianca, Air France, BA and other airlines. None of it proved to be accurate. It became clear that he was not genuinely cooperating but was passing on just enough to keep himself registered as an informant, for protection if things went wrong. Through other informants I tried to catch him out and to seize one of the consignments that he facilitated, but was never successful.

ANOTHER DUPLICITOUS informant was CI Judas, so named because I knew from the outset that he was a dangerous character who would readily betray me either to the mafia in Cartagena or to the Cali Cartel, for whom he worked. I had heard of him before I met him. He was a senior manager in one of the ports in Cartagena. Intelligence from police intercepts, and from CI Mike, had told me that he was corrupt. I subsequently met him in an official capacity to arrange training courses, and from the outset he seemed keen to offer his support. Over the following three years he frequently told me about possible drug shipments, and went to great lengths to be seen to be collaborating with the authorities in the fight against trafficking. It was all a sham. Whenever we met, he wanted to know what information the UK received about the port, whether we had informants, and whether we were making any inroads. Several times, after a seizure in Europe, he tried to wheedle from me whether it had come from an informant. I had no doubt that he was feeding information back to the cartel.

For three years we both played out a charade. He pretended to help and passed me false information, and I pretended to believe him and passed him false information back. He became a discreet way of spreading disinformation about our work, and of letting it be known, falsely, that the DLOs did not have a single informant in the port.

One day he disappeared. No-one knew where he went or what became of him. He had no doubt fallen foul of the cartel or been held responsible for some loss. I never heard of him again.

17

THE BOGOTÁ AIRPORT MAFIA

BOGOTÁ AIRPORT WAS home to a powerful mafia that controlled the illicit transport of prohibited goods by air. It was not a single organisation with a single leader or command, but rather a complex alliance between several powerful groups that operated within the airport and worked together on criminal activity.

One of the main elements in the mafia was the police themselves. They had a base at the airport and worked in both the public areas and airside, carrying out searches of cargo and baggage. They were the lead agency responsible for detecting and seizing drugs. They were also the lead agency controlling and facilitating drug shipments. Another important component of the mafia was the employees of companies who provided ground-handling services and catering. These firms employed hundreds of baggage hands, cargo handlers, tractor drivers and ramp workers, many of whom were recruited by the mafia to ensure the smooth transport of drugs. These workers had free movement around the airport and were adept at switching suitcases or implanting drugs in baggage or cargo. Other key players were the airport security staff and employees of the airlines themselves.

It was a nest of vipers; a network of corrupt officials in key positions who worked together to form an efficient and highly professional mafia. They could arrange the transport or theft of almost anything imaginable within the bounds of the airport.

The extent of the problem at the airport was well known; indeed I had been briefed about it even before my arrival in Bogotá. British Airways had two direct flights every week from there to London, and we knew that drugs were frequently sent on them. Intel told us that the police, in collaboration with security staff, smoothed the passage of drugs and that employees of the airline itself might also be involved. Without being able to trust the cops or the airlines, it was going to be difficult to find out more.

We did have a few trusted contacts, in particular a DAS employee who managed immigration at the airport, and the country manager of BA in Bogotá, Keith MacGaul. Keith would leave Colombia in 1996, to be replaced by Carlos Carbonell. Both he and Carlos were British nationals posted to Colombia for temporary periods, after which they would return to London, whereas the other BA employees were all Colombians with family ties there. For that reason, Keith and Carlos were the only people at BA who I could ever trust and speak with openly. Our focus was on flights to Europe, which meant KLM, Iberia, Air France, Alitalia and BA, plus Avianca went to Spain and Germany. In total there were around fourteen relevant flights per week, with each one carrying some 200 passengers and many tonnes of commercial cargo. Avianca later started flying direct to London too.

The security system at Bogotá Airport was actually impressive. Just a few years earlier, the Medellin Cartel had blown up an Avianca aircraft in mid-air by putting a bomb on board. The Government was also fighting two large guerrilla groups, FARC and the ELN. Because of the combined threats from drugs, cartels and terrorist groups, airport security was as tight and effective as anywhere in the world, – or so it appeared.

When passengers checked in, all suitcases were put through X-ray machines manned by police and airport security. Luggage was then subject to random police search after check-in, and drugs detector dogs would make last-minute sniffs of cases on the tarmac before loading. Passengers themselves went through a scanner and two full body frisks, one in the security hall and another at the gate, and might be subjected to additional random searches. On the surface, it seemed impossible for anyone to take a suitcase of contraband onto a flight, or to carry cocaine in their hand luggage or on their body. Yet that is precisely what happened every day.

Although the police and security were the main protagonists in the airport mafia, I reckoned that they would also be the best people to try to recruit as informers. Among the many corrupt staff would be good people who knew what was going on but were too scared to speak out. It was a small, and tight community, so I didn't expect to recruit many, but I believed that there must be some who would be willing to talk – and I only needed a few of them.

Following the model I had used in the ports, I arranged for HMCE to deliver several training courses. We taught groups of customs, police and security staff to profile passengers and cargo. It was a great way to meet the people at the workface and have a quiet word without attracting attention. Over time, we succeeded in establishing a small number of people at the airport who would pass on intelligence. Their secret codenames were Stern, Sonya, David, Alberto, Pedro, Rocio, Jean-Michel and Saddam. This group of eight would give us a deep insight into how the Bogotá Airport mafia operated.

DURING MY FIRST month in Bogotá, CI Alberto told me that an airport baggage handler known as Ismael was conspiring with someone in British Airways to send suitcases full of cocaine. This was something that I would hear of frequently over the next few years, concerning KLM and Iberia as well as BA flights. The cases would not be allocated to any passenger or recorded on the flight's manifest. This was known as the rip-on/rip-off, and was one of the most effective methods of sending drugs. A suitcase packed full of coke was taken airside, normally by corrupt police or ground staff. It would not be checked in by a passenger and so would not go through the X-ray machine. Once it was airside, baggage handlers or cops would slip the case into the hold of the aircraft. A similarly corrupt handler would recover it and take it out of the destination airport.

On other occasions they would steal a genuine case that had been checked in by an innocent passenger, remove its baggage tags and put them onto the suitcase of drugs. The dirty case would be delivered along with all the others on that flight. Corrupt staff at destination would then recover it, either airside, from the baggage carousel, or in left luggage. The legitimate passenger's real suitcase would be disposed of and would end up being reported missing by its owner. It was noteworthy that a large number of suitcases seemed to go 'missing' on the flights from Bogotá.

All that the rip-on/rip-off method required was corrupt workers at the airports at both ends. Unfortunately for us, both Bogotá and London Heathrow had whole teams of bent employees, and they worked closely together as an efficient conveyor belt.

MY FIRST SPECIFIC tip-off about a baggage rip-on was on 6 November 1994. It was a Sunday, but CI Sonya sent me a pager message saying that she had something and needed to meet me. Sonya was a young Colombian who worked for one of the airport ground service providers. She was intelligent enough not to get involved with the mafia, but knew everyone and what they were up to. She was very observant and had a fantastic memory for detail.

Her message said, 'Can we meet for a drink tonight? Some friends are having a party.'

I sent a pager message back: 'Yes, great. I'll pick you up at the Spanish Bar at 10 p.m.'

The 'Spanish Bar' was an agreed code for the counter-surveillance route she must follow. Having checked her for surveillance as she followed the set route, I picked her up in my car at around 10.15 p.m. in a quiet side street near the Unicentro shopping mall. Sonya told me that earlier in the day she had seen airport workers bring a green suitcase airside. The case had been put into an igloo baggage container with other luggage going on BA flight

248 to London. She saw two police officers nearby just watching, presumably as security, and another policeman with a dog then stood by the igloo to protect it until it was loaded on the aircraft. Sonya was certain that the case must contain drugs.

This was a great tip. It might take a bit of work by the customs guys at Heathrow to find the green case, but the information was precise enough for them to get it. I just hoped that there weren't too many other green cases on the flight.

I dropped Sonya back at her car, made sure that she wasn't followed when she left, and went home. London was six hours ahead and by now it would be 5.30 a.m. in the UK, so I passed the information to ID Control, which was staffed around the clock. They would ensure that it was actioned when the teams came into work in two or three hours' time.

The next morning, the staff at Heathrow Investigation Unit were told. Unfortunately they did not have enough time to mount a full surveillance operation to catch the rip-off team, but they watched all the cases being unloaded when the plane landed, and quickly spotted the green one. It had a baggage tag but was not assigned to any passenger on the flight. When officers opened the suitcase, they found it contained twenty-five one-kilo bricks of pure cocaine, and nothing else.

Similar rip-on bags were going to other European airports. I heard that some baggage handlers were working with the head of security for Iberia to send suitcases full of drugs to Madrid. In January 1995, another informant told me that a large yellow box had been put in the cargo hold of KLM flight 774 for Amsterdam. The box was not on KLM's manifest of cargo but had been slipped on board at the last minute by a cargo handler. London ID Control notified the Dutch, and when their customs went straight to the aircraft on landing, they found 30 kg of cocaine.

A few weeks later, I heard that police officers at Bogotá Airport had been seen to put a large black case onto a flight bound for Rome, and that Alitalia staff in Bogotá were in collusion with them. I again told our Control and they warned the Italian authorities. The Guardia de Finanza recovered the suitcase and found another 30 kg. A short while later, I received information that two boxes had been ripped-on to a Lufthansa flight to Frankfurt, and as a result 37 kg cocaine was seized.

Within just a few months, we had seized four rip-on cases in Europe with 122 kg of narcotics, and I was receiving similar intelligence on an almost weekly basis. Clearly the Bogotá Airport mafia was very busy. Even more alarmingly, it was obvious that similar mafias were active in the airports of London, Amsterdam, Madrid, Rome, Frankfurt, Paris and other European capitals. There was an entire network of well-coordinated rip-on teams in each airport, and we were detecting just a small fraction of their runs.

THE POLICE AND ground staff were key to the airport mafia, but fortunately they had disgruntled members who felt they were not getting a slice of the cake. These were ripe for recruitment. On 8 October 1995, one of them passed me a tip about a piece of luggage on the BA flight to London.

A ramp supervisor had brought a large, hard-sided case into the secure area earlier that day and arranged for it to be given a yellow security band to show that it had passed through the X-ray machine. Then, with the help of the police, it was put into an igloo baggage container with the other luggage. Acting on our information, the case was located by customs officers on arrival at Heathrow the next day and found to contain 24 kg, again without any clothes or personal belongings to cover it.

Suitcase rip-ons continued non-stop over the next four years whilst I was in Colombia. The problem was that although we seized some of them, we were not making any impact at all upon the organisation itself. Each time we learned of a run, law enforcement officers in Europe were simply seizing the case instead of trying to identify and arrest the rip-off teams. As we recruited new sources amongst the baggage handlers and police, it also became more complicated. It transpired that two of the informants were duplicitous and were only telling me fragments of the truth. None of them knew that we had others passing information to us, and it suited me to let each informant believe that they were the only one working for us at the airport. This was useful because at times they would name and implicate each other, not realising that the other person was also informing about them. Consequently I had a flow of information coming in from different sources, which was a useful health-check.

My intelligence clearly identified that one of the sources, who I later re-named 'Saddam', was telling me about the occasional suitcase ripped-on by others, but was also doing it himself. Saddam knew that by giving us an occasional seizure he would be registered as an informant and could use us as insurance if ever things went wrong and he got arrested. I carried on receiving his information, but I knew that he was playing for the other side and that I would have to handle him with great care.

It was always reassuring to be able to independently verify the information given by informants. This helped me to check that they were being truthful. No matter how good they were, I never ever trusted any of them. It was important to remember that an informant might at any time receive a better offer from the traffickers, or a threat to himself or his family, and could turn against me.

I was pleased, therefore, when one of our cases with the ANP crossed over the rip-on teams at the airport. We were working with them against an important Cali trafficker, Roberto, who was targeting the UK. He regularly sent large shipments by sea and was now planning something by air. Roberto had access to a rip-off team at Heathrow and was going to send 50 kg on a flight. The ANP intercepted his calls to corrupt contacts at Bogotá Airport, and it was reassuring for me that the people he spoke to were the very people that our informants had identified. I also felt reassured when one of my informants told me about the calls, and said that a big Cali trafficker called Roberto was planning to send 50kg to London. I would now get information from both angles: intercepts and informants.

IT WAS DIFFICULT enough to track drugs in suitcases and cargo, or with passengers, but when the traffickers started concealing drugs in areas of an aircraft's body and fuselage, it really did become a major cause for concern. It was a potential threat to the safety of the aircraft and the passengers on board.

We first heard of this development in December 1995, when CI Saddam said that a big Cali trafficker had recently sent 40 kg of cocaine in a space in the front section of a BA flight to London. According to Saddam, the drugs were in two holdalls that had been hidden inside an inspection hatch somewhere near the nose of the aircraft, beneath the pilot's cockpit and beside the front wheels. He said that an aviation maintenance worker at Bogotá Airport had put them there and that similar workers at Heathrow had recovered them. This was the first time I'd ever heard of putting drugs in the nose of a plane. Although we had missed it, I promptly passed the intelligence to the ID team at Heathrow.

A few weeks later, CI Stern told me that drugs were being hidden in a space inside the wall of cargo hold five of the regular BA flight, and that corrupt maintenance workers were recovering them at Heathrow. This was another new concealment area, and it seemed that the rip-off group at Heathrow was now using mechanics and maintenance staff as well as baggage handlers.

In the early hours of Saturday, 10 February 1996, I received an urgent call from Sonya. She couldn't meet me, as she was at home with her family, but she told me that a large quantity of cocaine had been hidden somewhere on the BA flight, and that corrupt mechanics employed by the airline would recover it at Heathrow. The drugs belonged to an important Cali trafficker, German Rodriguez, who had customers in the UK. Sonya didn't have any idea where it was hidden, but had heard ramp workers talking about the 'nose'.

It was 1.30 a.m. in Bogotá and 7.30 a.m. in London when she called, and the flight had taken off seven hours earlier. We had only a few hours to act before the aircraft landed. I rang Poddy at his home in London and woke him up. He immediately roused himself to coordinate action with the Heathrow investigation unit. When the BA flight landed at Heathrow, a search team was waiting with a sniffer dog. They led the dog around the known concealment areas. It found nothing in the hold, but when it went near the nose of the aircraft it went barmy. No one could at first pinpoint the precise location, but on further examination the searchers opened up an inspection hatch in the fuselage, beneath the cockpit, and found 40 kg of cocaine in the nose-cone area.

The use of BA mechanics at Heathrow to recover drugs was confirmed beyond all doubt shortly afterwards by the ANP investigation. Their telephone intercepts revealed that a representative of the Heathrow team was coming to Bogotá, and would meet with the airport mafia to plan future runs. They would agree new concealment places, codewords, payment shares, and other details of their future shipments. I knew that this was going to be a hugely important meeting, and we needed somehow to find out what they agreed.

I tasked all of our sources at Bogotá Airport to tell me immediately if they heard anything about a Heathrow rip-off man coming. Several of them picked up gossip about it, but it was the ANP intercepts that again gave us the best intelligence: the man from London came and brought with him photographs and diagrams showing several places on the plane where drugs could be hidden and the main-tenance team could recover them. Each was discussed in detail, and it was agreed that three places would be favoured. The first was inside the rear wheel housing, in a large space where the wheels are located when the under-carriage is up. It was said that up to 200 kg could be stashed there. The second was inside hold five, a wall cover sealed with retaining screws, which had a space inside for up to 15 kg. The third was inside the nose, reached by an inspection hatch in the front of the fuselage, below the cockpit and by the front wheels, where up to 40 kg would fit.

I passed this on to the BA country manager, and he immediately notified his head of security in London. The following week, Alun Evans, head of BA Global Security, flew to Bogotá and met me in the embassy. His bosses were extremely concerned that the mafia were now planning to conceal drugs inside the structure itself, which posed a huge security risk and a threat to the integrity and safety of the aircraft. Alun said the concealment area in the nose contained delicate wiring for the electronic control systems. If the traffickers put drugs into this space the wiring could be inadvertently damaged, and might cause a malfunction of the aircraft systems. The same applied to the space inside the wall of hold five. Likewise, he said that if they put a large quantity of drugs into the rear wheel area as described, it might become dislodged during the flight and cause the landing gear to jam and fail. All of these proposed concealments could cause the aircraft to crash, with unthinkable consequences for the several hundred passengers and crew on board.

BA were extremely worried. Alun asked me to try to get as much information about this new modus operandi, and to tell him as a matter of urgency if I heard of concrete plans to use any of the proposed concealments. He said they would consider cancelling BA flights from Colombia if the mafia went ahead.

We both agreed, however, that the real long-term solution was to tackle the rip-off teams at Heathrow, especially within the maintenance staff. If we could take them down at the UK end, the Colombians would not send the drugs. The Investigation Division already had a team based at Heathrow dedicated exclusively to tackling rip-off teams. Alun said that BA would start their own investigation into the mechanics and maintenance staff at the airport.

IT WAS SHORTLY afterwards, in April 1996, that I heard that a trafficker called Carlos was planning to send 200 kg of cocaine to the UK using the space in the undercarriage of the BA248 flight. Carlos was a major narco from Cali who kept a suite in the luxury Fontana Hotel for his use when in Bogotá. He planned to send an initial 50 kg and if all went well the rest would follow on the next flight. I notified Keith and Alun at BA so that they could take additional security measures.

The following Friday, on 19 April, whilst the BA plane was at Bogotá waiting to load, I received a telephone call from Keith.

'Tom, I think you need to get out here as quickly as you can,' he said. 'We have a big problem.'

'Okay. I'll leave the embassy now and should be at the airport within the hour, but what's it about?'

'The buggers have put something in the undercarriage. We saw them. I can't let this happen, and I need your help

on what we can do. We have to stop them, but it's a dangerous situation.'

At the airport I went straight to the BA office. In his
private room at the back, Keith told me what had happened. The first officer of the flight had been walking
around the aircraft doing checks when he saw two
ground staff near the rear landing gear, putting some
bags up inside the space above it. They also saw him. He
reported the incident to Keith immediately.

As the BA country manager, Keith MacGaul was
responsible for not only the commercial operations but
also the safety and security of the flight. He insisted that
he would not allow the flight to take off until he could be
certain that nothing had been put inside the aircraft that
might be a danger. We guessed that it was almost certainly drugs that the first officer had seen – most likely
the 50kg of cocaine that Carlos from Cali was planning
to send – but it could be a bomb, and he couldn't take
the risk.

'What do you reckon?' Keith asked me. 'I can't let the
flight take off with those bags there. I think I'll ring the
airport police and tell them what's happened. I'll tell
them to come and search the undercarriage and seize it.'

'Jesus, no,' I said. 'The airport police run the mafia.
It's probably them who have arranged it all. What if they
send someone to search the undercarriage like you ask,
but then say there is nothing there? What could you do
then? The drugs would still be there, but you won't be
able to do anything.'

'Then maybe we should ring DAS and ask them to
come and seize it,' suggested Keith.

'Bloody hell, that will really piss off the police and the mafia,' I said. 'If DAS seize the drugs, they'll be furious. They'll kill people in revenge. It will put you, the first officer, and all your staff at huge risk. Even if they don't shoot you, they'll take revenge against you. These are evil and powerful people. They could plant drugs and arrest you both. You could spend years in a Colombian jail.'

Keith was worried, and so was I. This was a dangerous predicament. Following big seizures in the past, airport employees had been assassinated, and the head of American Airlines in Colombia had recently had to flee the country because of death threats from the mafia. On the other hand, Keith couldn't allow the bags to stay on the aircraft and he had to do something quickly. Meanwhile, the passengers had now all checked in, the luggage was being loaded, and the flight was being made ready for departure. The pressure was on.

We discussed the various options and after a short while Keith made a smart and courageous decision. He arranged for a public announcement that the BA flight was delayed due to a technical fault, and let it be known that the landing gear was going to be thoroughly inspected before the plane was allowed to take off. He asked me to discreetly feed this message back through my police contacts as well, to make sure that the mafia heard. Then we waited and watched to see what would happen.

About forty minutes later, with torrential rain pouring down outside, we saw two ground staff in waterproof capes arrive at the side of the aircraft in a tractor unit. The tractor unit parked beneath the aircraft, its yellow lights flashing and beepers sounding, and two shadowy figures were seen to climb up into the undercarriage and remove what looked like several large canvas bags. They would no doubt be stashed airside somewhere, ready for a second attempt at a future date.

We never knew what happened to that consignment. The drugs were probably sent to the UK shortly afterwards by a different means and without us hearing about it. But at least we had temporarily stopped them from using the dangerous undercarriage area. From the viewpoint of the Cali traffickers it would have been a costly failure. They had paid the airport mafia to put the drugs onto the aircraft, and then had to pay them again to take them off. Apart from the wasted time and money, they had also come very close to losing 50kg of cocaine.

In the following month, Keith MacGaul received several death threats from anonymous telephone callers. Fortunately he was about to retire from British Airways anyway, and he left Colombia two months later, in June 1996. I subsequently received information almost weekly about planned drug shipments, either in suitcases or in cargo, but I never again heard about any further attempts to conceal drugs in the nose-cone or the undercarriage.

ACCORDING TO OUR sources, it was not just individual airport workers and cops who facilitated the movement of drugs, but the managers of airport service providers and senior police officers too. Indeed, I was told that they controlled the whole business, with each senior manager taking his slice. It was said to be a powerful and well-run organisation. The power of the mafia at Bogotá airport was demonstrated by what they did on the igloo job.

An igloo is the colloquial term for the aluminium container into which airlines put suitcases and checked-in baggage. They are easier to load into the hold of an aircraft than loose baggage, and more secure. Their uniform shape helps avoid wasted space inside the aircraft's hold, and they carry both suitcases and loose cargo. Igloos are lightweight, have solid roofs and floors, and very thin aluminium skins for the sides. The front is a pull-down canvas that seals closed.

On 12 August 1996, I heard from an informant that several weeks earlier a group of traffickers from Cali had stolen three igloos from BA. The theft had been perpetrated by corrupt airport workers and police, assisted by private security staff responsible for the airport perimeter. The igloos were taken to Fontibon, a working-class *barrio* near the airport known for its seedy bars, nightclubs, and side-streets offering prostitutes and other shady services. Many airport workers lived in Fontibon and it had become a service centre for many needs, both legal and illegal. In the backstreet workshops people made false-sided suitcases to carry drugs, impregnated fabrics with cocaine and made pellets for couriers to swallow. There were even cocaine laboratories. It was a whole narcotic sub-industry linked to the airport. In one of its workshops, false compartments were skilfully made in the roofs of the stolen BA igloos. Cocaine had been packed into the false roof of one of the igloos and it had been returned to the airport and then sent to the UK. My informant said that the remaining two igloos would be sent with drugs in the coming weeks.

The information about stealing igloos was something new to me. If it were true, it meant that the group had already successfully sent a large amount of cocaine to the UK. However, sometimes informants hear stories that are not true, or get the facts completely wrong. I needed to first verify with BA whether any of their igloos were missing. I phoned Carlos and arranged to meet him later that day. He had just taken over as their country manager a few months earlier, and was the only person in BA I could trust. I told him what I could and asked if he would check whether any igloos were missing.

It was possible, he said, but it would take some time to do an inventory and he'd need help. In the absence of anyone else we could trust, several days later Carlos and I carried out an inventory of all the BA igloos at Bogotá Airport ourselves. It took a whole afternoon to check each container and its tag number, but we listed them all and finally confirmed that two were missing. We were both baffled, because in theory it was impossible to steal three igloos like this without being detected. Each one had a unique number tag so that it could be tracked, and empty igloos were stored securely in the BA cargo area, which was enclosed by a steel fence, locked and with security cameras. Somehow, presumably at night, they had managed to unlock the gates to the BA cargo compound, load the three igloos onto a truck, and then drive them out of the airport. They had somehow gone past the security cameras, the twenty-four-hour guards who were supposed to check all vehicles in and out of the airport perimeter, and various police and mobile patrol units. Then, having taken the igloos to a workshop, made a false compartment and filled one with cocaine, they had repeated this entire operation again in reverse to put one of them back in its place – all without being detected. This was a clearly slick and professional operation, executed by various arms of the airport mafia working together on behalf of the gentlemen from Cali.

After discussing it with Carlos, we agreed that all we could do was to count the igloos each day, keep observing, and wait for the other two to be returned. I knew that when they reappeared in the BA compound, they would almost certainly contain a sizeable quantity of cocaine. We knew their unique numbers, and so during the following weeks Carlos monitored his internal IT systems to look out for the igloos. We had the situation under control – or so we thought.

THE MESSAGE FROM Sonya arrived with a 'ping' on my pager at about 9 p.m. on Sunday, 8 September 1996. It was several hours after BA flight 248 had left Bogotá for London.

'A big party is happening tonight. I need to see you.'

I sent a short reply with the meeting instructions: 'OK. See you at your sister's place at 22.30.'

It was always risky meeting late at night. Bogotá was too dangerous to go walking about darkened streets, so I couldn't ask Sonya to take a counter-surveillance route. It would look strange to see a single female strolling around at that time. The code 'sister's place' was a vehicle route that Sonya could follow, in a very quiet residential area of northern Bogotá. At 10.30 p.m. there were never many vehicles driving about there.

I got there ten minutes early and drove around the adjacent streets, looking for any cars with people in them, before parking in a dark, secluded spot that gave a clear view of any vehicles entering the estate. Sonya's car appeared at 22.30 on the dot, came slowly down the street and went past me. Then she turned left and parked out of sight. I could see for a long way back that no other vehicles had followed, but I watched and waited in the darkness for a while. All was silent, except for the sound of dogs barking in the distance; first one, then another in reply, then others joining in. After five minutes I started my engine and moved off, drove past Sonya's car and pulled up next to it. She jumped into the passenger's seat and we drove to a quiet car park to talk.

'Señor the igloo job has taken place tonight,' she said, flushed with excitement. 'There was a lot of police activity, they were out back all the time that the igloos were being loaded onto the BA flight. A lieutenant and the guy with the drugs dog were there also.'

'That can't be right. We are monitoring the igloos and the two stolen ones have not yet been returned.'

Sonya laughed. 'Ha, señor. The mafia are smarter than you think. They can do anything they want at the airport and you won't ever know about it. That's why you need people like me to tell you.'

We spoke for around fifteen minutes. Sonya said that the mafia had sent both igloos and that coke was packed inside the roofs or floors. The mafia had seen Carlos and myself doing our inventory of the igloos several weeks earlier and knew that we must have discovered that two were missing. They knew that we were checking the numbers and would detect the missing ones as soon as they were returned. So they had returned the igloos the previous night but had then stolen two others in their place, and switched the unique number tags so that we would not detect anything.

This was like a complex game of chess, and they had outwitted us. They had returned the dirty igloos beneath our very noses. Sonya had no idea of how much drugs were in the igloos, but she said that because of all the police watching and minding it, she thought they probably contained a large quantity.

It was about 11.40 by the time I had dropped Sonya back at her car and seen her safely onto her route home without anyone behind her. I was back home by midnight, which was 6 a.m. in London. This was too important to pass via ID control, so I waited an hour and then woke up Poddy at home. We had about four hours to plan some action before the plane landed at Heathrow.

Poddy coordinated with the ID team at Heathrow and they scrambled the whole team to do surveillance on the aircraft and cargo when it arrived. From the tag numbers of the two dirty igloos, they were able to discern that they contained a cargo of fresh flowers. When the aircraft landed the next day, the surveillance team patiently watched as all of the igloos were offloaded. Those with suitcases and baggage were taken to the terminal. Several with cargo were taken to the freight area, and the two with flowers were taken by a tractor unit to a cargo area that was used for perishable cargo. The ID team planned to watch while the flowers were taken out, and then follow the empty containers to see where they were taken. Hopefully, they would eventually see the narcotics being removed. The aim was to identify and arrest the rip-off team and the criminals behind the venture.

The surveillance team watched as the two igloos were taken to the cargo shed. However, once there they were deliberately put into a blind spot and it was impossible to keep them under observation. Without being able to see them, there was a serious risk that they might disappear, so a customs team with a dog was quickly sent in to do a 'routine' inspection. When taken near to the igloos, the dog immediately indicated and alerted its handlers. The igloos were then searched by uniformed staff and 180 kg of cocaine were found inside false compartments in the roofs. It was the biggest cocaine seizure ever at Heathrow up until that time, with a street value of about £27 million.

As always, it was important that no one should ever know that information had been passed from Colombia. To protect my informant, and also Carlos and myself, the press were told that the drugs had been found during a routine inspection and a dog called Jasper took all the credit. Jasper was a handsome young Springer spaniel who had worked for HMCE at Heathrow for several years and who now held the record for the dog with most cocaine seizures under his collar.

I did not receive any more information about drugs in igloos going to the UK. Having lost the second consignment, the cartel knew that BA and HMCE were now aware of the method and would be on the lookout for it in future. However I did hear several months later that the Cali organisation were using the same method of sending cocaine in false roofs of igloos on American Airlines to the USA.

Just a week after the igloo seizure, I received information from CI Pedro that yet another suitcase packed full of cocaine was being sent to the UK. This time it was with an accompanying passenger, although the suitcase was not checked in as normal but was taken airside by ground staff to avoid the X-ray and security measures. We tipped off Heathrow and the following morning 28 kg of cocaine were seized and the passenger arrested.

By January 1997 two separate informants, CIs Sonya and Rocio, were both telling me, independently of each other, that CI Saddam, a baggage handler, was facilitating cocaine shipments in rip-on suitcases and in air cargo. CI Rocio said that Saddam was working with the head of security at Iberia Airlines and that together they were sending a suitcase with 25 kg cocaine every week to Madrid. She said that he had also recently sent a large shipment to the UK in air cargo, and that corrupt BA staff were involved. Despite the intelligence that he was working for the mafia, several weeks later Saddam told me about two suitcases that had just been ripped-on to a Lufthansa flight to Frankfurt. Acting on this, German customs managed to arrest four baggage handlers when they recovered the two suitcases at Frankfurt, and seized 33 kg. That was an excellent result, and at last a rip-off organisation had been arrested, but Saddam was clearly playing it both ends, and was only telling me about the cocaine runs by his competitors but not the ones that he facilitated himself.

WE KNEW THAT the cartels were also sending large quantities of drugs by air cargo. Most passenger flights to Europe had large cargo holds, which would be filled with exported Colombian flowers, ceramics, personal effects and other material. I frequently received intelligence about cocaine in air cargo, but we could never get sufficient detail to find it. We knew that a Cali trafficker called Guillermo R. was working closely with Efrain, a cargo supervisor, and had sent consignments of 30 and 50 kg to the UK in fruit, but we were unable to detect them in time. In addition to the main passenger airlines, Martinair had cargo planes flying to the UK several times a week. We received frequent information that cocaine was being sent with consignments of flowers on Martinair, but my informants couldn't get close enough to get details. It was extremely frustrating to know what was going on, but not be able to seize any of it.

Despite our success in gathering intelligence at Bogotá Airport, the police and ground staff were always rotating and being moved to new positions, so it was important to recruit new sources. In October 1997, Steve came up with the idea that we should try to implant one of our own trusted sources at the airport, either as a baggage handler or airline security. Steve had been cultivating CI Pele for some time and thought he was ideal for the task. He was a sharp-witted young man and had previously worked for DAS intelligence. We duly met with Pele in Café Oma and proposed that he infiltrate the airport mafia. Pele liked the idea and agreed to apply for a job there. If the plan worked, we hoped to have a reliable long-term source working undercover at the airport.

Pele's application was successful, and he started work as a baggage handler in December 1997. We had hoped that he would quickly establish himself as a person willing to do anything for money. Steve met him regularly and mentored him on how to interact with the traffickers. It was important that he appeared to be willing and corrupt, but he must not commit any crime himself. In the event he exceeded our expectations. Within weeks, and without getting himself involved in any way, Pele started to see suspicious activity. In February 1998 he told us about a suitcase being ripped-on to a flight to Los Angeles. In April, he spotted four unaccompanied suitcases being ripped-on to a flight to London. A few weeks later, he saw a consignment being sent to the USA in cargo.

But criminals never trust newcomers or accept them into their group until they have proved themselves by getting their hands dirty. After he had been in the job just two months, the Bogotá airport mafia gave Pele a test. Pele told Steve that they had offered him $20,000 to facilitate a rip-on suitcase. Steve told him that he could not accept the money. We couldn't allow Pele to commit any criminal acts, because if anything went wrong we wouldn't be able to protect him. He was working completely in the black, and had to stay within the law. Also, if he accepted the payment he would be on the mafia's payroll, and they would control him. He was instructed to decline but to reassure them that he was happy to turn a blind eye to help, although he did not want to get directly involved. Deep down, we knew that having turned down the offer to join them, Pele would not have their full trust.

Over the following months, the mafia offered Pele $20–25,000 on several occasions to join them and facilitate smuggles of drugs. Each time he had to refuse, saying he was happy to ensure the coast was clear but not get further involved. We knew that his refusal would limit his access, and while he was able to tell us in general terms about rip-on activity over the following months, he could never get precise details. Then, on 27 July, Pele told Steve that a suitcase with 20 kg had been ripped-on to the Avianca flight going to London. The case was seized on arrival at Heathrow, his information was spot-on and the cocaine was found inside.

Shortly afterwards, Pele's manager installed someone else in his job and he was frozen out. We realised that unless we could authorise him to participate, he would never get further access and it was becoming dangerous for him to remain. Steve took the sensible decision to pull him out. It was a shame, but in six months Pele had given us several seizures and a wealth of intelligence about the airport mafia.

IN ADDITION TO suitcases, there was a continuous flow of passenger couriers through Bogotá airport carrying drugs either in hand luggage or concealed on their person. Whilst the quantities were small, the sheer number of couriers made this a highly successful method of sending drugs. And like everything else, it was arranged and controlled by the airport mafia.

After check-in, passengers would go through immigration and then a security check. The police and airport security officers searched all hand luggage, and did a body search of all passengers, patting them down to find anything hidden in their clothes. When they reached the airline waiting area at the boarding gate, there was another final check and body search by antinarcotics police. The security was impressive, and to any external observer these robust checks would clearly detect any passenger foolish enough to carry drugs on their person or in hand luggage. But for those who paid an appropriate fee, the mafia simply circumvented the entire process.

Pre-arranged drug couriers would often go through this entire process carrying drugs but without having any problem. Having been paid off, staff would only do a superficial search or frisk, ignoring anything they might see or feel. On other occasions, the courier would go through without any drugs, and would be handed the drugs by police or security staff in a toilet near the boarding gate. The police did sometimes catch couriers and seize drugs at the airport, but these were individual chancers, the ones who were working on their own and not part of any mafia, and who had foolishly not bribed the right people.

During my four years in Colombia our informants identified hundreds of couriers, often carrying 5–10 kg on the body, or up to ten in hand-luggage. Of these, more than fifty were intercepted on arrival in Europe, which was probably only about a fifth of the ones we identified. This might seem a low hit-rate, but it was not easy to identify them amongst the thousands of passengers going through controls upon arrival. We might tell Customs at Heathrow that a passenger called Maria Suarez would be arriving on the BA248 from Bogotá and had 8 kg strapped to her body beneath her coat, but it was not an easy task for them to find Maria Suarez, plus the other dozen or so names they might be looking out for, amongst the sea of people that flooded through controls. Such was the success in sending couriers that we would often receive information about the same courier doing a second or third run.

18

ONE THAT GOT AWAY

M Y INFORMANT PACHO generated some huge seizures of cocaine, but his most valuable case was one that slipped through the net without a single gramme being found. It would, however, open the eyes of law enforcement agencies in the UK and Spain to the true scale of the flood of narcotics into Europe and to the tonnes that were arriving beneath our noses. It would also receive considerable publicity, none of it good, and result in a scandal for senior customs officials in Spain. It was the case of the *Orto-I*.

As the Cali and North Valley cartels increased in power, they started to use fishing boats and cargo ships to transport bigger loads, sometimes several tonnes at a time. During the 1990s several multi-tonne shipments, such as that on the *Limerick* in Cuba, had been intercepted en route to the USA, but it was unheard of for the cartels to send such amounts to Europe. The European market was smaller than that of North America and the distributors were less developed and more localised. No-one doubted the power of Cali or the North Valley to shift a single load of five tonnes in the States, where they had well-established networks that could quickly break down the loads on arrival and disperse them to distributors for cutting and onward sale. But in Europe we did not believe that there were any criminal organisations big enough to receive even one tonne, let alone several in one go.

So I was intrigued, but sceptical, when Pacho first told me in February 1997 that a large cargo ship called the *Nova* was going to take five tonnes of coke to Spain. He claimed that the organisation behind it had already sent five tonnes there the previous year on a ship called the *Hefan*. I might not have believed him, but everything he had ever given me had been spot-on, leading to big seizures on the *Limerick* and the *Gold Star*. According to Pacho, the *Nova* would set off from Panama towards Europe. As it passed by the coast near Cartagena, several fast launches would take cocaine out to the ship at night and load it. I did checks on maritime information systems and found that a cargo ship had previously been registered under the name *Hefan* and had recently been re-named the *Nova*. Furthermore, I found that it made several cargo runs from Panama to Europe in the past year. Pacho's information was looking good.

In early March 1997, Pacho told me that the five tonnes had been brought to Cartagena and were concealed in a stash near the coast, ready for onload to the mothership. The *Nova* was expected within the next few weeks. Unfortunately I could not locate the ship anywhere and our contacts in Panama said it had not passed through the Panama Canal. To make things worse, Pacho lost contact with his sub-source and could not get any further information. The case dried up.

Six months later, in September 1997, Pacho suddenly came up with more information, and explained why his sub-source had previously lost contact. Two weeks before the transfer of drugs to the ship, everyone involved in the loading operation was invited to a meeting. They were searched, and had their mobile telephones taken and the SIM cards removed. They were then driven to a remote *finca* several miles outside Cartagena, where they were isolated and not allowed to communicate with the outside world, not even their families. They were only allowed out when it was time for them to transfer the cocaine to the passing mothership, after which they were returned to the *finca* and again held in isolation for a further week. All of this was to prevent anyone leaking information about the operation, either deliberately or accidentally through loose talk. The cartel took great care to ensure security, and their precautions worked; without any specific information about the onload, we had missed the *Nova* shipment.

Since then, Pacho had established a well-placed contact within the organisation. He had managed to confirm that the ship *Nova* had indeed successfully taken five tonnes of cocaine to Spain back in March. It had also done a previous run before that, when it was called *Hefan*. This organisation, said Pacho, had successfully transported no less than ten tonnes of cocaine to Spain in the previous ten months.

The good news, Pacho said, was that another five-tonne shipment was being planned and should take place within the next month, but that this time they would use a new ship called the *Orto-I*. As it sailed past the north coast of Colombia, several fast speedboats would take the drugs out to it. The traffickers feared that the CIA had spy satellites watching the area and could detect if the ship stopped to load drugs, so the *Orto-I* would neither stop nor slow down. Instead it would keep to its normal course and a cruising speed of around twelve knots. The speedboats would come alongside, would fire ropes to the *Orto-I* and would transfer the cocaine in sacks tied to ropes, like strings of sausages. All of this would take place during the night, in complete darkness. Pacho said that a similar method would be used to offload the drugs. As the *Orto-I* approached the Galician coast of north-western Spain, speedboats would come out to meet it. The drugs would be passed to the speedboats, again with the bags of cocaine tied to lines like sausages, and the speedboats would take the drugs to land. When the *Orto-I* arrived at its first destination port of Bilbao, it would be clean. Pacho had infiltrated right to the heart of the transport organisation and was able to give an amazing amount of detail. I set to work to find out more about the *Orto-I*.

When I passed the information to London, however, they had grave doubts. In fact they did not believe me. Our maritime experts said that to load the drugs in this way was unheard of. For speedboats to flank a large vessel whilst it was moving would be extremely foolhardy, not just because of the risk of collision but also because the large bow waves pushed out by a cargo ship could easily swamp or capsize a small boat. To come alongside at night in complete darkness, without lights and at full speed, and to load five tonnes of bagged powder by ropes, would be incredibly risky, if not impossible. UK maritime experts said that such a manoeuvre would require the highest level of skill and seamanship, the kind of operation that only Special Forces trained for. I believed Pacho completely, but London thought the suggestion that untrained fishermen could do this was simply not credible. I was hugely disappointed.

A few weeks later, after researching maritime information

sources, we were able to identity the *Orto-I*. It was a large general cargo ship of 5,600 gross tonnage, built in 1979 and registered in Panama. It had previously been registered under the names *Kolpinsee* and *Corto*, and it had changed its name from the latter to *Orto-I* just a few months earlier, in June 1997. I knew that the recent change of name was a great indicator of a potential smuggle, but I couldn't find out its current location. Our DLOs in Panama had no trace of it.

'Señor, I have some good news,' Pacho said, when he called a few weeks later. 'Write down this number. It is the number of the big man behind the *Orto*. He is a big trafficker, working for the North Valley Cartel. He is the one arranging the transport.'

It did not take long to identify the phone number, and it led us directly to a narco called Hernan, from the town of Armenia, north of Cali. This was fantastic news. Hernan was already known to both the Colombian Drugs Police and the DEA as a trafficker, and had known links to the Cali and North Valley cartels. We coordinated with DAS, who immediately commenced an intelligence operation and intercepted his phones. Within a week, DAS told me that Hernan had spoken to an unknown male who seemed to be in charge of a ship somewhere in Chile. They had discussed when the ship would finish loading and be ready to go. This was all great intelligence – but I needed to find that ship.

I had worked with Chilean Customs several years earlier when I was based in Peru, so I telephoned a contact I knew in the port of Valparaiso and asked if he could discreetly check if a ship called the *Orto-I* was in any Chilean port. The following day my friends in Chilean Customs confirmed that the *Orto-I* was in Antofagasta, loading copper ore to take to Germany. Once it had finished, they told me, it was scheduled to go to Arica in northern Chile, where it would load eighty empty containers for delivery to Bilbao, Spain. It appeared that the ship had been recently re-painted, because earlier photographs of the *Corto* showed it as having a grey hull and red-coloured cranes and deck machinery, whereas the Chileans told me that *Orto-I* had a dark blue hull and yellow cranes. This last-minute change of name and appearance was another classic indicator that the ship might be used for a drugs shipment.

Over the following weeks, Steve, Bernie and I worked with DAS while they intercepted Hernan's telephones in Armenia, and gathered more and more intelligence about the organisation behind the motherships. DAS found evidence that clearly linked Hernan to the North Valley Cartel and to the ship. The captain of the *Orto-I* telephoned him regularly and gave updates on the ship's progress. Hernan was also in contact with people in Barranquilla who were getting ready for something big. Whilst they didn't spell it out over the phone, this was clearly the onload team. Hernan also had some interesting conversations in which he spoke to the captain in code, and sent a fax in which he told the captain that he should load simultaneously at the front and rear, 'two at the front and two at the back'. They were clearly not talking about the ship's legitimate cargo of copper; this had to be the cocaine. From the intelligence obtained by DAS, it seemed that the *Orto-I* would be loaded by four fast launches about eighty miles north of the coast of Barranquilla. Despite London's initial doubts, Pacho's information was looking good and had been corroborated. But just like the last time, Pacho lost contact with his sources as the run became imminent and was unable to get any more information. The cartel had isolated everyone involved, for security.

My customs contact in Chile rang me when the *Orto-I* set sail from Arica on 5 October 1997 and headed north, carrying eighty empty containers for Bilbao and 5,000 tonnes of copper ore for Hamburg. It had a crew of sixteen Peruvians and one Ukrainian. Unfortunately we had not been able to put a beacon on it, so would have to track it the hard way. On 13 October, it arrived at the Pacific end of the Panama Canal, went through and came out at Cristobal on the Caribbean side the following morning. Our DLO in Panama rang me to confirm that it had left Cristobal at 6 a.m. and was heading out into the Caribbean Sea towards the north coast of Colombia. Then we lost it.

For three days, we had no sightings of the ship and no updates from Pacho. The telephone intercepts were silent. I was starting to think that we had lost it completely when, on the 17th, Pacho called.

'Señor, I am very sorry but I couldn't find out sooner. They did it. They loaded it on the fifteenth. It was five tonnes.'

Pacho explained that during the night, several go-fast fishing launches had set off from a beach a few miles to the north-east of Cartagena and had delivered the cocaine to the *Orto-I* as it sailed past, approximately 170 miles off the coast. The drugs were inside 200 canvas sacks, each containing 25 kg, tied together by ropes. I passed the update to London. Despite their initial scepticism, the NIS now believed that Pacho's information was correct and that the *Orto-I* was on its way to an unloading rendezvous off the coast of Spain. They passed the intelligence to the Spanish Police, and together mounted a joint operation to try to locate the ship.

The Spanish had coastal surveillance aircraft themselves, but their range and capabilities were limited. Fortunately the UK had a Nimrod maritime plane available, and it was agreed it could be temporarily sent to assist. Whilst designed for military purposes, Nimrods were deployed by the Royal Air Force in peacetime to support civilian law enforcement operations such as fisheries protection and customs operations. They had a world-leading capacity to locate small targets at sea, such as hostile submarines, and were frequently used to support HMCE in drug cases. Flying from airbases in Madeira and Portugal, the Nimrod started the meticulous task of searching for the *Orto-I* in the middle of the Atlantic. It was like looking for a tiny, moving needle in the vast haystack of the North Atlantic Ocean.

Meanwhile, the Spanish were mounting a preparatory operation, and their Customs Service put to sea its maritime intercept vessel, the *Petrel*. It was a fairly old, slow patrol ship, but it carried three rigid-hulled inflatables on its rear deck. The RIBs could be launched within ten minutes and could move at speed to take armed boarding teams to intercept suspect vessels. Our own NIS had sent a maritime expert, Raymond Furlong, to Spain to coordinate, and he was taken on board the *Petrel*. He would act as the link between the UK assets and the Spanish intercept boat, feeding intelligence updates as they came in.

We had passed all our information to the Spanish Police, including details of how the drugs would be offloaded. It was rare to have such precise details about how a large shipment would take place. We told the Spanish that as the *Orto-I* passed close to the coast of Galicia, several speedboats would come out, draw alongside the ship as it sailed, and receive the drugs. These speedboats would then take the drugs ashore to mainland Spain. Galicia is an area renowned for its smuggling tradition. The coastline is rugged and marked by hundreds of small coves which are often inaccessible by road. It was infamous for its smuggling families and mafias, heavily involved in the illicit importation and distribution of cigarettes, alcohol, marijuana, and now cocaine.

The Spanish police would lead the investigation but would rely upon their Customs Service to control the *Orto-I* at sea as it approached. However, Spanish Customs did not trust the police, and did not believe our information. They thought that the *Orto-I* would probably be met by a fishing boat. They had no solid reason to think this, but later justified themselves by saying that this was the most common method being used at that time by the Galicians. The *Petrel*, therefore, planned on taking up a position behind the *Orto-I* and following it at a distance, waiting until it detected a fishing boat approach before launching two of its RIBs to intercept after it had loaded from the *Orto-I*. They chose to ignore our information that speedboats would be used.

What next unfolded can only be described as a shameful disaster.

ON 20 OCTOBER 1997, the RAF Nimrod crew spotted the *Orto-I* as it passed the Azores in the mid-Atlantic, more than a thousand miles west of Portugal and heading towards Spain. Two Nimrod crews flew in turns over the following days to continuously track the ship as it sailed towards northern Spain. Also in the area was a British Navy warship, which supported the surveillance operation with its long-range radar and communication systems. An NIS officer called Micky was on board the warship and communicated with the Nimrod crew and with Ray on the *Petrel*, so that everyone was kept up to date as events unfolded. Mick's call-sign from the warship was 'Argonaut' and Ray's on the *Petrel* was 'Cerberus'.

By the 28th the *Orto-I* was just sixty miles off Cape Finisterre on the Galician coast. It stopped its engines, dropped anchor and waited. We all held our breath. *What was the captain doing?* I imagined the various reasons why he might order his ship to stop. Perhaps this was it, and the handover was about to take place, or perhaps they were waiting for something. Maybe they had arrived earlier than planned, and were waiting for confirmation that the Galicians were ready to come out. Or perhaps the cartel had informants within Spanish Customs and had been warned that the *Petrel* was out on patrol. Whatever the reason, after a wait for most of a day, and much nervous nail-biting, the *Orto-I* moved off again and continued towards Bilbao.

On the 31st it changed course slightly and moved closer towards the Spanish coast. It was now just fifteen miles off northern Galicia, sailing at roughly ten knots towards Bilbao. This was far too close to the coastline for our comfort, and meant Spanish Customs were no longer in control. They still expected a handover to a fishing boat further out at sea, but on the radar screens of the Nimrod up above, four blips appeared coming out from the coast toward the ship. The blips were moving fast. Micky contacted Ray on the *Petrel*.

'Cerberus from Argonaut,' the radio crackled. 'Relaying from MPA, four unknown objects departed the coast and now moving at speed towards the target.'

Ray immediately told the Spanish captain of the *Petrel*, and urged him to get the RIBs and boarding teams ready to launch. Amazingly, the captain was not at all concerned. He said that it was probably just pleasure craft, normal marine traffic for that area. He said he would consult with his headquarters in Madrid, and disappeared below deck.

The radio calls from Micky became more urgent.

'Cerberus from Argonaut. Four unknown objects now identified as day-fisher type speedboats, moving at speed and now approaching the stern of *Orto-I*.'

Ray could now see the four objects on the *Petrel*'s radar. He rushed below, found the captain in his cabin, persuaded him to come back up to the deck and again urged him to launch the inflatables, before it was too late. Again the captain said he thought it was routine traffic, sports boats out for the day. He was still expecting the *Orto-I* to rendezvous with a large and much slower fishing boat. His mind was fixed, he would not accept what appeared to be happening, and he declined to launch the interceptor RIBs. Ray was frantic, but he was a guest on board the ship and had no power to make them act.

Micky's sharp, concise radio calls continued.

'Cerberus from Argonaut. Four targets are now with the mother. Believed to be handing over front and rear.'

The surveillance crew on the Nimrod later reported

how they saw four speedboats come alongside the *Orto-I* as it sailed along, two at the front and two at the rear, just as Pacho had said they would. Each one fired lines to the mothership and strings of bags were transferred to the speedboats like sausages. The crew must have had the bags prepared and securely tied together on deck at the front and rear, ready to go. It took less than fifteen minutes to transfer five tonnes of cocaine to the four boats. The Nimrod crew then watched as they broke away and sped in different directions towards locations on the Galician coastline. The smugglers were clearly well organised and professional. They knew that even if law enforcement started to chase them, they would only be able to pursue one of the speedboats, not all of them, so the four boats, each with 1.25 tonnes of coke, headed for different landing points in small, remote coves. In the event, no-one followed them at all.

In no more than thirty minutes, from start to finish, the narcotics had been offloaded, taken to land and safely stashed. Meanwhile, the patrol vessel *Petrel* was still lagging behind the *Orto-I*, badly positioned, too slow and completely impotent. Five tonnes of cocaine, worth over £150 million at wholesale price and around £750 million at street value, had just been safely landed beneath our noses.

I was furious with the Spanish Customs, and so were the Spanish police. We had been working the case with the UDYCO, the organised crime and drugs division of the Spanish Judicial Police in Madrid, who dealt with international trafficking investigations. The UDYCO had relied upon Spanish Customs to provide the boats for the interception and felt that the captain of the *Petrel* in particular had let them down. The failed interception had been a debacle, and things were to get even worse. Shortly afterwards, someone leaked the whole story to the Spanish press. It was most likely someone from the police or the prosecuting magistrate, but was clearly someone who was angry with the way Spanish Customs had bungled the job, and wanted the world to know about it. Press reports appeared in early November in both Spain and the UK, telling how British aircraft had kept surveillance on the ship as it crossed the Atlantic, and how Spanish Customs had bungled the operation. The *Daily Telegraph* reported the story under the headline '£1 billion drugs haul slips through police net'. Worryingly, it also referred to 'detailed intelligence provided by the British authorities', which caused me some concern.

Worse was to come. On 16 November, the Colombian newspaper *El Espectador* ran a full-page article about the case. Their reporters had clearly picked up on the reports in Spain and investigated further. Their article revealed in great detail how the *Orto-I* had left Chile with a legitimate cargo of copper before being secretly loaded with drugs as it sailed by the northern coast of Colombia. It told how British aircraft followed the ship as it crossed the Atlantic, and how the crew of the Spanish Customs vessel *Petrel* had allowed five tonnes of cocaine to be collected by four speedboats and brought ashore. Whilst no mention was made of informants, *El Espectador* said that information had come from the British liaison officer in Colombia. It was clear that this had been leaked by the Spanish police; no one else had such detailed information. I was furious. Pacho was still infiltrated within the transport organisation, and we still had an intelligence operation with telephone intercepts ongoing in Colombia against the North Valley cartel principals. The leak of the whole story in the Colombian press not only disrupted our investigation, but also put Pacho, myself and the other DLOs at great risk.

HMCE lodged a strong complaint with the Spanish. The country's leading drug prosecutor, Baltazar Garzon, had been leading the case with the Spanish police and had authorised the boarding of the *Orto-I*. He too was furious, both at the leaks to the press and the bungling of the operation by Customs. Following strident complaints from all sides, the captain of the *Petrel* 'retired' shortly afterwards.

ALTHOUGH THE *Orto-I* case did not lead to a seizure of drugs or arrest of traffickers, it was probably the most useful of all the cases that Pacho gave us. His information about the huge shipments made by the *Hefan*, *Nova* and *Orto-I* opened our eyes to what was happening. The authorities in the UK and Spain had been completely unaware that the Cali and North Valley cartels were shipping such huge bulk loads to Europe. If we accepted that the *Hefan* and *Nova* shipments were five tonnes each, as Pacho said, and added the *Orto-I*, it meant that this transport organisation had successfully imported fifteen tonnes to Spain, worth around £450 million at wholesale prices, and with an eventual street value of more than £2 billion. The size of these shipments was mind-boggling, and previously unheard of in Europe.

Following all the press coverage in Colombia, we thought that the cartels and their transport organisation would be spooked and would pause for a while before sending another shipment. We were wrong. A few months later Pacho reported that they were getting ready to send another five tonnes. He said he would infiltrate and try to get details of the ship. Unfortunately, events overtook him, and he never did. Interestingly, the Panamanian-flagged ship known as the *Orto-I* changed its name five times in the six-year period from 1996 to 2002. Our research showed that it was successively registered under the following names: *Corto, Orto-I, Kolpin, Khensu I* and *Falcon I*. One might wonder why a legitimate owner would keep changing a ship's name, as well as frequently re-painting it in different colours. Drug traffickers knew that the US and other authorities had 'lookout' lists of suspect drug ships. When we identified one, it would be put on a watch list at JIATF in Florida and on other databases. The authorities also took photos of these vessels. So before embarking on a large drug run, the cartels often changed the name and appearance of motherships. The five name-changes of the *Orto-I* in just six years might give an indication of how many drugs runs it was used for over this period.

Pacho was never aware of the scandal and inter-agency fighting that had been caused in Spain by the *Orto-I*, nor the long-term impact of the case. His information had opened a window of opportunity and revealed a scale of bulk shipping that up until then we had never imagined. His information led to a change of tactics by the UK and Spain, and we started to work together to target the big mothership loads and the organisations behind them. Although the *Orto-I* case was itself a failure, it would lead to many other operations and the seizure of dozens of ships and hundreds of tonnes of drugs over the following years.

19

THE VETTED UNIT

I N THE EARLY 1990s the British DLOs and Customs ID helped the ANP to develop an intelligence unit and a telephone intercept capacity. We played an important role in providing the ANP with technical equipment and training so that they could tap phones, pagers and radio communications, and technicians from the UK came out frequently to repair recorders and upgrade their kit.

The ANP's special intercept unit was located in a secret hidden section of their headquarters on Avenida El Dorado in Bogotá. I remember clearly my first visit. An officer guided me through the ANP main building and up several flights of stairs to the top floor, then out onto the flat roof. We crossed to another stairway, then went down these stairs and turned right into a separate area at the back of the building, where the intelligence unit was located. We walked through the unit until we came to a small meeting room, with wood panelling and bookshelves on the far wall. The officer went to the bookshelves and slid aside one of the wooden back panels, to reveal a hidden doorway. Stooping down to avoid banging our heads, we stepped through the narrow opening and into a hidden den, occupied by the intercept suite. Therein sat half a dozen ANP staff with headphones on, listening to the phone conversations of drug traffickers.

Dan and Anne would spend many hours sitting in the suite, running joint cases with ANP staff, as would Bernie and Steve later on. Very few people knew of its existence, and the British DLOs were the only foreigners allowed to see it, let alone work inside.

When traffickers started using encrypted cellphones around 1995, the intercept suite was stymied. At first law enforcement agencies could not crack the new digital mobiles at all, but within a few months specialists in the UK and US developed equipment that could break the encryption. However we could only intercept calls within a short range of several kilometres, so portable units were required to carry out the listening. We tested the British equipment with DAS during Operation Papagayo, and it worked well, but because of the limited range of the technology it was clear that if the ANP wanted to investigate traffickers in Cartagena and Santa Marta, we would need an intercept team based on the north coast, as well as one in Bogotá.

Because of the threat from corruption, the British DLOs had always worked with just a very small number of people in the ANP and DAS. When Colonel Leonardo Gallego Castrillon took over as head of the ANP in April 1994, he instigated a major purge to clean up the force and remove dishonest staff. Gallego was highly respected and had earned his reputation fighting the cartels. He was a hard man with strong values and would not accept anyone who he considered corrupt or inefficient. We worked closely together and became good friends. Over the following three years he sacked or transferred hundreds of cops. Simultaneously he launched recruitment drives to bring in a fresh generation of officers and managers who could impose new standards of moral rectitude and professional conduct. Slowly the level of dishonesty within the ANP fell, and it became possible for us to work with a wider group of people.

Colonel Gallego had already identified a small group of reliable ANP officers who we could work with. Major Buchelli, and Lieutenants Portilla and Barrios had worked closely with me in developing intelligence in Cartagena and Santa Marta. Buchelli had even spent several months undercover in Cartagena docks and had gathered intelligence about how the mafia operated and the main security staff involved. Portilla and Barrios had developed a network of good contacts in the ports and had helped me to recruit several informants. During most of my time in Colombia these three were the only ANP officers, apart from Gallego himself, who I really trusted, but I realised that we could accomplish far more if we had a larger group of reliable people in the north.

In mid-1997, I decided that we should try to establish an elite team of ANP officers on the coast. This unit could help recruit and handle informants in the ports, and carry out surveillance and intercept work against known traffickers. I approached Colonel Gallego and put a proposal to him: would he select fifteen motivated, capable and trustworthy officers to work with us against the networks that controlled drug shipments from Cartagena, Barranquilla and Santa Marta? They had to be hand-picked and of the highest integrity. If he agreed, the UK would supply the equipment, training and funds. Gallego agreed.

Over the following months, Gallego personally selected thirty of his best staff, all carefully vetted by himself. From these we picked the best fifteen, plus five reserves. In years to come, we would introduce a more formal selection process with vetting and polygraph-testing, but at first we had to rely upon Gallego's judgment. He also secured the use of a large house in a residential suburb of Cartagena, and an apartment in the smart Boca Grande district. Both properties had been seized from narcos several years earlier, and would eventually be sold by the Colombian state, but in the meantime Gallego obtained authorisation for the ANP to use them. The large house became the primary base for the intelligence unit. It had beds for ten officers, secure parking for several surveillance cars and storage for equipment. The two-bedroom apartment was on the fifth floor of a luxury block and would be used as a listening post. For security reasons, we agreed with Gallego that no one must know of the existence of the new unit, nor its location.

The NIS provided specialist training to the fifteen officers, with courses in the UK and ongoing mentoring in Cartagena. They learned how to recruit and handle informants, as well as interception, surveillance and intelligence. In March 1998 a new DLO, Andy, arrived in Colombia and took over responsibility for the development and day-to-day operation of the unit. Andy and I supervised the arrival and installation of the British-supplied intercept equipment in the Boca Grande listening post. At one stage we both climbed precariously on to the roof of the apartment block, five floors up, to install antennae for the kit. At least the view of Cartagena was awesome from up there. Shortly afterwards the team at the main house received vehicles, mobile radio equipment, and a budget for running expenses.

By April 1998 our special team was fully operational in Cartagena. It proved to be a tremendous asset. Instead of working on my own to recruit port informants, we now had a dedicated, vetted unit of well trained, handpicked Colombian officers. Over the following years they would build their own network of human sources, supported by intelligence from intercepts, and would be hugely successful. They would also manage to remain a small and secretive unit, operating from covert premises and unknown to the rest of the ANP and other agencies. The work of the vetted unit would become of critical importance two years later, when the UK's informant network in Colombia was dismantled.

20

THE END OF THE NETWORK

J UST A SHORT distance inland from Albornoz, where the *Zeeland* was beaconed, lies a residential district of Cartagena called Blas de Lezo. It is named in honour of a Spanish naval commander. A large square and avenue in Cartagena also bear his name, and his bronze statue stands proudly in front of the Castillo San Felipe in the old town. He is one of the great heroes of Spanish naval history, and of Cartagena.

Born in the Basque region of Spain, Admiral Blas de Lezo became famous for his astute strategies as a naval commander and for his tenacity and courage in battle. In 1704, as a junior officer, he lost his left leg, blown off by cannon shot, whilst fighting the British at the battle of Vélez Málaga. In 1707, he lost his left eye in the defence of Toulon against British and Dutch forces. In 1714, at the siege of Barcelona he lost use of his right arm. Thus by the age of twenty-seven he had only one eye, one leg and one working arm, but had gained a reputation as a fearless commander.

In 1741, the British were fighting Spain in the so-called War of Jenkins' Ear, and were keen to use it as an excuse to seize Spanish-held territories in the Americas. Admiral Edward Vernon was dispatched with a huge invasion force of 124 ships, 27,600 men and 2,600 artillery pieces to attack Cartagena. Blas de Lezo, by then fifty-two years old, was in charge of the Spanish forces there. He was vastly out-numbered, with just six ships and 2,300 men. Vernon had carried out several small raids on Cartagena during the previous year, to test the defences and learn the terrain, and when he returned that March he was confident of victory. In the first month of battle he captured the gun batteries on Tierra Bomba island and the forts of San Luis and San Jose, which guarded the entrance to the bay. This allowed the British to sail into Cartagena unchallenged and land forces to occupy the outer part of the town, while the remaining defenders retreated to the Fortress of San Felipe. Vernon was so confident of victory that he sent word to London that Cartagena was about to fall. Such was the joy that special commemorative coins were minted in celebration; the coins depict Don Blas de Lezo kneeling before his tri-umphant conqueror, with the words 'The Pride of Spain humbled by Admiral Vernon' on one side, and on the other, 'Vernon Conquered Cartagena, April 1741'. Such a victory would have changed the history of Colombia, making it an English-speaking colony of Great Britain. But the celebra-tion was premature.

By mid-April the British were preparing to make their final assault on the fortifications of San Felipe. But the cunning Blas de Lezo sent fake deserters to offer information to the British. They gave false details about the weakest part of the fortifications, where, they said, the walls were low, vulnerable and difficult to defend. Having laid the bait, Blas cunningly ordered his men to deepen the dry moat around these walls and to dig a network of defensive trenches. The

British attacked on 20 April, sending a large force towards the walls at the rear of the town in a direct assault. They expected to scale the walls and overwhelm the defenders by force of numbers, but because the moat had been deepened, they found that their scaling ladders did not reach the top of the walls. Unable to advance, they were trapped in a killing field with no protection. The Spanish laid down heavy fire, and the attacking force suffered huge losses. Vernon was forced to withdraw from Cartagena shortly afterwards in shameful retreat, his army decimated.

Don Blas de Lezo himself died four months later but remains one of the great heroes of Cartagena. When British tourists now visit Cartagena, city tour guides take great pleasure in recounting the tale of de Lezo's heroic defence, of how his small force defeated the British, and of the victory medals that the British prematurely made. It makes me smile to think that he had sent fake informants to the British, just as the Cali Cartel did in modern times.

It was near the district of Blas de Lezo that CI Pacho lived, and where he was drinking a beer one day in October 1998, a few months after I had left Colombia. Pacho was a highly successful informant, but was completely unaware of the enormous impact that his information had. He infiltrated transport organisations and passed us intelligence, but he had no idea of the bigger picture or of the strategic importance of his work. He knew nothing, for example, of the geopolitical impact of the *Limerick* case, or that it caused a stand-off between the American and Cuban authorities over whether the US Coast Guard could enter Cuban waters to recover the sinking vessel with drugs, or of the diplomatic breakthrough when American officers were allowed to search the ship in Santiago de Cuba. He had no clue that the presidents of the USA and Cuba had both been personally briefed about the case, or the huge contribution it made to improving US–Cuban relations and law enforcement cooperation.

He was also completely unaware of our secret beaconing missions, the first time that the UK had carried out covert ops to put tracking devices on ships in Colombia, which had always been considered far too dangerous. Pacho's cases on the *Zeeland* and *Marshall* had enabled the first such operations, and set in train the close relationship that would develop between the NIS and the Colombian Navy.

He was unaware that his information about the shipments on the *Hefan* and *Orto-I* had opened our eyes to the multi-tonne motherships that were arriving in Europe beneath our noses, and enabled Great Britain and Spain to shift focus and target them. His information about motherships would kickstart a series of extremely important international joint operations over the following years. One, Operation Journey, involved the UK, USA, Spain, Greece and several other countries and resulted in the seizure of over forty tonnes of cocaine. Joint operations by the UK and Spain between 2000 and 2005 would also result in the seizure of dozens of motherships and over fifty tonnes.

Pacho was also not aware of the motorcycle that pulled up outside the bar while he was having a beer with his friends near his home in Cartagena on 3 October, nor of the two men who dismounted and entered. They walked across the bar and came towards him. Without saying a word, they drew guns and fired four or five shots into Pacho at close range. Bottles and tables went flying as the other drinkers in the bar scattered in panic, hiding wherever they could. As Pacho lay on the floor they calmly fired two more bullets into him to make sure, and then left. Pacho died on the spot.

We found out several weeks later that Pacho had been sold out by one of his own sub-sources, who was in trouble with the mafia and desperately needed money. He betrayed Pacho for cash and told the traffickers that he had been the informant responsible for the seizure of 540 kg on the *Gold Star* twenty months earlier. These people have long memories and do not forgive. They took their revenge.

I was gutted when I heard about Pacho's death. I had worked with him closely for more than two years and had come to really like him. He was always smiling and always positive. When I'd first met him he was just a young rogue, ducking and diving around the port, earning money handling stolen goods or however he could. But he wasn't a bad person. I had got him into this business, telling him about the cocaine transport methods and where to look. I had guided him towards the cargo ships and trained him to work as my informant. He was a nice guy, with a wife and young kids, and he didn't deserve to die. And to some extent, at least, I was to blame.

FROM 1994 TO JUNE 1998, I handled more than fifty informants in Colombia, most of whom I recruited personally. Some were not very productive, and a few were time-wasters or treacherous individuals working for the other side. But the majority were serious people, who worked professionally to infiltrate the cartels. They all knew that they were doing extremely dangerous work in a volatile and high-risk environment. I was lucky that despite the huge risks involved, none of my informants were killed during the time I worked there, although two of their sub-sources were murdered and we did have some scary close shaves. CI Pacho was executed several months after I left, and Mike was assassinated the following year. Alberto simply disappeared. We never found out what happened to him, but he joined the list of many thousands of Colombians who simply disappeared without trace amid the violence of criminal mafias, guerrillas and paramilitary groups.

During my four years, our team of informants identified hundreds of consignments of drugs. More than 290 tonnes were seized, worth over £3 billion. Those figures did not include the *Orto-I*, the Black River case, or the hundreds of tonnes that we identified but which got through the net. Perhaps more importantly, we caused huge damage to the criminal organisations behind the trade, with over 300 traffickers arrested, and disrupted the flow of drugs to Europe. I had started with no informants in the Colombian seaports. I ended up with an effective network in all of the main ports that exported drugs to Europe. After four years, the cartels still controlled the ports, and still had effective transport systems to ship drugs to Europe and the USA. We had not stopped them, but we had infiltrated their transport organisation, caused instability and weakened them. They could no longer feel secure or guarantee safe deliveries. Over the following years the UK intensified its activities against the maritime transport organisations, causing the cartels huge losses, disruption, and forcing them to change their methods and routes.

However, because of two big changes to come, the UK would eventually turn away from informants and disband the network of sources that had been so carefully established in the Colombian ports. Those two big changes were RIPA and SOCA.

The Regulation of Investigatory Powers Act (RIPA) came into force in October 2000 and, amongst other things, changed the rules governing how law enforcement agencies like HMCE should handle informants. Prior to RIPA, Customs ID (later the NIS) had a simple but robust process for handling informants overseas. Every meeting or contact was recorded in the DLO's official notebook at the time, and dated and signed. The pages of the notebooks were photocopied and sent to London management by secure diplomatic bag. Notebooks were also regularly examined by managers during inspection visits. This process ensured that all contacts were properly recorded and could not be altered after the event.

In 2000, RIPA imposed a new process that required a great deal of additional paperwork. More critically, it required all meetings and contact with informants to be pre-authorised by a manager in London. The law had been designed to regulate activities in the UK, and the difficulties of working in distant overseas locations had not been taken into account. Because of the time difference with Colombia, and insecure communications that might be tapped by the cartels, it was not possible to seek approval from London before each contact. I would often receive a pager message late at night from an informant, asking to speak with me or meet urgently to tell me about a shipment arriving in the UK within the next few hours. I often met CI Sonya and other sources at very short notice, and at a time that was in the middle of the night in the UK. It was simply not possible to ask London for approval before every such contact.

The changes introduced by RIPA, the extra paperwork and the requirement for pre-approval before contact, made it impossible to continue handling the large number of informants that we had developed in Colombia. Consequently, NIS London instructed that only the most important and productive informants would continue, and that all other informants would be de-authorised, or in other words, sacked.

Many informants only made contact when they had specific useful information, perhaps only two or three times a year, and these less active sources were all dispensed with. CI Eddy, for example, never wasted time and only contacted me when he had some specific reason to do so. But each time that he did contact me, it was to pass precise information that led to a seizure of drugs. In the last year of my posting in Bogotá I spoke with Eddy only twice, yet he gave me information that led to the seizure of 3.6 tonnes of drugs in the UK. He was deemed to be insufficiently important to continue, and was de-authorised in 2000. We never heard from him again. Because of RIPA, the network of informants that had been so carefully built up in Colombia was reduced to less than half the number.

Then, in 2006, the Government created the Serious Organised Crime Agency, or SOCA. HMCE lost its remit as the lead UK agency responsible for the investigation of international drugs trafficking. That responsibility, along with management of the international DLO network, was taken over by SOCA. In the early days of SOCA there existed considerable inter-agency rivalry and a mistrust of HMCE and its legacy. Senior directors of SOCA ruled that the new agency would not take on any of the informants previously handled by the NIS.

In the preceding years, the handling of informants by the NIS had been heavily criticised during two major investigations. In the London City Bond case, irregularities came to light regarding the way in which investigators had handled participating informants. Officers were accused of malpractice and consequently several court cases were appealed, and convictions quashed. The *Butterfield Review*, published in July 2003, was a judicial report by Mr Justice Butterfield into the irregularities and mishandling of these excise duty and VAT investigations by HMCE in the late 1990s. Whilst it acknowledged that significant improvements had been made since then, the Butterfield report laid bare major failings in the way that HMCE had handled informants.

Operation Brandfield was a separate, four-year investigation by West Midlands Police into alleged malpractice by a number of HMCE drug investigators. It focused on alleged sting operations and the handling of participating informants in so-called 'controlled deliveries' of mainly heroin from Pakistan during the 1990s. Three HMCE investigators were found guilty of misconduct in public office, and the reputation of the NIS was severely tarnished.

Because of these problems, when SOCA started in 2006 it did not take over any informants previously handled by the HMCE Investigation Service. SOCA senior directors wanted the agency to start with a clean slate, without any hidden skeletons in cupboards that might accompany precursor-agency informants. All of the informants in Colombia were therefore de-authorised and sacked. When I left Colombia in June 1998 we were running twenty-six active informants. They were identifying several shipments each week, and generating five or six seizures every month. More importantly, they were passing us a constant flow of rich intelligence about major cartels and criminal groups in the UK, Europe and Colombia, how they operated, their latest transport methods and planned future shipments. When SOCA started in April 2006, the entire informant network was dismantled, and the flow of intelligence from them stopped.

The impact of these changes on the UK's ability to gather intelligence in Colombia was significant. The information flows were shut down overnight and we no longer received accurate intelligence about maritime shipments from Colombian ports. Several years later, a senior intelligence officer in SOCA's 'Knowledge' section, dealing with drugs intelligence, told me that they had no information about rip-ons from Colombia, and did not even understand how rip-ons worked!

Now, more than a decade later, the UK still does not have informants in Colombian ports or airports. The mafias still control these places and cocaine is still being transported to Europe in considerable quantities. But we no longer have a network of reliable sources to tell us about it. I returned to Colombia in 2016, and I spoke with one of my former informants, the person who had been known as CI Sonya. Sonya was now a senior manager at Bogotá Airport. She told me that drugs were still being sent on flights to Europe on a regular basis, in suitcases, with passengers and in cargo. She said that the airport mafia still controlled the flow of cocaine through there. The only difference now was that she had no-one to pass information to. Nothing had changed, we were just no longer aware or informed about it. The most worrying detail about this was something that Keith MacGaul of British Airways had said to me back in 1996: 'If they can put ten kilos of cocaine onto an aircraft, they can just as easily put ten kilos of explosives.'

The cultivation of coca and production of cocaine in Colombia fell significantly between 2000 to 2015 because of a crop eradication programme and strong law enforcement actions. In 2015 the Colombian government stopped crop fumigations, and consequently the coca cultivations increased again. According to the United Nations Office on Drugs and Crime, in 2016 Colombia had 146,000 hectares of coca cultivation, sufficient to produce 866 metric tonnes of pure cocaine a year. This was an increase of one-third over 2015. This huge surge in cultivation and production in Colombia will without doubt have a big impact upon availability in consumer countries. At the time of writing this book, in 2018, Colombia is said to be producing more cocaine than ever before.

During 2017, I spoke with former informants and colleagues who were working in the maritime domain in Cartagena and Santa Marta. They told me that large shipments of cocaine are still being sent to Europe from Cartagena, Santa Marta and Turbo. Indeed, I was told that shipments from Turbo port have increased significantly since we ran informants there in the 1990s. The flow of cocaine from the ports continues unabated, but the difference now is that the UK no longer has a network of informants to give us a reliable intelligence picture.

EPILOGUE

T HE DLO TEAM in Colombia was the jewel in the crown
of the UK's overseas network. In 1998 there were sixty
British DLOs operating in forty-two different countries.
The ones in Colombia were producing more intelligence
and more seizures than the rest put together. We had the
advantage, of course, of being at the very source of the
world's cocaine production. Most of those seizures came
from the intelligence passed by informants.

The UK still has law enforcement liaison officers based
overseas. In 2017, the National Crime Agency had over
150 in fifty countries, dealing with serious crime, including drug trafficking. These officers work closely with
foreign law enforcement to exchange information and
develop investigations against major criminals and organised crime groups. But working methods have changed.
Nowadays liaison officers do not recruit informants in
ports and do not work in the same way as depicted in this
book. I have not revealed any sensitive current working
practices or methodologies because British liaison officers
no longer work in that way.

Because the Colombian cartels were so powerful in
the 1990s and had corrupted law enforcement agencies,
the DLOs had to work independently and recruit sources
themselves. How we operated back then was unique. We

had freedom to use our imagination, to take risks, to go into hostile places and find and recruit sources alone. Now things have changed. Health and safety concerns preclude such actions. The Colombian Police are also now relatively free from corruption and are a professional and respected force. The UK has a strong relationship with agencies there, and they now run their own informants.

I have deliberately not described informants in any detail in this book, because to do so might identify them and put them at risk. I have also not given the names of the corrupt people who were part of the transport mafias in the ports and airport. The names of the police, baggage handlers and security staff who facilitated shipments of drugs through Bogotá airport are known; likewise the names of corrupt port workers, police and those who arranged maritime shipments from Cartagena and Santa Marta. But to publish their names so many years later seems pointless.

I have described how corrupt the Colombians were, and how violent. I have not exaggerated. During the 1990s the country was engulfed in carnage. The people had become accustomed, and de-sensitised, to the extraordinary level of violence. Human life seemed to have lost its value. Criminal groups would lob grenades into a busy restaurant just to assassinate one opponent, with complete disregard for the dozens of ordinary people killed and injured. A car bomb would be detonated at a wedding reception to kill one enemy, ignoring the scores of other victims. A jetliner was blown up in mid-air, killing hundreds, in an attempt to kill one man, a presidential candidate. Mutilated bodies were dumped at the side of main roads. For four years my family and I lived with armed guards, police and soldiers all around us, and were constantly looking out for threats. My children, like many from expatriate families, were taken to school by armed guards in a bulletproof jeep. Their school had watch towers and guards with pump-action shotguns. Restaurants and shopping malls had armed men on their doors and car parks. In addition to the ever-present private security, the police and army were always visible on the streets, in the shopping centres, indeed everywhere.

As DLOs we had to live in this hostile environment with our families, but so did the good citizens of Colombia. Whereas we could escape back to normality after a four-year stint, for Colombians this nightmare *was* their normality, their home, their reality.

In the early 1990s all of the agencies had been infiltrated and it was impossible for us DLOs to know who we could trust. But it must have been even more difficult and perilous for the Colombian police and DAS officers themselves, never knowing whether they could trust their colleagues or senior managers; never knowing, if they did their job correctly, who might betray them and get them killed. That was the sorry situation back then, and how the country had become after years of fighting against the cartels. Against that backdrop it is important to outline also the positive aspects.

The small number of Colombian police and DAS officers who we came to trust, and with whom we worked closely, were amazing people. They were highly motivated, dedicated, and very brave, working in difficult and dangerous circumstances to deliver results. Once we had earned their respect, our Colombian colleagues became true and reliable friends and gave us tremendous support and loyalty. They were decent and honourable people trying to do their jobs efficiently against overwhelming odds. They eventually succeeded in defeating the cartels, and in reducing corruption and restoring the integrity of their institutions. I am still friends with some of them today, twenty years later.

To the outside world Colombia is often known only for cocaine, cartels and violent drug lords. But Colombia is an amazing country. To the east it has tropical Amazon rainforest, with bounteous biodiversity, and in its centre the Andes range traverses the country from south-west to north-east, providing spectacular mountain scenery. In the north, the Caribbean coastal region has stunning nature reserves, beautiful beaches and magical, little-known islands off-shore. It is a country rich in natural resources, with coal, emeralds, coffee, fruit, flowers, and vast expanses of agricultural land. Above all Colombia has its people, the majority of whom, despite the years of hell inflicted upon them, are honest, welcoming and friendly.

THEY ASKED ME to stay on one more year, and I was very tempted to accept. It was all going incredibly well. Luisa was happy and loved the diplomatic life, and at work I was managing a fantastic team. Our network of informants worked like a well-oiled machine, and we were sending back a continuous flow of quality intelligence, churning out drug seizures every week. But deep inside I knew that I was burned out. I had gone to South America nine years earlier as an energetic young investigator. Now my hair and beard had turned grey and I felt increasingly drained. Luisa said that South America had changed me, made me colder and less sensitive. That was no doubt true. Conversely I also found myself getting upset at trivial things. I became short-tempered, and my emotions were all over the place. I was exhausted, and I knew that if I stayed on I would start to make mistakes.

I had been under massive stress in Colombia, and it had taken its toll. I knew that something was wrong, but it was very hard to tell anyone. I was meant to be a tough investigator and boss. I was managing the UK's top DLO team, working with the hardnosed Colombian Police, handling front-line informants and tackling the world's most dangerous criminal groups. ID officers and DLOs were supposed to be tough. We worked hard, played hard, drank hard. Stress was looked upon as a sign of weakness, even of failure, and something that no self-respecting ID officer could admit to. So I kept it to myself.

It was flattering to be invited to stay on another year in Colombia, but I had been away for nine, the first four working completely on my own in Peru, and I was exhausted. I turned down the offer. It was time to go home.

It took me a long time to settle back to a normal life. I had spent years living under threat, carrying my pager and mobile phone night and day; always checking carefully when I went to my car; always looking out for people watching me; working with people who I could never trust; always knowing that someone might be listening to my telephone calls, be it corrupt police working for the cartels, or DAS intelligence, or our own secret services and internal security. It was a long time before I could relax again. The impact on my family was also huge. My son Seb had grown up with armed guards all around. He had never played outside in the street, nor walked to school or gone for a bike ride with friends like kids in the UK would. He had spent his early life enclosed in secure areas, with guards watching, and being driven to school in bullet-proof Jeeps. It took him several months before he could get used to walking outside on his own without security. These were the hidden impacts that I had not appreciated at the time.

Several years later, while I was managing an operational drugs team in the UK, I went on a senior management course. Part of it involved a session on how to identify stress in my staff. As I listened to the list of indicators, I was not really surprised to recognise most of them.

I WAS FREQUENTLY asked the same one question about my work. I heard it from Government ministers when they visited Colombia, from diplomats, from members of the public. It was even the first question the Queen asked me when she gave me an MBE, an award that I was immensely proud to receive on my return from Colombia.

'Are we winning the war against drugs?'

It was often followed by another question: 'Is it worth so many people being killed to stop drugs?' If the answer to either question is, 'No,' then it leads to the really big questions, the ones that people often think but are sometimes afraid to articulate: 'Should we not just give up and legalise drugs? Why not let people use them, if that is what they want to do?'

For many years I would reply, 'No, we are not winning.' Then I would add firmly, to dispel any doubt, 'But we should definitely not give up or legalise cocaine. That would be utter madness.'

In some ways the first question is over-simplistic, even naive. It is rather like asking if we can ever stop robbery or theft. There will always be bad people out there who want to make easy money, and they do this by robbing other people. On the other hand, it would be unthinkable to legalise robbery. If we ignored robberies or legalised them, or left criminals to get on with it, society would soon crumble into anarchy and disorder.

I always believed firmly in the need for robust law enforcement against trafficking. We might not be winning the war, but we weren't losing it either. By seizing large amounts of drugs and putting traffickers in jail, we were at least keeping it under control and stopping it from getting worse. By disrupting supply we also kept the price high. As I saw it, without enforcement action the price of coke would drop so low that everyone could afford to buy it. We would have schoolchildren buying it with their pocket money. Law enforcement and criminalisation at least made people fearful of being arrested and kept the price of drugs high.

I am not so sure any more.

Are we winning? Most certainly not. The quantities of cocaine being produced and exported, along with the huge profit margins, mean that that the cartels can afford to lose a sizeable percentage of what they send. It is factored into their business models and profit margins. When we seized six tonnes of cocaine from the *Limerick*, the cartel simply arranged to send another six tonnes. During 2005 and 2006, cocaine seizures in Europe soared, with more confiscated than ever before. Did this have any significant impact? No. The cartels did feel the pressure a little, and changed their routes, opening up new transport through Africa. But it had no effect at all on street prices or availability. In fact, the price continued to fall. No matter how much we seized, they just absorbed the loss and sent more.

No, we are not winning. Our governments have spent many billions of pounds fighting drug trafficking during the past twenty-five years, yet we have nothing to show for it. According to the UNODC, Colombia is now exporting as much cocaine as ever, and the number of drug users in Europe is at its highest level.

Was it worth so many people losing their lives? When I think of people like Mardoqueo, and our many friends in DAS and the Colombian police who were killed, the answer can only be no. Then there were the informants who didn't make it, like Pacho, Mike, Alberto and their sub-sources. These were people with families and children, killed because they gathered intelligence for us. Did they change anything? The answer is a resounding no. How can we justify all these people losing their lives, to achieve nothing?

Cocaine itself is not the cause of violence, murder and corruption. These are the consequences of criminalisation. I do not believe that cocaine itself causes any significant harm to our society. When alcohol was prohibited in the USA in 1920 it brought a decade of violence and corruption by criminal groups who fought to control the illegal trade. Yet once legalised, it became a source of legitimate trade and welcome revenue for the government. The same applies to cocaine. Were it to be legalised, that would remove the criminality, the mafias, the corruption, murders and violence. Naturally its abuse would have to be managed in some way: by taxation, age restrictions, and other social boundaries, just as for tobacco and alcohol. But the violence and corruption generated by criminality would be gone, and the huge revenues from taxation could fund more meaningful programmes of education and social awareness. The long-term solution for our drugs problem must surely lie in education.

Perhaps the time has come for us to stop the so-called 'war' against drugs, and instead legalise them, just as we have done with tobacco and alcohol. Tax them heavily, which would keep prices high and generate revenue, and then spend that money on an extensive programme of education, media advertising and addiction support.

In the 1970s around half of all adults in the UK smoked tobacco. By 2016 this had fallen to under sixteen per cent. This massive fall was achieved by a strategy of high taxes, mass media awareness campaigns and educating people about the adverse health effects. It used to be considered trendy and cool to smoke; now it is the complete opposite. Unfortunately in many social groups it is still considered cool to take drugs. We must change this perception. Surely the answer lies in the power of social media and education, not criminalisation?

The war against drugs will not be won with bullets. It can only be won through a strategy of education, coupled with mass media and social media campaigns. These are our most powerful weapons. The weapons of the future.

APPENDIX

Codenames of the Colombian Informants, 1994–1998

Alberto	Jorge	Pacho II *
Alfredo	Jose	Pacho (F) *
Andy *	Judas	Pacho (H) *
Angelica	Julia	Pacho (N)
Apollo	Lech	Paco
Barry *	Lech II *	Paddy
Bates	Lucho	Patricia
Chepe	Luis	Pedro
Daniel *	Luis Eduardo	Pele *
Dario	Manuel	Pepe*
David	Maria-Cristina *	Popeye
Eddy *	Maribel	Raquel *
Emilio *	Maritza *	Roberto *
Fidel *	Marta *	Rocio *
Franco	Martin *	Rodrigo
Gerardo	Mike*	Roy *
Helmut *	Nancy	Saddam *
Henry	Noriega	Sierra
Hernando	Oma	Sonya *
Hilda	Orlando	Stern
Jairo	Oso *	Wally
Jean-Michel	Pablo	Walter *
Jean-Paul	Pacho	

The 26 informants active at June 1998 when I left Colombia are denoted with *

GLOSSARY

ANP	Anti-Narcotics Police of Colombia
CI	Confidential Informant
CIU	Collection Investigation Unit
CROPS	Covert Rural Operations
DAS	*Departmento Administrativo de Seguridad*. The Colombian Security and Intelligence agency. Disbanded in October 2011.
DEA	Drug Enforcement Administration
DIAN	*Dirección de Impuestos y Aduanas Nacionales de Colombia*, the Colombian Customs Service
DIJIN	*Dirección de Investigación Criminal*, the Criminal Investigation Directorate of Colombian Police.
DIRAN	*Dirección Antinarcoticos*, the Anti-drugs Directorate of the Colombian National Police
DLO	Drug Liaison Officer
FBI	Federal Bureau of Investigation
FCO	Foreign and Commonwealth Office
FLIR	Forward-Looking Infra-Red
Go-fast	A speedboat or fishing boat with powerful outboard engines, used to transport drugs in the Caribbean.
HMCE	HM Customs and Excise
HUMINT	Human Intelligence (Intelligence obtained from informants and human sources)
ID	Investigation Division. The Investigation Division

of HMCE consisted of approximately 1,000 specialist investigators who dealt with serious crime involving Customs matters. This included drug trafficking, the importation and exportation of prohibited goods, VAT fraud, and Customs fraud. In 1996 the ID and the CIUs were merged into a new National Investigation Service (NIS).

Igloo · Colloquial term for the containers used to transport air cargo and baggage on commercial aircraft.

JDF · Jamaican Defence Force

JIATF(S) · Joint Inter-Agency Task Force (South).

NIS · National Investigation Service of HMCE, created in 1996.

Rip-off · The method of receiving prohibited goods by removing them from inside a legitimate container, cargo or aircraft.

Rip-on · The method of smuggling prohibited goods by putting them inside a legitimate container, cargo or aircraft.

RIB · Rigid inflatable boat

SAS · Special Air Service

SIGINT · Signals Intelligence (Intelligence obtained from Intercepted communications)

SIS · Special Intelligence Service

SOP · Standard Operating Procedure

UNODC · United Nations Office on Drugs and Crime

DUDLEY PUBLIC LIBRARIES

The loan of this book may be renewed if not required by other readers, by contacting the library from which it was borrowed.

CP/494

FUNNY BY NATURE

FROM THE GOVERNMENT DEPARTMENT OF TOP SECRETS

If you are reading this, it means that you've gained access to one of the worst kept secrets in the history of the secret service.

Before continuing, I need you to carefully check that no one is reading over your shoulder—go ahead, do it now.

First off, that was terrible, really obvious. If I'm going to tell you top secret government information, you're going to have to be a bit more stealthy. Try again.

Was anyone looking? No? Right, then I'll begin.

This year the Secret Service made a major mix-up: they mistook a 13-year-old boy called Kevin for a secret agent. (I know, so much for an 'intelligence' agency.)